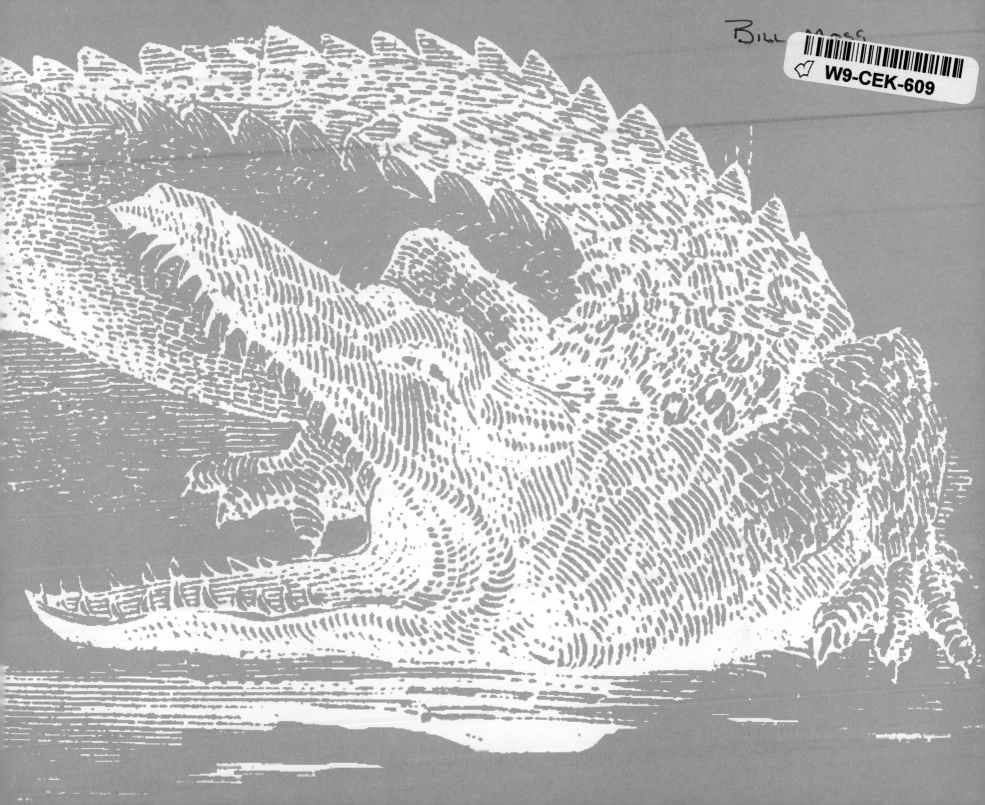

A SOCIAL HISTORY
OF THE AMERICAN
ALLIGATOR

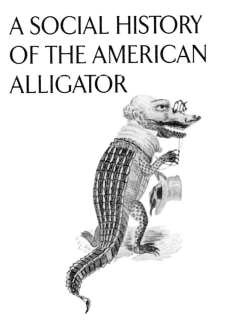

A SOCIAL HISTORY
OF THE
AMERICAN
ALLIGATOR

The Earth Trembles with His Thunder

VAUGHN L. GLASGOW

WITH THE SUPPORT OF THE LOUISIANA MUSEUM FOUNDATION

ST. MARTIN'S PRESS   NEW YORK

Design by Carol Haralson

Library of Congress Cataloging-in-Publication Data

Glasgow, Vaughn L.
    A social history of the American alligator /
Vaughn Glasgow.
       p.   cm.
    ISBN 0-312-06287-7—ISBN 0-312-06288-5
(Limited ed.)
    1. Alligators—United States—Folklore.
2. Alligators—United States—History.
I. Title.
GR740.G53   1991
398' .369798—dc20   91-18235
                       CIP

First Edition: September 1991
10 9 8 7 6 5 4 3 2 1

Half-title page: Alligator Costume from the 1873 Comus Parade. Detail of a carnival costume plate, collection of the Louisiana State Museum, New Orleans, gift of Mrs. Zulma Young Salaun.

Frontispiece: View of Lake Cocodrie. Oil on canvas by Hypolite Sebron, ca. 1861, collection of the Musée National de Coöperation Franco-Américaine, Blérancourt, France. Photograph © photo R. M. N., courtesy, photographic service of the Réunion des Musées Nationaux, Paris.

Second half-title page: Alligator Chorus (New Orleans), ca. 1910. Postcard illustration by the Curt Teich Co., Chicago. Courtesy, Lake County Museum, Curt Teich Postcard Archives, Wauconda, Illinois.

Chapter Fifteen title phrase *Gimme Some Skin* courtesy of Rebecca Venable.

Quoted materials written by Diane Ackerman are from her book, to be published by Random House in September of 1991. Reprinted by permission; © 1988 Diane Ackerman. Originally in *The New Yorker*. Quotations from *Madame Sarah* by Cornelia Otis Skinner © 1966 by Cornelia Otis Skinner. Reprinted by permission of Houghton Mifflin Co. Passages quoted from the novel *V* by Thomas Pynchon © 1961, 1963, 1989 by Thomas Pynchon. Reprinted by permission of the Melanie Jackson Agency. Quotations from E. A. McIlhenny's *The Alligator's Life History* are reprinted from the edition published by Ten Speed Press in 1987 and are reproduced by kind permission of the E. A. McIlhenny Enterprises, Inc. and Ten Speed Press.

This work is dedicated to the memory of the late Dr. Leslie L. Glasgow, professor of both forestry and wildlife management and assistant director of the School of Forestry and Wildlife Management at Louisiana State University, director of the Louisiana Wildlife and Fisheries Commission, assistant secretary of the United States Department of the Interior, husband, father, educator, international ecological consultant, published author, and president of many professional wildlife and game-management organizations. Recipient of numerous prestigious awards, Dr. Glasgow was a highly respected ecologist twenty years before the nation became widely aware of the word. His strong support encouraged the development of aquaculture studies at LSU. His uncanny ability to work with legislators was instrumental in obtaining authorization for the funding to plan and construct the university's current facility, renamed the School of Forestry, Wildlife Management, and Fisheries. Dr. Glasgow's interests and concerns with wetland ecology encouraged initial studies that were major contributions to the establishment of the state's highly successful crawfish industry.

Professor Glasgow first expressed his concern for the American alligator in the 1950s, and he was instrumental in early protective measures, both in Louisiana and nationally. His firm belief was that well-researched, professionally planned management would allow the alligator to survive as an important element in southern fauna. He foresaw the development of a $25 million Louisiana industry if the alligator were properly conserved.

Dr. Glasgow's high standards are maintained by the graduate students whose theses he directed and who devised and carried out the management programs that are responsible for many of the successes of the great American alligator adventure. One of those former students, Ted Joanen, has written, "It was largely through his efforts the Rockefeller alligator program was established and the encouragement he gave us in the early years kept our interest alive. . . . Largely through Dr. Glasgow's efforts, the alligator is alive and well in Louisiana."

While this is not the book Dr. Glasgow would have written about alligators, it is one he would have enjoyed.

CONTENTS

That remarkable reptile, the American alligator (*Alligator mississippiensis* daudin), has intrigued explorers, scientists, residents, writers, artists, filmmakers, and others for nearly half a millennium. Before that, it was well known to Native Americans. This denizen of southern wetlands is one of our most successful life-forms, along with the shark, cockroach, and fly, and has been with us in one form or another for at least 70 million years. Its closest relative is Chinese.

Drawing on scientific observation, speculation, imagination, exaggeration, affection, fear, historic resources, artistic inspiration, hunger, and economic motivation, Americans have found an astounding number of ways of integrating the alligator into their lives. It has become symbol, totem, medicine, mascot, pet, handbag, saddle, main dish, hors d'oeuvre, nightmare, and souvenir. Our resident crocodilian has been hunted, researched, photographed, published, managed, farmed, sold, tanned, and eaten.

Concurrent with these developments, the alligator was anthropomorphized, mythologized, sensationalized, filmed, drawn, engraved, painted, and sculpted. It is the basis of various children's books, folktales, horror stories, novels, magazine articles, newspaper columns, and fine literature.

As a result, by their dynamic, changing relationship with the alligator over time, Americans have endowed it with a rich and significant social history. It has become an element of national life, part of our collective identity—a notable achievement.

The saga of man and alligator is indeed a rich story, written in many languages and involving several continents. Each time that a new scientific discovery was made, another song was written, or an alligator-related film premiered, our perceptions of the United States's predominant saurian were changed. These perceptions differed from community to community. Alligator hunters have never looked at their quarry in the same way that biologists and game managers have regarded it. Film audiences, thrilled and titillated by the emotional osmosis that is the magic of the movies, built within themselves a silver-screen image of the alligator vastly different from the objective view of a laboratory scientist. Wealthy and fashionable ladies clutching alligator bags have seen the alligator as the source of the sensual pleasures of very fine and exotic leather, while youngsters have been charmed by the alligator fantasies of children's authors. Every segment of U.S. society has been touched in some way by the alligator.

FEEDING HER PET,
POSTCARD ILLUSTRA-
TION BY THE CURT
TEICH CO., CHICAGO,
CA. 1912.

ALLIGATOR LAMP,
CA. 1955.

The touch has varied with time. Alligators functioned differently in different eras. Poverty and deprivation in the past have led Americans to eat the alligator for want of other foodstuffs; while today, alligator meat has become an expensive gourmet delicacy with worldwide distribution. Alligators provided oil for superstitious medicinal application, indigo refining, and the lubricating of early steam machinery long before the alligator's belly appeared as novelty upholstery on Victorian furniture.

Tracing these permutations in the perception and utilization of the alligator unfolds in a fascinating multifaceted story of the alligator's cultural impact on the American people. It explains why William Bartram could say "the earth trembles with his thunder" in the 1790s, and why that phrase, with altered meaning, is just as apt today.

A SOCIAL HISTORY
OF THE AMERICAN
ALLIGATOR

ALLIGATOR CHORUS DOWN IN LOUISIANA. NEW ORLEANS.

LOST IN THE MYTHS OF TIME

AMERICAN ALLIGATOR LEGENDS

"THE NATCHEZ." ENGRAVING BY LEFÈVRE THE ELDER AFTER A DRAWING BY TONY JOHANNET, CA. 1834 (DETAIL, FACING PAGE.)

NATIVE AMERICAN AWL (PLAQUE-MINES-MISS-ISSIPIAN CULTURE) AND VIAL (COLES CREEK CULTURE) MADE FROM ALLIGATOR BONE AND TOOTH.

Native Americans of the Gulf Coast held many natural phenomena in reverence, including the alligator. These tribes had a healthy respect for alligators, but they achieved a familiar, comfortable relationship with them. At least five tribes performed an alligator song or dance, including the Seneca in faraway New York. Many tribes ate alligators and used teeth and bones for a variety of purposes. Avocational archaeologist Benward Treadaway, Jr., has identified alligator artifacts of the Archaic, Coles Creek, and Plaquemines-Mississippian period cultures found in St. Bernard Parish, Louisiana. These include

awls of alligator bone, a tooth dressed as a vial, and a remarkable atlatl weight carved of chlorite schist with an alligatorlike creature spread-eagled across the top.

Among early explorers' accounts concerning Indians and alligators is that penned by Father Paul du Ru, who accompanied Iberville in 1700: "This beast, which passes for something so terrible in Europe, is seen here [that is, on the Mississippi] as another fish, the Savages, while bathing, play with it, without coming to any harm." A very similar story was reported by Andrew Ellicott, a traveling civil engineer, exactly a century later. In 1831, Forest recorded a

superstitious medicoreligious belief: "The aborigines have blind confidence in the healing power of crocodiles' [*sic; that is, alligators'*] teeth . . . they always have a crocodile's tooth hanging around their neck."

The most prominent manifestation of alligator worship in the United States is the seven-hundred-foot-long alligator-shaped effigy mound built by Native Americans at Grand Lake in Cameron Parish, Louisiana. Another very large mound at Shell Beach has been suggested as having once been alligator-shaped, but is so badly eroded that identification of its original form is difficult. The Choctaw word for alligator, *hachunchuba* (meaning "without hair") has been transliterated into English as Chinchuba and is used to designate towns, creeks, and bayous on the Gulf Coast.

European encounters with American crocodilians (encompassing the caimans, crocodiles, and alligator) began with Christopher Columbus in 1492. On Crooked Island in the Bahamas, that intrepid Italian went in hot pursuit of a six-foot "serpent" that "threw itself into the lake." Columbus, of course, personally had never seen a Nile crocodile, let alone one of its new-world cousins. It was a natural mistake that occurred when those early European explorers of the fifteenth and sixteenth centuries first found the alligator and confused it with what little they knew of the old-world crocodile. They promptly imbued the alligator with all the attributes—true, false,

and legendary—with which science and mythology had endowed that denizen of the Nile. Slaves, brought from Africa, also credited the alligator with all the lore that tribal wisdom had furnished them about crocodiles.

Europeans looked to the Bible and found Ezekiel speaking of "the great dragon that lieth in the midst of Pharaoh's rivers." From the Book of Job, they dredged up the Leviathan, which despite its lovely "eyelids of the morning" was a fierce fighter with an impenetrable covering of scales: "The sword of him that layeth at him cannot hold . . . the arrow cannot make him flee . . . he laugheth at the shaking of a spear." To this they annexed Marco Polo's observations on the Chinese alligator, brought home in the thirteenth century at a time when crusading knights were still defending fair maidens from fire-breathing dragons.

Thus it is no surprise that the Iberville expedition of 1699 discovered "crocodiles" of "prodigious size" in the Mississippi, and ran "very great risks because of the infinite number of alligators." In 1753, DuMont de Montigny reported them "very difficult to kill because of the hard scales and skin," a description reminiscent of Job's commentary on the Leviathan. Even the Diderot *Encyclopédie* stated in 1754 that "its mouth is so big, its jaws are so strong, its teeth are so pointed that it is claimed that it can cut through a man in the middle of his body."

In 1758, LePage du Pratz told readers, "this animal always has a body covered with slime . . . it covers its path with this slime"; and in 1777, Jean-Bernard Bossu described alligators "so big and so old they have moss on their head and back." William Bartram enthralled his reading audience in 1794, saying, "Clouds of smoke issue from his dilated nostrils. The earth trembles with his thunder . . . the floods of water and blood rushing out of their mouths, and the clouds of vapour rising from their wide nostrils, were truly frightful." Biblical scholars, of course, had known for years from Job that "his teeth are terrible round about. . . . Out of his nostrils goeth smoke, as out of a seething pot or cauldron."

As these and other myths, exaggerations, and partial truths grew and spread, Dr. Bennet Dowler set out in 1846 to correct the errors that "have been accumulating until the herpetological account of this saurian has, at length, become as fabulous as that of the Griffin." Or, as the Baton Rouge *Morning Advocate* put it in 1973, "Each tale-bearer would strive to make his story a little more exciting than the last, and it was difficult to tell where fiction ended and fact began." Good copy brought good sales, so despite scientific effort, as late as 1937 the popular press could report on "a vicarious dragon hunt," and in 1948 the alligator was still described as a "Medieval looking beast, something that might have crept out of the catalogue of the devilish Bestiaries compiled by religious monks of the middle ages."

VISIONS OF MONSTERS AND THE BIBLICAL LEVIATHAN: *ORCA BALENAM MORSU LACERANS*. WOODCUT FROM *ULYSSIS ALDROVANDI*, 1638.

FACING PAGE, ABOVE: PRE-COLUMBIAN CROCODILIAN FIGURINE, ECUADOR.

FACING PAGE, BELOW: "MEDICINAL" ALLIGATOR TOOTH.

LOST IN THE MYTHS OF TIME 3

Such imagery proliferated throughout following decades in the work of novelists and screenwriters, intent on thrilling audiences at the expense of accuracy. In the prologue to *Alligator,* published in 1977, Shelley Katz expounded on "a gator as big as an elephant that eats little children and attacks men in boats with the power and ferocity of a landlocked Moby Dick."

European settlers were quick to note that Native Americans thought alligator teeth prevented snakebite, and speedily added an impressive number of additional alligator cures and remedies to the colonial pharmacopoeia. Alligator blood was thought to cure ophthalmia (irritation of the eyes) and to assuage the ravages of the bite of poisonous snakes (possibly because the alligator ate such snakes without harm, and remembering that the hapless victim shouldn't have been bitten in the first place if he had been wearing his alligator tooth as the Indians said to do). Fever was relieved by rubbing the sufferer with alligator fat.

M. F.-E. Guérin wrote in 1834 that "The blacks [in the United States] have great esteem, it is said, for the fat of the caiman [*sic*], used as liniment in the treatment of rheumatism and sprains . . . ." This may have been a survival of African crocodile-related traditions, adapted to new-world alligators. Others thought that alligator fat or oil also cured arthritis. Guérin saw through such treatment, accusing practitioners of "confusing the action of the application, that is to say of rubbing, with that of the auxiliary agent."

At one time, ashes of burned alligator skin, steeped in oil, were believed to have narcotic effects. The gastroliths or "stomach stones"—those bits of extraneous matter such as rocks, wood, and even glass, worn smooth by corrosive digestive juices and gastric action—from an alligator's belly were alleged to possess unidentified medicinal properties, as well. These "stomach stones" also reminded settlers of another old Nile crocodile legend: that the Egyptian animal swallowed a stone every time it ate a person in order to keep count of its victims. Contrary to popular belief, alligators do not maintain an internal abacus. In North Carolina, the teeth of an alligator's right jaw (never the left) were eaten (which must have been difficult unless they were powdered) by sterile or impotent male colonists, "to provoke Venery."

Some of these superstitions have remained current in American folklore and folk medicine. Alligator oil was in use as recently as the 1970s in Louisiana's Cajun country to relieve rheumatism. One elderly patient asked local alligator hunters to stop giving the stuff to his wife, who, he was sure, was poisoning him by making him drink it.

The "alligator horses" tale may have begun in the eighteenth century when William Byrd, colonial official in Virginia, wrote that Native Americans would surprise napping alligators, "get astride upon their Necks, then whip a short piece of wood like a truncheon into their Jaws," after which they rode them to exhaustion, dragged them to shore, and ate them.

Throughout the nineteenth century, many stories were told of men riding alligators. John J. Audubon was quoted by Dr. Bennet Dowler as saying, "When alligators are about to go into winter quarters [that is, becoming torpid in low temperatures], a child may mount them as a

THE HOME STRETCH IN FLORIDA.

ONE MILE

wooden rocking horse." Dr. Dowler also recounted in 1846 that road-building and canal-digging crews often inadvertently penetrated alligator dens, and "on one occasion, an Alligator had been wounded by a man who was not aware of it[s presence] at the moment—the animal ran some distance with the man, who had accidentally fallen astride its back." By 1855, this tale had become "a man . . . mounting on the back of an alligator, and using the two

LOST IN THE MYTHS OF TIME 5

fore legs—which he drew over the reptile's back—as one does the reins of a bridle." The anonymous writer didn't put much credence in it, even though he said it was the subject of many depictions.

Other versions existed, such as the boast of a drunken sailor in Natchez, reported by Christian Schultz in 1810: "I am an alligator; half man, half horse; can whip any *on the Mississippi,* by G-d." Shortly afterward, a song commemorating the Battle of New Orleans in 1815 said, "No matter what his force is / We'll show him that Kentucky boys / Are alligator horses." This may be the variant that led journalist Charles "Pie" Dufour to rewrite history in 1951, proclaiming that British troops at the battle were tripped up in a veritable mine field of alligator holes, where they had been lured by a scurrilous relative of one of Jean Lafitte's pirates.

Both literature and oral tradition abound with stories of the alligator and its relationship with the dog, covering the past quarter millennium. In 1737, John Brickell reported in *The Natural History of North Carolina,* "they frequently kill swine and dogs," and forty years later, Bossu found them "eager for dog flesh." The dogs of the Native Americans, however, outwitted the alligators in Bossu's narrative: "dogs that belong to savages have a peculiar way of saving themselves from being eaten by these cruel amphibians [*sic*] when they want to cross a stream or channel of the Mississippi. They approach the banks and bark very loudly, striking the water with their paws to attract all the crocodiles [*sic*] from surrounding territory." Then they ran farther along the bank, crossing at a considerable and safe distance from the congregated alligators "at a place where they will not meet the enemy."

J. J. Audubon would not risk sending his retriever into the water if alligators were about. Baron Cuvier, writing in 1831, repeated Bossu's story of the doggy decoys. In the 1850s, it was attributed to a particularly intelligent pack of hunting hounds near Opelousas, Louisiana. E. A. McIlhenny said that as children in the 1870s, he and his companions would call alligators at Avery Island "by imitating the barks and cries of dogs."

Numerous bloody accounts of alligators consuming dogs have been published. Among pets eaten are the Pekingese, dachshund, and poodle. Perhaps the most sensational alligator-dog encounter was that at Belle Isle, in France, a place to which actress Sarah Bernhardt had shipped an alligator she had acquired near Lake Charles,

Louisiana, about 1900 on one of her American tours. As described by Cornelia Otis Skinner: "Sarah uncrated it herself. The tiny Manchester terrier she then had, excited by the strange reptilian, barked madly and started snapping at its nose. The alligator, alas, came suddenly out of its long winter's sleep and snapped back and the small dog disappeared down the tooth-lined maw. Madame's secretary, Pitou, grabbed a gun and shot the monster, and Sarah, grief-stricken over the loss of her terrier, had the 'gator's head dissevered, mounted and hung in her hall. She would point it out to her guests and say mournfully, 'My beloved little dog—his tomb!'"

"I knew a French woman, who was washing clothes on the river bank; an alligator tried to drag her away," wrote DuMont de Montigny in 1753; and in 1777, Bossu declared, "Louisiana lakes and rivers are infested with such big and dangerous crocodiles [sic] that they often devour Negresses who without taking precautions go to wash clothes in places frequented by these animals."

Thus began yet another of the great eighteenth-century alligator legends, branding the alligator as the occupational hazard of the colonial laundress. Alligators seem to select prey by size, and a kneeling figure might resemble a large dog or pig, both of which were particular favorites. Tall figures that are standing are seldom attacked. The laundress legend persisted in various forms throughout the nineteenth century until the early Maytag supplanted the Mississippi on wash day.

Bossu launched the tale of alligators raiding lost arks, writing in 1777 about a slave sent to get preserved meats from a beached pirogue: "Immediately the slave came back, all excited and almost beside himself, to tell us that the evil spirit had taken all our provisions. But the evil spirit proved to be nothing more than a crocodile [sic] . . . ." He may have been inspired by DuMont de Montigny, who had written a quarter of a century earlier that "this voracious and carnivorous animal even gets into the pirogues of travelers to get at any meat that might be there . . . ." William Bartram's 1794 account included a similar tale, which, he concluded, "may be sufficient to prove the intrepidity and subtilty [sic] of those voracious, formidable animals."

In 1808, Thomas Ashe, who also possessed a vivid imagination, had the alligator attacking an occupied boat in midstream, intent on stealing ducks, and "on one of the men cleaving the claw with which he sustained himself, he made a dreadful flounce, uttered a tremendous cry, beat in the upper plank of the boat, knocked us all three from our situation, and carried off the coop as the reward of his victory." As late as 1831, Forest claimed, "If the hunter discovers a prey, immediately it becomes victims of crocodiles [sic] which only leave the plumage." Dr. Dowler said he was "credibly informed" in 1846 that alligators nosed around hunters to "watch for offal of the camp."

There is one modern account that substantiates tales of this sort. It is that of professional biologist Archie Carr, writing in 1967 of an alligator hard-pressed for a meal during flood season that was "so hungry that she broke into the strong cage we had built for a new flock of mallards and ate two of them."

OCCUPATIONAL HAZARD OF THE COLONIAL LAUNDRESS. PEN AND INK SKETCH BY CHUCK SILER.

By the mid-eighteenth century, a legend circulated that alligators preferred to eat black men instead of whites if presented with a choice. Supplementing oral tradition, this myth was published at least fifteen times between 1777 and 1929 in the United States, France, and England. In his third letter, Bossu wrote in 1777, "It has been observed that they [alligators] attack Negroes especially, because of a certain exhalation discharged from their skin when they perspire," and proceeded to illustrate with a tale in which an alligator (Bossu still called them crocodiles) singled out a black who was swimming across a river with a group of Indians. The Indians were unmolested. French traveler and

"WAITING FOR A BITE IN NEW ORLEANS." POSTCARD ILLUSTRATION BY THE CURT TEICH CO., CHICAGO, CA. 1936.

Waiting for a Bite in New Orleans

6A-H1418

author de la Coudrenière followed customary practice of the day, summarizing Bossu's contention (but not giving him credit) in 1782 by writing that this animal feeds on men, "particularly the negroes."

In 1800, Ellicott noted an alligator attack on a black man near New Orleans as the only authenticated injury to a human by an alligator that he knew about, maintaining that Indians of all ages bathed in alligator-infested waters "without any apparent dread or caution." The English even imputed that French recountings of the legend proved French racism. The offensive Thomas Ashe published in 1808, "The French believe that they [alligators] have a decided predilection for negro flesh. This idea prevails so much, that negroes dare not venture into the water," and he proceeded to support the argument by another tale in which a black man and a white man, pushing a boat off a sandbar, were inspected by an alligator that selected the black for lunch and "crushed his bones in the presence of the white man, whom he neither attacked nor regarded."

The change in the legend from Indian and black to Caucasian and black was aped by Timothy Flint, writing in 1828, "It is said, they [alligators] will attack a negro in the water, in preference to a white." This sort of unconfirmed hearsay also appeared in the works of noted scientists such as François-Marie Daudin (1803), Baron Cuvier (1831), Dr. John Edwards Holbrook (1842), Dr. Bennet Dowler (1846), and Remington Kellog (1929). Their professional stature lent the story unintended credibility, as they simply repeated it as hearsay without taking the position of confirming it.

During the late nineteenth and early twentieth centuries, many pejorative images, particularly on souvenir postcards, were issued depicting alligators attacking or devouring blacks. Their validity, especially in the popular mind, was bolstered by all the previous retellings of the myth. Historically, this imagery began to appear shortly after the end of Reconstruction and the return of home rule to the southern states. This encompassed the time when blacks began to lose their previously federally protected rights due to the passage of legislative acts during the late nineteenth century that provided for separate but equal railway coaches and other accommodations, which introduced legalized segregation to the South. Most of these images were created and produced by northern souvenir manufacturers but were intended to be retailed in the South, largely to tourists.

It was the alligator's large size that first seems to have suggested great age—and led many into conjecture concerning its probable life span. In the mid-1970s, Ruth Gross summarized a two-hundred-year-long divergence of

"A Race for Life or a Solution of the Race Question," scriptwork exercise, Soulé Business College, ca. 1890.

"FIGHT BETWEEN
ALLIGATOR AND
BEAR." WOOD
ENGRAVING FROM
HARPER'S NEW
MONTHLY MAGA-
ZINE, 1855.

wild." One of the functions of saurian basking is to expose such accumulations of algae to the sun, which destroys it. Bossu's "mossbacks" may have been sporting nothing more than a temporary layer of floating duckweed or some other aquatic plant acquired by swimming through it, but his observation (or misobservation) was among those that automatically equated great size with great age in the minds of early commentators.

Daudin was nearer the mark in 1803 when he reasoned, "It is nevertheless easy to presume that they [alligators] must live a great number of years, perhaps nearly a century, especially when one reflects that growth is very slow in these animals and they must have a great period of time to reach their inordinate size . . . ." But even as big a name in nineteenth-century science as John J. Audubon could be misled by that "inordinate" size. Describing a seventeen-foot alligator about 1827, he wrote in a British journal: "it was apparently centuries old; many of its teeth measured three inches." Audubon's opinions were generally highly respected; publication of that remark helped establish the alligator's reputation for overestimated longevity. Baron Cuvier, also a scientist of repute, held a divergent opinion, admitting that the life span of crocodilians "is not exactly known; but there are facts which tend to prove that it is equal, if not superior, to that of the life of man."

Various thoughts on the subject of the length of an alligator's term among the living were voiced, generally with little or no basis, for the next eighty years. Then biologist Alfred Reese found that at early twentieth-century tourist-attraction alligator farms, "a large specimen may be

opinions, saying, "Most scientists think a crocodilian can live for only 50 to 75 years. Others think that 100 years must be right, but they can't prove it." Fully two centuries earlier, Jean-Bernard Bossu had seen "crocodiles [*sic*] so big and so old they have moss on their heads and backs . . . ." Frank and Ada Graham, however, found that " 'moss' is not a sign of age at all. It is an algae that grows on unhealthy alligators and is not usually seen on healthy animals in the described by the exhibitor as more than a century old. . . . Even scientific writers of reputation have not been free from this error in their writings." Among the thorny facets of the problem were that few if any had actually kept track of specific alligators from hatching to demise; that Mother Nature (being no formal statistician) had not issued birth and death certificates to demonstrate the age of her saurians; and that the older the scientist, the more likely that his alligator subjects (especially if they were young ones) would actually outlive the inquirer, resulting in a legacy of unanswered questions.

A few documented cases were available to those still wondering in the 1920s and 1930s. An example was found in England, where, E. T. Bennet reported, "One kept in the London Zoological Gardens lived 34 years, 10 months, and 27 days . . . ." E. A. McIlhenny kept tabs on the alligators in the marshlands surrounding his Avery Island domain, and he could authoritatively say by 1934 that he had seen alligators "twelve feet long that were certainly no more than twelve or fifteen years old, and alligators that were ten feet long that were certainly twenty-five years old." The apparent discrepancy is probably explained by the more recently available knowledge that male alligators will grow much longer than females, which seldom exceed the nine- or ten-foot mark. Growth rates (of about a foot a year) of both sexes slow considerably after reaching six or seven feet. McIlhenny's conclusion was that to obtain fifteen feet, an alligator must "live for at least thirty to forty years."

The Baton Rouge *State-Times* cheerfully confounded fact with fantasy in 1943 by reporting that "One [alligator] that died a natural death after being captured in Bossier Parish was said to have weighed over 500 pounds and his age was estimated at 171 years." The operable word in that piece of trivia was *estimated.* The paper appended this: "One method of estimating the age of a 'gator is to count his teeth, add two to that number, divide by the number of feet in the length of his tail, and add six—to reach the correct number of years he has roamed the swamps." Just where and how this magic formula was originated were not revealed. It indicated, however, the uncertainty that was more succinctly worded by biologist Archie Carr in the *National Geographic* in 1967: "No one knows the life expectancy of an alligator in the wild. Tagging studies may provide answers in years to come."

Two decades later, Jack Scott had had the benefit of some of those studies, which empowered him to pontificate: "It is a fallacy that alligators live to be one hundred years or even older. They do not live as long as a man, and are fortunate if they reach fifty. And studies of captive alligators conclude that females may not live much beyond thirty." Some 212 years had passed between Bossu's "mossy" commentary and this resolution—or about triple the life span of an alligator. Alligators are now believed to parallel human life, reaching about seventy, but more statistics (which will take years to collect) are needed to be absolutely sure.

Among the legends that were transplanted from the Nile to the Mississippi was that of "crocodile tears." In Africa, according to Faith Medlin, "When crocodiles make a weeping sound and produce large tears by crying, they are not expressing sorrow but rather are ridding their bodies of excess salt through special glands in the head." And, as Frank and Ada Graham explained, in the New World, "some writers told of hearing wild sobs and cries near swampy places at night. Such cries reminded them of the Old World legend that when a crocodile ate a human being it felt so guilty it lay down and wept 'crocodile tears'—until the next time it ate somebody and wept hypocritically again."

The often regrettable Thomas Ashe provided one of the most colorful tales of such nighttime sobbing in the swamps near Natchez in 1806:

> I was started up by the most lamentable cries that ever assailed the human ear . . . they issued from so many directions, and expressed such a variety and number of persons afflicted with the deepest grief, that our reason and judgment were dissipated in wild conjecture . . . at times the cries sunk [sic] into the feeble plaints of expiring infancy, and again gradually rose into the full and melancholy swell of an adult tortured by fiends destitute of mercy and humanity. The lamentations, turn by turn, touched every string capable to vibrate excess of misery, and denoted the variety of sorrow incident to individuals from the loss of health, friends, fortune, and relatives. Above all, they denoted calamity in the act of supplicating relief in the strong language of sobs, sighs, and tears, and moans of inexpressible anguish and length. . . . This violent outcry was followed by plunges in the water and a rustling among the trees, which at length explained the objects of our dismay and apprehension. They were a host of alligators.

No wonder the Grahams were impressed!

Ashe began his investigation into the alligator version of crocodile tears that same year, looking at some baby alligators he had caught: "Much has been said of the *crocodile lacrimae*, or deceitful tears. . . . I carefully watched to discover whether the melancholy cries of my young alligators were accompanied with tears. I can attest they are not . . . nor does any moisture whatever fill the eye, though the plaints are piteous to the most distressing degree."

Dr. Bennet Dowler took up the inquest in 1846, taking this crocodile version as his premise: "Among the many fabulous accounts of this reptile [crocodile], not the least defamatory and false is that concerning its want of *sincerity*. It is said to be a hypocrite, and that its tears are false." Dowler had heard that a crocodile could be forced to cry by exposing it to saffron, and he set down this account of an American equivalent: "I have seen the detestable juice of tobacco tried, by a negro, who, spirted [sic] his saliva in its eyes, as correctly as Boz could wish, but without producing any tears; it only enraged the animal." His conclusion was: "An alligator has no deceit. If he hates you, he will hiss you to your face." Closely following him was the correspondent for *Harper's New Monthly Magazine*, who wrote in 1855, "The species are honest in their indignation, and shed no tears at all. . . ."

Thomas Ashe also began the circulation of one of the most preposterous of the alligator legends, publishing in 1808, "They open their mouths while they lay [sic] basking in the sun, on the banks of rivers and creeks, and when filled with all manner of insects, they suddenly let fall their upper jaw [only the lower moves] with surprising noise, and thus secure their prey." To this tale of a reptilian Venus's-flytrap, *Harper's New Monthly Magazine* added in 1855, "If our swamps, instead of being crowded with a rich, tropical vegetation, which render[s] them majestic aisles of dim twilight even at mid-day, were more open to observation, it is probable that our alligators would be found to have their little bird which performed the friendly office of 'winged toothpick,'" recalling the legendary relationship between the African crocodile and the trochilus. That oddly named bird is supposed to have entered the crocodile's open mouth to peck out leeches that congregated inside the reptile's jaws. The crocodile suffered such ignominious treatment in a mutually profitable symbiotic relationship, according to ancient historians, notably Herodotus.

In 1939, Harold Smith speculated that, in the case of the alligator, perhaps the bird (and not the insects or other incumbents) was intended as the meal: "One story is that of the gator in search of a more tasty morsel than the usual crab, fish, or turtle, lying patiently on the edge of some stream with jaws agape and mouth full of shrimp or other water life, until some hungry blackbird, spotting this tempting offering and ignorant of the wiles of the tempter, who will remain unmoving for hours on end, will alight with the intention of consuming the food, only to be made a meal of himself when the gator's teeth come together with a snap."

However, five years earlier, after a lifetime of careful observation, E. A. McIlhenny had already debunked the legend, saying, "When taking sunbaths on the bank, it is usual for alligators to hold their mouths partly open. I have never in all my experiences seen them snap their jaws together at such times, although flies and mosquitoes swarm around them. I believe the reason they open their mouths is to let the leeches and small water lice which frequently attach themselves inside of their mouths along the tongue to have a chance to dry out in the hot sunlight, which perhaps would rid them of these pests."

Alligators will investigate any potential meal, which led to a sort of sport for naturalist John J. Audubon in the 1820s:

> I have frequently been very much amused when fishing in a bayou, where alligators were numerous, by throwing a blown bladder on the water the nearest to me. The alligator makes for it at once, flaps it toward its mouth, or attempts seizing it at once, but all in vain. The light bladder slides off; in a few minutes many alligators are trying to seize it, and their evolutions [*sic*] are quite interesting. They then put one in mind of a crowd of boys running after a foot ball. A black bottle is sometimes thrown, also, tightly corked; but the alligator seizes this easily, and you hear the glass give way under its teeth, as if ground in a course mill.

Glass, including Coke bottles, has often been noted in alligator stomachs among the gastroliths. One early alligator hunting account tells of corked bottles used as lures to draw alligators to a snare. Dr. John Holbrook found glass in alligator stomachs in 1842, writing, "there is [*sic*] at all times found in the stomach of the Alligator, various extraneous substances [such as] stones, pieces of wood, fragments of glass, broken bottles, &c. . . . ." In 1846, Dr. Dowler accused alligators of "errors of diet," and he told of a bottle that so lacerated the 'gator's innards that it died of the wounds: "A gentleman of the State of Mississippi . . . finding that the whiskey bottle, which he had been carrying, was now empty . . . threw it to an alligator. . . . On returning to the same place in a few days after, the animal was found dead, with its abdomen greatly distended. . . . Broken fragments of the bottle, with putrid fish, were found in the stomach and bowels." E. A. McIlhenny recalled that a bottle was used as a float for alligator fishing when he was a boy on Avery Island in the 1870s and 1880s: "The alligator would grab the bait and float, and if the float was a bottle, would crush it with its jaws as if it was paper, and then swallow the remnants of glass and baited hook."

In 1940, Will Branan suggested that to avoid killing alligators with whiskey bottles, "It is therefore advisable for sportsmen to transport their liquid refreshment in kegs, or barrels, instead of a flask, as Mr. Gator is on our conservation list of picturesque exhibits."

One aspect of alligator behavior that early legend mongers reported correctly was fear of fire. In 1720, Christophe Weigel advised "they can be kept away easily with a stick of burning fox's brush since they avoid fire." This was taken as gospel by later writers, who repeated it ad infinitum. LePage du Pratz added a nice twist in 1758, saying of a night-visiting alligator in his Bayou St. John garden, "his gaze was so fixed on the [cooking] fire, that all of our movements were not capable of distracting him."

J. F. D. Smith warned in 1791 that voyagers in open boats, "are obliged to land every night, and light a large fire to discourage the approach of these voracious animals." Alligator investigator J. D. Mitchell chronicled some refugees during the Texas Revolution, saying that in 1836 "Dr. Kerr was aroused during the night by the screams of the negro boy, and on investigation found that an alligator was dragging him by the foot toward the [Sabine] river. He ran to the fire, and seeing a burning faggot, thrust it into the alligator's eyes, when the animal released the boy and escaped . . . ." By the late nineteenth century, "fire hunting" was a common method of procuring alligator hides for the market, a torch being used to blind or hypnotize alligators so that hunters could come within easy range to dispatch their prey.

One nineteenth-century story, which apparently never made very great inroads into the popular concept of alligators, was that of Baron Cuvier, who tried to explain why the freshwater animal wasn't found in the sea. In his words, "It is afraid of the shark and the great tortoises, and consequently avoids the neighbourhood of salt or brackish waters." Some crocodilians, notably the lengthy seagoing crocodiles of southeast Asia, spend a great deal of time in saltwater. An American alligator occasionally makes a marine excursion; one was sighted in the Gulf of Mexico off the Louisiana coast near Grand Isle in 1990. Such forays, though, are rare. The most likely explanation is that alligators have a low tolerance for salt, and simply do not expose themselves to unnecessary quantities of it without some compelling reason.

Various nineteenth-century stories have been told of gladiator-type alligators, locked in mortal combat with other predators. Chief among the reported enemy are cougars, jaguars, and bears. A particularly lurid version, allegedly an eyewitness account, was published in 1855: "Seized with desperation, the amphibious beast fetched a scream of despair; but being a warrior 'by flood and field' he was not yet entirely overcome. Writhing his tail in agony, he happened to strike it against a small tree that stood next [to] the bayou—aided by this purchase he made a convulsive flounder, which precipitated himself and Bruin, locked together, into the river."

It was alleged that true alligator baiting had its prototype in India, where there was a traditional entertainment in which Indian princes set starved crocodiles against tigers or bulls. Usually the tigers lost, but the bulls won. This apparently entertained many a maharajah and his guests. The SPCA would have been horrified by a version told by William Bartram, which squared off his American Indian guides and a twelve-foot alligator about 1790:

> It was a rare piece of sport. Some [of the guides] took fire-brands and cast them at his head, whilst others formed javelins of saplings, pointed and hardened with fire [exactly how they had time to make these javelins during the heat of battle was not explained]; these they thrust down his throat into his bowels, which caused the monster to roar and bellow hideously; but his strength and fury were so great, that he easily wrenched or twisted them out of their hands, and wielding and brandishing them about, kept his enemies at a distance.

. . . Some were for putting an end to his life and sufferings with a rifle ball, but the majority thought this would too soon deprive them of the diversion and pleasure of exercising their various inventions of torture. . . .

Numerous stories of this sort, although none quite so rich in imagery, were published in the ensuing century. For example, in 1875, Edward King claimed that a professional alligator hunter in Jacksonville, Florida, had told him, "When the boys want sport, sir, they get a long green pole, and sharpen it; 'n then they find a 'gaiter's [sic] hole in the marsh, and put the pole down it; then the 'gaiter [sic] he snaps at it, 'n hangs on to it, 'n the boys get together, 'n pull him out, 'n put a rope aroun' his neck and set him to fightin' with another 'gaiter [sic]. O Lord! reckon t'would make you' har [sic] curl to see the tails fly."

Man's capacity for cruelty is certainly well illustrated by these vicious memories, but it is more likely they were created by imaginative writers for the value of the reader appeal of the vicarious thrills they imparted rather than for documenting any genuine or widespread tradition of 'gator baiting.

The best-known twentieth-century American alligator legend asserts that vacationing Manhattaners brought home large numbers of live souvenir baby alligators from Florida and flushed them into the sewers of New York City when it became apparent they were not suitable apartment dwellers. There the 'gators allegedly grew to large sizes, feeding on rats, terrorizing sewer workers, and occasionally emerging from their underground haunts to spread panic in the streets. Some versions said the alligators, like cave animals, had become blind and white, having lost sight and pigmentation from generations of living in total darkness.

This choice example of urban folklore seemingly finds its origins in a 1935 report in *The New York Times* that a large live alligator was fished out of the sewer by youngsters on 123rd Street near the Harlem River. The reporter speculated it had escaped from a passing ship and entered the sewer from the river in search of warmth. A variant story was recalled by Sewer Commissioner Teddy May. Reported in 1959 by Robert Daley, it said that alligators in the two-foot range had been discovered in Manhattan sewers in the 1930s, but this infestation had been eradicated fully by 1937.

In his novel *V* (published in 1963 but set in the mid-1950s), writer Thomas Pynchon devoted an entire chapter to the alligator patrol at work in the New York City sewer system, building on May's account. Folklorist Loren Coleman judged that Pynchon "brought this tale into modern popular culture as no one before him had." The story continued to grow and to provide a subject for comment.

When Americans became conservation-minded, Asahel Cooper, Jr., of the Wyvern Club in New Orleans, suggested in 1972 rounding up the occupants of the New York sewers and using them to repopulate depleted marshlands. In 1974, Calvin Tomkins pled for misidentification in *The New Yorker,* insisting that "those long menacing objects are minisubs of uncertain origin, perhaps Bolivian." In 1980, the film *Alligator* appeared, starring in the title role a huge saurian named Ramone, who lived in a midwestern sewer. A second change of venue was suggested in 1990 when reporters for "Real New Orleans," a locally produced magazine-format television series, used the white alligators at Audubon Zoo in a segment devoted to "them sewer 'gators."

Folklorists began to investigate seriously in the late 1970s. Coleman discovered the *New York Times* article from 1935 that seems to have given birth to the legend; and in 1981, Jan Brunvand presented a thorough analysis. More recently Diane Ackerman debunked the myth in a *New Yorker* article of 1988, agreeing with prevailing scientific opinion that alligators could neither survive nor propagate in such an inhospitable subterranean environment. Peter Lippman provided those New York alligators with an imaginative escape route in his children's book of 1973,

The Great Escape, or The Sewer Story. In that charming fantasy, the sewer dwellers got together, settled on disguising themselves as tourists, and heading for Florida on a vacation charter flight. Equipped with parachutes, they intended to bail out over the Everglades.

As a footnote to the New York myth, alligators do come in various colors. Writers in the 1930s told of a "yellow" color phase, and albinos, or partial albinos, have been found (but only infrequently) since the 1920s onward. These albinistic saurians are generally almost white with a yellowish (or darker) mottling, and golden eyes. A very dark "black" alligator has been seen by the author on Lake Hatch, near Houma, Louisiana. In the 1980s, rare leucistic

FACING PAGE: NEW YORK LEGEND: COVER DRAWING BY ARTHUR GETZ, *THE NEW YORKER,* NOVEMBER 29, 1952. COPYRIGHT © 1952, 1980 *THE NEW YORKER* MAGAZINE, INC. COURTESY, WALTER WADE WELCH, NEW ORLEANS.

BELOW: LEUCISTIC ALLIGATOR.

alligators occurred in Louisiana. These unusual specimens are pure white—they look like walking patent leather—with normal dark eyes, and no patterning whatsoever.

As if all this wasn't enough to stamp the alligator's legend(s) deeply on the impressionable minds of the American public, cannibalism is occasionally seen among saurians. The very small number of fossil vertebrae and osteoscutes found at the Wannagan Creek Quarry excavation site in North Dakota suggested to Dr. Bruce Erickson that they might have disappeared because even ancient crocodilians may not have been adverse to devouring their next of kin. Mark Catesby noted among the alligators of the Carolinas as early as 1771 that "while young they are a prey, not only of ravenous fish, but of their own species."

Baron Cuvier, who repeated much of Catesby's information, recycled that tidbit as well, and it appeared in editions of Cuvier's works as late as the 1830s. A popular reading audience learned to be grateful for saurian cannibalism from the *Book of Reptiles,* published in London in 1835, because "The number of eggs produced by them [alligators] is so great, that if they were not subject to many casualties, the countries they inhabit would be completely overrun with them. The Alligator itself is also said to lessen the number of its progeny, by destroying many when very young." A French publication of 1883, *Histoire naturelle,* somewhat overdramatized Catesby's story by saying, "The smallest push into the thick bushes, where the large ones cannot penetrate and where they take cover from their murderous teeth."

By 1929, a federal researcher had collected stories of larger-scale intraspecies predation. Charles Hallock, we are told, recorded an eight-foot alligator in the maw of another. In 1928, F. M. Uhler saw a seven-foot alligator in the zoo at Sanford, Florida, "in the act of swallowing a smaller individual that measured about half its length. The smaller alligator was swallowed whole, but he could hear the bones being crushed by an occasional snap of the jaws."

By 1937, alligators of different sizes at the Luthi farm were segregated into separate pens, Katharine Daly explained, "as the larger eat the smaller when they grow hungry." Thomas Barbour knew in the mid-1940s that "by common reputation they are cannibals," which explained that hunters killed large old ones "because they were supposed to be destructive of younger and hence more valuable gators." In 1947, the Audubon Zoo in New Orleans suffered a repeat performance of the 1928 spectacle at the Sanford Zoo. The *Times-Picayune* mustered out a photographer in time to cover the event, running the picture of saurian chomping saurian over this grievously anthropomorphized caption: "Papa Alligator, arriving home and finding dinner not ready, eats the little woman instead."

The full extent of alligator cannibalism has not been seriously studied. It is known, according to the Baton Rouge *State-Times*, "that alligators [in captivity] are highly cannibalistic under crowded conditions. . . . This makes it imperative to keep their numbers in balance, accomplished by careful management." It also seems clear that adult alligators will eat very small ones encountered in the natural habitat, which may demonstrate nothing more than a somewhat indiscriminate selection of foodstuffs—anything that moves seems to be fair game, as long as it's of manageable size.

For over four hundred years, writers have argued about the relative dangerousness of the alligator to man. Many of the myths and legends grew up around this theme, or exploited it for vicarious emotional effect. Early European explorers, mentally preconditioned by myths and legends pertaining to crocodiles, called the alligator a "monster," and commented that it makes "sudden attacks on the unsuspecting." Crocodilelike voraciousness was attributed to the alligator by eighteenth-century colonists and visitors, who claimed it would attack "anything that comes within its reach." Others differentiated it from the crocodile by saying, "they attack men in the water, but never on land."

The more imaginative gave free reign to their descriptive powers. Early alleged attacks were reported anecdotally. DuMont de Montigny gave this account in the 1750s: "A soldier of the Company of the Indies was asleep one afternoon under a tree below Bayou St. John, when one of these animals caught him by the leg and dragged him into the water. Also, a young surgeon, experienced in his profession, named Aubert, brother of a jeweler of the same name living in Paris near the Palais [Royal], was bathing one day in the river, and was devoured by an alligator." In 1771, Mark Catesby wrote, "they cannot be more terrible in their aspect [appearance] than they are formidable and mischievous in their nature, sparing neither man nor beast."

Bartram's near-gothic 1794 account of his confrontation with alligators in Florida could well have served Mary Shelley as model when she composed *Frankenstein* only a few years later: "suddenly a huge alligator rushed out of the reeds, and with a tremendous roar came up, and darted as swift as an arrow under my boat, emerging upright on my lee quarter, with open jaws, and belching water and smoke that fell upon me like rain in a hurricane. I laid soundly about his head with my club, and beat him off; and after plunging and darting about my boat, he went off on a straight line through the water, seeming[ly] with the rapidity of lightning . . . ." Such versions caused others to draw misleading conclusions. J. F. D. Smith had already written in 1784, "they are a species of crocodile, and equally, if not more dangerous than those of the river Nile in Egypt; these also devouring men, oxen, or whatever else they can get within their horrid jaws."

Alligators found their defenders early on. Brickell wrote in 1737 that alligators "are never known to devour men in Carolina, but on the contrary, always strive to avoid them as much as they possibly can." A resurgence in defense of the alligator occurred in the early nineteenth century during a time when alligator populations were drastically declining. In 1827, Williams reported this fact concerning West Floridian alligators: "nor have they been known, in this country, to injure any human being"; and the naturalist J. J. Audubon observed, "they are afraid of man if he shows no fear of these reptiles." Both Timothy Flint and Captain Alexander noted, however, that alligators had no objection to some rather audacious child snatching.

Detractors continued to abound. With more dramatic effect than veracity, the intrepid Mrs. Frances Trollope claimed that a settler, awakened by noise in the night, "beheld the relics of three of his children scattered over the floor, and an enormous crocodile [*sic*], with several young ones around her, occupied in devouring the remnants of their horrid meal." The settler ran for help but returned too late, finding "the wife and her two babes lay mangled on their bloody bed." Remington Kellog recognized that these tales had been reduced to formula writing, as he expressed in 1929: "Conflicting and in many cases unreliable versions of alligators killing human beings appear in books by early travelers in the Southern States. The sympathy of the reader is gained for the victim by a recital of horrible and gruesome details, as is the case in Mrs. Trollope's story. . . ."

It is apparent that the formula was successful. Proof lies in the similar horror stories circulated by word-of-mouth and in the popular press. An especially striking example appeared in the *Chicago Tribune* in 1900. The heroine was Miss Savannah Walston, described as "a pretty Texas girl," from the small town of Tunis on Bayou Sarah, which sounds a great deal like a twisted reference to Bayou Sarah, which passes through the Tunica hills of Louisiana (noting that a cursory examination of turn-of-the-century Texas maps located neither Tunis nor Bayou Sarah in that state). She and her mother were alleged to have been attacked by two large alligators that barged into a bedroom in the middle of the night. A young black boy ran in to see what was the matter as the two women stood on the bed, preparing to fend off the invaders. He stumbled over one, falling into the jaws of the other, and "The women were helpless to defend the unfortunate little African. The monster crushed the little negro's head between its jaws, and the two women could plainly see the child's blood streaming over the carpet." Savannah, who had seen her brother use a gun, managed to dodge the 'gators long enough to grab one, and luckily she aimed for the eyes in her literal "maiden" shot. Such tabloid journalism made no-risk vicarious thrills available to a turn-of-the-century reading public. We feel sure that a romp through the back issues of the *National Enquirer* and its kind would yield a similar harvest.

All of these tales and the diverse opinions they supported were repeated in variant versions until the 1920s, when the need for alligator conservation became ever more apparent. Karl Schmidt maintained, "Human beings are rarely attacked by alligators." In 1929, Remington Kellog stated that the alligator defended itself when threatened, and in 1933 Percy Viosca, Jr., added that it would also protect its nest and young.

Isolated attacks continued to occur, especially in Louisiana and Florida. They were seriously investigated by T. C. Hines and K. D. Keenlyne in the 1970s, as alligator populations increased because of protective legislation and excellent resource-management programs. They concluded that as alligator numbers increased and expanding human populations began to compete for the same residential territory, "provoked" attacks were on the upswing, abetted by the circulation of incorrect information that alligators were harmless. Furthermore, "unprovoked" attacks did occasionally happen when alligators were hard-pressed by hunger.

Among the most unsettlingly graphic of recent stories is that of Kermit George, Jr., of Florala, Alabama. In July 1986, George was cycling through the Conecuh National Forest near the Florida-Alabama state line. It was a hot southern summer, and understandably, he stopped at a roped-off swimming area to cool down. In chest-deep wate[r] the forty-two-year-old man was attacked by an eleven-and-a-half-foot alligator, which bit off his arm. He later brought suit against the federal government. The case was settled in 1990, when U.S. District Judge Robert Varner in Montgomery, Alabama, awarded George $772,807 in literal "damages," to be paid by the U.S. National Forest Service. The federal agency was found liable because it had not posted warning signs, despite an established history of complaints about alligators in the forest.

It must be stated that an adult alligator is a large and powerful predatory reptile that does not necessarily distinguish between man and other edible prey. Some scientists have speculated that between the eighteenth and twentieth centuries, alligators came to recognize man as a dangerous foe rather than as a potential meal, and modified their aggressive behavior. Irresponsible authors of children's literature often have portrayed the alligator as a cute and cuddly creature, investing children (the most vulnerable of possible human alligator victims) with false and potentially dangerous impressions. Caution should always be exercised by persons confronting alligators or trespassing in alligator habitat regardless of what tales may be in current circulation. Will Branan agreed in 1940, being "constitutionally and temperamentally opposed to a journey through its digestive tract, however in[teres]ting and exciting that experience mi[ght] ...

... , frequently based on partial truths ...ften changing and growing by ...sion over time (depending on the ...raconteur), do reach an enormous ...bable that every reader of this ...[w]n't think of peeking between its ...e of the tales that have been ...[ne]w pages. Their effect has been ...p[...] for the alligator in the ...po[...] recognized, the pervasive ...inf[...]s subconsciously affected the[...]about alligators. It is good to be[...]orm opinions or draw concl[...] southern saurian.

CHAPTER TWO

THE GREAT AGE OF DISCOVERY

OR HOW TO TELL AN ALLIGATOR FROM A CROCODILE IN SIXTY-FIVE EASY LESSONS

"Those who first attempted serious studies of alligators," wrote Herbert Zim, "had problems in sifting out the facts. Details . . . were not easy to observe first hand. Scientists often did not have enough experience in the field to know if the reports from hunters and local people were true. Data . . . often included legends and half-truths." In addition, Darwin had not yet intervened with his theory of evolution, and many did not question religious teachings (of whatever faith) of their day. The "scientific method" was still in its infancy and was neither widely nor universally applied.

Early observers at first actually thought they were seeing crocodiles, and continued to use that word for literally centuries. Sixteenth-century Spanish explorers christened the animal "*el lagarto*," meaning "the lizard." The Spanish phrase, corrupted into other languages, including English, became *alligator*. The preconception that the animal was a crocodile, however, saddled scientists with many incorrect assumptions about size, behavior, anatomy, and other aspects of the new but unrecognized species.

By attributing to it the new legends (albeit often unrecognized) associated with the Nile crocodile, and appending the legends that untrained field observers reported as truths about the North American alligator, scientists themselves sometimes unwittingly compounded fact with fiction. Their story is a tale of collecting and shipping hides, pickled alligators (in barrels of whiskey or rum), or live alligators (generally crated) to laboratories and menageries and studying them to determine just how to separate them from the crocodiles, if indeed that should be

FACING PAGE: "PIKE-MUZZLED CAIMAN." HAND-TINTED LITHO-GRAPH FROM *THE ANIMAL KINGDOM*, VOL. 9, BY BARON CUVIER, 1831.

done, as well as investigating habitat, behavior, life history, and related subjects. This was a slow process: it required nearly three hundred years.

By intertwining the various traveler's accounts, scientific observations, and fanciful descriptions, it is possible to re-create something of the bizarre picture projected of the alligator and the excitement of discovery as knowledge was simultaneously advanced and hindered by the efforts and arguments of those authors over a period of three and a half centuries. These pioneers might well have

taken as their motto the opening verse from the Book of Job, XLI: "I will not conceal his parts, nor his power, nor his comely proportions." That biblical text continues to describe the Leviathan, which some identified as an alligator/crocodile: "His scales are his pride, shut up together as a closed seal. . . . When he raiseth up himself, the mighty are afraid . . . he is a king over all the children of pride."

Among the earliest scientific specimens of the North American alligator sent to Europe for study was one taken

A llagatto. This being but one moneth old was 3 foote . 4 . ynches in length . and lyue in water .

72

in French Florida, a colony on the Florida–South Carolina coast, in 1564. This Renaissance alligator was described in a letter as "shaped like a lizard; but it has joints like a person with five toes on its front feet and four on its hind feet. Its skin is being sent to France. . . ." This initiated French knowledge of the North American alligator and efforts to describe, classify, and study its physiognomy and natural history. Twenty-two years later, de Laudonnière reported from the same location so many alligators that "often-times in swimming men are assayled by them," establishing supposed dangerous man-eating characteristics in the growing French body of alligator knowledge.

Jacques LeMoyne de Morgues, also writing from French Florida, called the alligator a "monster" and said that "they make such a frightful noise that it can be heard for half a mile." This 1591 remark is a particularly early mention of "bellowing," the loudest vocalization made by the alligator. Its complete function—territorial defense, mating call, long-distance communication—is still not fully understood. Later, writers of the eighteenth century compared the noise to the bellowing of a bull, and said it was just as loud.

Well-to-do and better-educated European gentlemen had been assembling natural-history collections since the Renaissance. These classical amateurs, or knowledgeable enthusiasts, used them both for serious study and to impress others with their erudition. Called "cabinets of curiosities," such protomuseums became the homes of alligator hides and stuffed or pickled animals. There they were frequently ranged with comparative examples of other crocodilians

from Africa and even Asia, and were generally confused with caimans from South and Central America. Such private collections were accumulated until the nineteenth century, when they often became the basis for public or university natural-history museums.

In the late seventeenth century, French explorers began to describe alligators in Louisiana. The logbook of Iberville's expedition of 1699 recorded sightings of "crocodiles," often of "prodigious size." About 1700, Dr. Bennet Dowler reported, "An alligator was sent to Louis XIV, [and] was examined by the French *savans,* who were quite astonished at not finding the Herodotian ears, though it is doubtful whether they believed their own senses in opposition to so great an authority." Dowler was referring to the inconspicuous, movable skin of the ear slits of crocodiles that the ancient historian Herodotus had said the Egyptians decorated with precious ornaments, leading later readers to think he meant large protruding ears. In fact, Dowler, writing in 1846, may have mistaken the genuine crocodile sent to Louis XIV in 1681 for this "alligator." Dowler's conclusions, based in part on his own historic research, show that he found no significant difference between the two animals.

Until the mid-eighteenth century, little new information became available. In 1751, the Diderot *Encyclopédie* (it was issued volume by volume over several years) introduced the word *alligator,* defining it as a "species of crocodile in the West Indies; it is up to 18 feet in length . . . it is an amphibian. It diffuses a strong odor of musk, which impregnates the air and water for a great

"SPECIES OF CROCODILE CALLED ALLIGATOR." ENGRAVING FROM A DRAWING MADE IN LONDON, 1739, FROM *HISTOIRE GÉNÉRALE DES VOYAGES*, PARIS, 1746.

FACING PAGE: "THE ALLIGATOR (*LACERTA CROCODYLUS*)." HAND-COLORED ENGRAVING FROM *THE NATURAL HISTORY OF CAROLINA, FLORIDA & THE BAHAMA ISLANDS* BY MARK CATESBY, 1771.

distance." Musk, from glands beneath the jaw and near the tail, had not been widely known until this publication. The function of distinctive alligator musk remains speculative, despite recent detailed studies. At the time this volume of the *Encyclopédie* appeared, the American Gulf Coast, located within the extended Caribbean Basin, was generally lumped with the West Indies; the *Encyclopédie* observations were thought, therefore, to apply to Louisiana, Mississippi, Alabama, and Florida, as well as to the islands. *Alligator* became more widely used after this publication, although the word *crocodile* remained popular and in incorrect usage for another half century.

DuMont de Montigny presented his alligator observations in 1753, adding to the stock of inaccurate data such items as "its ribs are placed lengthwise which keeps it from turning easily: where the head leads, the rest of the body must follow. . . . There are some of these animals twenty-five feet long and five or six thick. . . . If a bull comes to drink near it, the alligator catches him by the foot, drags him into the water, drowns him, and has a feast."

Anatomical errors concerning the alligator's neck, spine, ribs, and jaws proliferated as such remarks were repeated by later writers. Some even advised running in zigzag patterns to escape an alligator's attack because of its alleged inability to turn. Tracing such quasilegends is an entertaining illustration of the inaccurate field data upon which early scientists based erroneous statements that the public accepted as fact for centuries.

Remarks concerning the alligator's jaws are equally enlightening. Ancient crocodile misobservations, transferred to alligators by Europeans, are to blame. Herodotus, according to *Harper's New Monthly Magazine*, first gave voice to the misconception, "noticing that the crocodile invariable raised its head when opening its mouth, conceived the idea that it moved its upper jaw 'down on its lower one.' " He was followed in error by Pliny, who noted, "The crocodile only moveth the upper jaw or mandible, wherewith he biteth hard."

Father du Ru, on the Mississippi River in the year 1700, saw his first alligator and wrote in his journal, "I remarked as the Benedictines had observed in their *Saint Augustine*, that the jaws of this animal move equally." The misconception that either both move, or that only the upper moves, was repeated throughout the entire eighteenth century. As it ended, William Bartram wrote in 1794, "only the upper jaw moves, which they raise almost perpendicular, so as to form a right angle with the lower one." As the next century opened, Thomas Ashe came very close to plagiarism in 1808 by saying, "the upper jaw only moves, and this they raise so as to form a right angle with the lower one."

Only when taxonomists got to work was the true situation disclosed. Dr. Dowler described his methods in 1846, writing, "I have for hours forced the jaws asunder by levers . . . ." And what he found was that the upper jaw is part and parcel of the skull, while the movable lower jaw is hinged to it. *Harper's New Monthly Magazine* popularized

"CROCODIL[E]."
ENGRAVING FROM
*HISTOIRE DE LA
LOUISIANE* BY
ANTOINE SIMON
LEPAGE DU PRATZ,
1758.

the new knowledge in 1855: "anatomy proves that the lower jaw, as in all animals, alone moves in a socket." Fully a century later, Ezra Adams voiced an explanation for Herodotus's original error: "the alligator's jaw is 'hinged' on the bottom, but *appears* [emphasis added] to be [hinged] on the top because he is on the ground and must raise his head enough to open his mouth." More than a millennium separated their writings.

In 1754, the year following DuMont de Montigny's exposé, another volume of the *Encyclopédie* went to press, which included the alphabetical *C* listing encompassing *crocodile*. In that article, it was said that "In the Antilles the Crocodile is called cayman . . . the skin of the back resists the shot of a musket with a double charge. . . . It runs rather fast on land, but only in a straight line . . . the Crocodiles which are in fresh water have an odor of musk. . . . " It went on to note camouflage (resemblance to a dead log), but failed to distinguish caimans from alligators.

While eighteenth-century guns did not have the force of modern rifles, alligators were not so heavily armored as to be impenetrable. Such references established the reputation of their natural defenses, and were frequently repeated. They may have been founded on Job's Leviathan. That biblical chimera had scales, "shut up together as with a closed seal. One is so near to another, that no air can come between them. They are joined one to another, they stick together, that they cannot be sundered. . . . " Except for the final phrase, the description could well be of an alligator's hide.

The armored alligator's resistance to man-made projectiles was upheld for over a century. De la Coudrenière told serious scientific readers of the *Journal de physique* in 1782 that "to kill it with a rifle ball the gun must be aimed at the flanks or the eyes . . . ." Even Daudin reported in 1803 that many globe-trotters of the day had observed crocodilian skins to be "ordinarily bullet-proof, as long as the shot was not made at close range or the gun super-charged [with powder]."

Anecdote began to replace ex cathedra pronouncement in the early nineteenth century. Herman Ehrenberg went up the Red River on a steamboat in 1835, shooting at alligators along the way, "Although our bullets merely glanced off their stiff bone-plated hides . . . ."

Dr. Bennet Dowler examined alligator hide in 1846 and said, "I have found no difficulty in dividing it in the living state, and that too, with the common lancet, the edge of which was not injured or blunted by the operation. Here, at least, the maxim, that what every body [*sic*] says, must be true, fails completely." *Brewster's Encyclopedia*, though, seemingly contradicted him, telling the public that "Several leaden bullets, even when they penetrate, are sometimes insufficient to kill, unless they reach the brain, the spine, or some of the large blood vessels. Iron balls are recommended." The difference lay not in the material from which the bullet was made but, rather, in where the bullet lodged. *Brewster's* was correct about the placement but misleading about the substance.

It wasn't until the early twentieth century that scientists settled the matter. In 1915, the team of Wright and Funkhouser, according to Karl Schmidt, determined "The common supposition that the skin of an alligator will turn the bullet of a gun is, of course, unfounded." Guns, as Raymond Ditmars implied in 1920, had undergone many technological changes in the interim between those eighteenth-century observations and this twentieth-century determination.

Returning to the eighteenth century, one remembers that LePage du Pratz published his *Natural History of Louisiana* in 1758, noting, "the crocodile [*sic*] is very common in the St. Louis [Mississippi] River," and cited specimens of nineteen and twenty-two feet in length. He related an unusual alligator practice of ambushing fish by hiding in a dark cavern under the bank of a fast-moving stream where fish, seeking calm water, could not see the adversary in its obscure retreat and unwittingly became its next meal. He did find a difference in the various American saurian cousins, saying, "I can assure that the crocodiles [*sic*] of Louisiana are without doubt of another species than those of other regions," because they did not follow established behavior patterns for those of the Nile. He concluded, "if they are dangerous, it is only in the water . . .

where they have great agility; one can, in this case, take his precautions."

The Diderot *Encyclopédie*, that continuing compendium meant to encompass all eighteenth-century knowledge, brought out a volume of illustrations in 1768. The "crocodile" it depicts "was only twelve feet in length and had been brought from America. It perfectly resembles the crocodile of the Nile." During this time, the Acadians made their famous migration from Canada to Louisiana, bringing another French-speaking element to the colonial population. The colony, however, had become an official Spanish possession. The Spaniards had their own perfectly

"CROCODILE" AND "HATCHING EGG." ENGRAVED DETAILS, FIGURES 1 AND 2, PLATE XXVII, VOL. VI (PLATES), DIDEROT *ENCYCLOPÉDIE*, 1768.

good word, *el lagarto*, but instead of using it in Louisiana for the alligator, they chose *cocodrillo*, a variant of *crocodile*. To make matters worse, the newly arrived Acadians, who had both *crocodile* and *alligator* at their linguistic disposal, sought to emulate their governors, and corrupted *cocodrillo* into *cocodrie*. That term remains in Cajun use today, and also designates many lakes and bayous—places that were known as alligator territory.

Mark Catesby, writing in 1771 of the fauna of the Carolinas, was none too detailed in his taxonomy, finding that by then alligators were "often observed and described," thus relieving him of the responsibility "to be so particular in its description." He also accepted the African crocodile as an alligator, compounding an already rampant confusion. Catesby was concerned with the alligator's range, which extended "as far as the River Neus in North Carolina, in the latitude of about 33 [degrees], beyond which I have never heard of any." Remarks on the natural range of the alligator would soon become commonplace in the works that appeared about them.

Six years later, Jean-Bernard Bossu didn't do much to help matters. Having read (and copiously borrowed from) much of the earlier literature, he reinforced old legends and inaccuracies. Bison, after drowning, were dragged to the banks of streams to be eaten, "because these amphibians [*sic*] have such big mouths that they would fill themselves with water if they opened them." Actually, alligators have valved throats, allowing them to operate their jaws when submerged. Bossu called them *crocodiles* and *caimans* and suggested that bullet holes in their hides became filled with slime, mud, and stray seeds, resulting in strange-looking animals growing thickets on their backs. He added, "Moreover it is known that *caimans* are like rocks . . . all of a piece, unable to look behind or lean back like quadrupeds."

It was at this time that Carolus Linnaeus (Carl von Linné) published the twelfth edition of his *Systema naturae,* which first had appeared in 1735, a monumental work providing the foundation for biological classification as we know it today. Apparently, the Swedish scientist based his alligator entry on misinformation then in circulation. "He seems to have regarded it but as a variety of the Nilotic crocodile, in which opinion he was followed by many naturalists of the time," assessed Dr. John Holbrook, who issued his own alligator study in 1842.

J. F. D. Smith, writing in 1784, labeled alligators as "a species of the crocodile, and equally, if not more dangerous than those of the river Nile in Egypt. . . . " Shortly afterward, the French Count de Lacépède contributed to current, later, and continuing confusion, joining the taxonomists who were not as accurate in their observations as they might have been or did not utilize significant criteria or recognize critical features during their examinations of specimens. This led C. C. Robin to write in 1807, "it [the alligator] is nothing less than the true species of crocodile: which Monsieur de Lacépède has proved, by the comparison of individuals come from these [Louisiana] regions with others from the bank[s] of the Nile." De Lacépède himself found "numerous contradictions" in the previous literature, but he asserted, "all true crocodiles have five toes on the front feet, four webbed toes on the hind feet, and only have claws on the three inner toes of each foot."

De Lacépède then proceeded to confuse terminology by proclaiming, "The first [of de Lacépède's self-designated three species of crocodiles] is the ordinary or true crocodile, which inhabits the banks of the Nile; it is called *alligator,* primarily in Africa. . . . The crocodiles of America have been given the name *caiman* . . . which was borrowed from the Indians." *Cayman,* or *caiman* actually seems to have been of African origin, a word brought to the New World by slaves, who quickly used it to designate the crocodilians of the West Indian islands to which they had been shanghaied. De Lacépède continued: "With great care we have compared several of these of different ages with the crocodiles of the Nile, and we have come to believe that they are absolutely of the same species . . . they show no remarkable difference that cannot be attributed to the influence of climate. In effect, if their muzzles are a little less elongated, they do not differ sufficiently in their abridgement . . . to cause the caimans to constitute a distinct species. . . . The crocodile of the Nile and those of America thus form only one species. . . . "

Through the remainder of the century, popular writers and travelers continued to repeat each other's errors. At least by century's end, the majority of English-language authors were calling them alligators, although in 1794 William Bartram used the terms interchangeably, saying in one paragraph, "This crocodile," and in another, "the subtle greedy alligator."

Bartram's version certainly wins, hands down, any contest for colorful alligator writing, with such passages as: "the alligators were in such incredible numbers, and so close together from shore to shore, that it would have been easy to have walked across on their heads." His description was of alligators congregated in the shallows, all lying in wait with their mouths open to collect schools of fish moving with tidal change in the coastal stream. This vivid image so inspired a later screenwriter that it was actually attempted, without much success, using tethered saurians in the James Bond film *Live and Let Die.* Despite weights and lines, the rented crocodilians cut up so badly in protest of their bondage and ill treatment that the walk-on-water stuntman was injured and the botched scene made little sense in the completed movie.

Although Bartram erred with regard to the hinging of the alligator's jaw, as had many before him, he did note that "in the lower jaws are holes opposite these [large conical upper] teeth, to receive them." He got the placement wrong. The teeth about which he wrote are in the lower jaw, and the holes are above. This is a distinguishing characteristic separating alligators (with such pits) from crocodiles (with teeth exposed in grooves on the outer

THE CAYMAN CROCODILE AND ITS EGG. DETAIL, ENGRAVING FROM *OEUVRES DE COMTE DE LACÉPÈDE, COMPRENANT L'HISTOIRE NATURELLE DES QUADRUPÈDES, DES SERPENS, DES POISSONS ET DES CÉTACÉS. . .* VOL. I BY BERNARD GERMAIN ETIENNE DELAVILLE, COUNT DE LACÉPÈDE, 1836 (FIRST PUBLISHED 1788?).

surface of closed jaws). Impressionable readers were agape at his description of bellowing: "It most resembles heavy distant thunder, not only shaking the air and water, but causing the earth to tremble; and when hundreds and thousands are roaring at the same time, you can scarcely be persuaded, but that the whole globe is violently and dangerously agitated."

Ellicott, in 1800, wanted to determine whether "stomach stones" really existed. "For this purpose," he recorded, "two Alligators of about eight or nine feet in length were taken and opened." He found the sought-after gastroliths made from pine knots by the action of digestive juices and gastric grinding, and he concluded, "So far the report appears to be founded in fact; but whether these substances were swallowed on account of their tedious digestion . . . or to prevent the collapse of the coats of the stomach [during winter torpor], or by accident owing to their voracious manner . . . is difficult to determine." Even today, the function of "stomach stones" is not fully understood.

The beginning of the nineteenth century brought new breakthroughs in the alligator-crocodile controversy, and later researchers were grateful. "It is to [Baron] Cuvier that we owe nearly all that is worth knowing on this subject," wrote Dr. Holbrook; "it was he who first observed the differences of the Crocodiles of the old and new world . . . he recognized the peculiarly shaped head of the alligator— 'flat and resembling that of the pike,' and seems to have regarded it as distinct from the South American animal."

Another appreciative French analyst was François-Marie Daudin. By 1803, he had begun to pull things together by comparing all the written accounts and scientific specimens he could find. "If, as I think," he wrote, "the Florida crocodile is the same as that of the Mississippi, it must be identified with the very incomplete description that Williams [sic] Bartram has given of it. . . . " Daudin was exercising just critical judgment; Bartram's travel account of Florida was to be admired more for drama than accuracy. European-based scientists such as Daudin, however, had to take what was available in terms of eyewitness testimony and evaluate it as best they could.

The authors Daudin cited included Bosc, Cuvier, Michaux, Catesby (whose "crocodile" Daudin considered "badly drawn") and de la Coudrenière. From their accounts, the specimens they sent to Europe, the analyses of other scientists, and his own observations, Daudin began to separate the "Mississippi" crocodile from the caimans of other New World regions. He wrote: "it differs principally because its muzzle is a little wider, more flattened and similar from above to that of a pike [the fish]; . . . on its nape it has a single shield composed of four oval plates, ridged and arranged in a square. It is by these characteristics that the Mississippi crocodile differs. . . . " He agreed with Cuvier, saying, "only more numerous observations, made on a greater number of specimens will tell us if this crocodile is of a different species. . . . " Daudin corrected the earlier error concerning the jaws: "Its lower jaw is the only movable one." He also noted the alignment of the teeth, which separates alligators from crocodiles.

Daudin was correct in applying a more stringent

"scientific method" to his work, and he also was correct in identifying a separate species. His achievement is honored by the full scientific name of the American alligator: "*Alligator mississippiensis* daudin," although he himself called it *Crocodilus Mississippiensis.* Even in the nineteenth century, it was still tough getting those Frenchmen to say *alligator.*

Cuvier hadn't had his last say yet, either. Holbrook's copious praise continued: "having completed (1807) his most interesting observations on this family of animals [Cuvier] now described the Alligator as a new species . . . under the name 'Alligator lucius,' from the shape of the head resembling that of the common pike of Europe (Esox lucius)." In fact, the common term *pike-headed caiman* was put into play by many later writers as an alternative for *alligator.*

Among the old school was C. C. Robin, who persisted in calling the animal a *crocodile* or *caiman,* when he published his Louisiana travelogue in 1807. Since the alligator is the most powerful predator in its usual habitat, Robin found that "Having only to exercise empire on agile animals, weak in comparison to it, it has not been endowed with the hardiness and courage for combat, nor with the weapons correct for audacious attack." He repeated eighteenth-century errors concerning articulations of neck and jaw, and noted the alligator's inability to chew, having "only the faculty of harpooning its prey," which it must swallow in large pieces.

Robin defined the geographic range of his "crocodile" as from the thirty-fourth to thirty-fifth degrees of latitude. In 1810, Christian Schultz observed, "It [the Arkansas River] likewise seems to be a dividing line between the upper and lower climates; as the alligator is seldom seen higher up than this river, and at no time numerous." A thorough dissection of one specimen failed to locate its musk glands, and Schultz expressed the "opinion that it [musk] is diffused through the whole system of the animal." "Stomach stones," he interpreted as debris that stuck to prey, inadvertently swallowed because the alligator "never stops to separate the one from the other, but swallows the whole."

Renowned ornithologist John J. Audubon got into the act on several occasions, notably sending specimen alligators to colleagues for study. In 1821, he obtained a "bagful" of babies to be sent to such a researcher in New York. Alligators also contributed to his own work. He wrote that while on the St. John's River in Florida, he shot a "monstrous fellow," because he was "desirous of obtaining him to make an accurate drawing of his head . . . ." The whooping crane in his famed *Birds of America* is shown, accurately, eating baby alligators. While in England, working to have the *Birds of America* published, Audubon wrote to his close friend the Rev. John Bachman of Charleston: "Try to study the Habits of Alligators, the time of their propagation, number of eggs, form of the Nests &c &c &c—I long to possess all respecting this reptile (amphibian) for my article on the *Wood Ibis* and Sand Hill Crane, for it will make a fine picture on paper. . . ."

Royal alligators were usually kept in royal menageries, or zoos, where they were available for public as well as scientific consultation. Audubon might well have seen the

alligator of George IV, which was housed at London's Tower Menagerie. E. T. Bennet said of it: "Our specimen was apparently very young, not measuring more than three feet in length; but during two years that it was kept in the Menagerie it was not observed to have at all increased in size. It was fed once a week upon raw beef."

Bennet was also clear and exact in his separation of the alligator from the crocodile: "The alligator constitutes a natural subdivision of the genus (*Lacerta,* from Linnaeus) in which the snout is broad, blunt and less produced [*sic,* possibly "pronounced"?] than in the true Crocodiles; the fourth tooth on each side of the lower jaw enters a hole in the upper jaw when the mouth is closed; and the toes are only half-webbed. They appear to be only natives of America." Europeans had not yet studied and classified the Chinese alligator, so this statement was true within the limits of then-current knowledge.

Scientific specimens sometimes got their owners into trouble, and the nineteenth century was no less anecdotal in its approach than the eighteenth had been. General Power, dining with B. E. Hill about 1836, made the unexpected acquaintance of a preserved specimen when relish bottles were confused: "helping himself to the expected piccalilly, [he] discovered, to his extreme horror, that he had fished up a young alligator, whose juvenile form after having been immersed in rum for several days, now lay stiff and sprawling on the plate of the highly-offended general. . . . Good feeling was, however, shortly restored, and the evening passed away pleasantly."

The peregrinations of such specimens was also of

interest. Improved transportation during the nineteenth century allowed animals to be shipped relatively quickly, and arrive still living. This impact of technology on biology was dramatically related by an anonymous contributor to *Harper's New Monthly Magazine*, which recorded the mid-nineteenth-century transport of live specimens from Concordia Parish, Louisiana, to the vicinity of Gottingen, Germany, for a researcher "desirous of obtaining a living specimen of the *Crocodilus Mississippiensis* [cheers for Daudin!], for the benefit of science, by the better understanding of its habits and anatomy." The emigrating 'gators, with the aid of visas obtained "through different consuls . . . for safe conveyance . . . were simply secured in boxes affording plenty of air, and in this condition started on their travels. By the aid of steamboats, ships and rail-cars, they finally, after various adventures through the long period of nearly five months, in good health reached the destined owner. . . ."

Medical practitioners began to take the lead in alligator research in the United States, and to minutely investigate taxonomy. Dr. Holbrook became so specific as to say of alligators in 1842: "the opening[s] of the nostrils are superior near the snout, and directed forwards and upwards; and from the earliest moment, as was observed by Cuvier, are separated from each other by a bony plate, which happens in no other of the Crocodile family."

Shortly afterward, New Orleans physician and professor of medicine Dr. Bennet Dowler made significant contributions to the knowledge of alligator anatomy in 1846, "taken from five of these animals placed at my

disposal . . . ." He was not disposed, however, to separate the alligators from the crocodiles: "Even those naturalists who have labored most to establish a difference, have admitted directly or indirectly, that there is none of a radical character." Dr. Dowler wished to "leave the question of scientific classification open, as it ought to be, until vague and contradictory descriptions shall be replaced by exact observations." His opinion was popularized in *Harper's New Monthly Magazine* by the correspondent who had tracked the Concordia Parish 'gators to their German destination: "The idea is very general that there is a radical difference between the crocodile and the alligator; but such is not the case. The inhabitant of the East is the same as his prototype of the Western world."

Cuvier's designation, *Alligator lucius*, also remained in vogue. As late as the 1880s, C. G. Wheeler could state quite inaccurately, "American alligator. 'Alligator lucius.' Native of Southern and Central America . . . malicious and dangerous. Rounder head [than other crocodilians], short, blunt snout. Musky smell. Live in large herds, rendering the vicinity unsafe [shades of Bartram!]. . . . The head of those in the United States nearly resembles [illustration] No. 8 [which is of the Nile crocodile!]."

At about the same time, another Louisiana alligator departed for Washington, D. C., John Avery shipped a seventeen-foot specimen to the Smithsonian in 1886 "as the authorities of that institution had requested some member of my family to secure for them a very large alligator. This alligator was put on deck of one of the Morgan line steamers going to Philadelphia. During the trip up, there

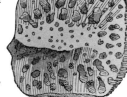

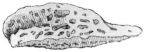

ANATOMY OF THE SCUTE: "OSSEOUS PLATE OF THE ALLIGATOR'S SKIN." LINE DRAWING IN "CONTRIBUTIONS TO THE NATURAL HISTORY OF THE ALLIGATOR," BY DR. BENNET DOWLER, OFFPRINT FROM *NEW ORLEANS MEDICAL AND SURGICAL JOURNAL*, NOVEMBER 1846.

"HEADS OF
ALLIGATOR AND
AMERICAN CROCO-
DILE." PHOTO-
GRAPH FROM *THE
ALLIGATOR AND
ITS ALLIES* BY
A. M. REESE, 1915.

BELOW:
CROSS SECTION OF
CROCODILIAN
TOOTH. LINE
DRAWING FROM *THE
ALLIGATOR AND
ITS ALLIES* BY A.M.
REESE, 1915.

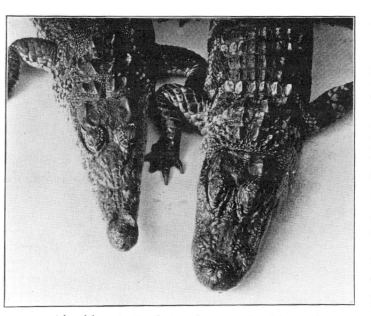

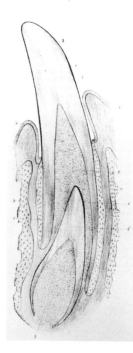

was considerable painting being done on the ship, and one of the sailors poured part of a can of green paint over the alligator's back, rubbing it in with his brush. The alligator died and was thrown overboard before reaching its destination."

During this period, the "alligator farm" developed, as did the late-Victorian craze for "pet" baby alligators. Some travelers demanded and got larger live specimens. This led to some entertaining confusion concerning the alligator's full geographic range, although it had been pretty well established much earlier. Isolated escapees, jettisoned "pets," and rare venturesome specimens who exceeded their normal range received considerable coverage in the Victorian press. Remington Kellog said that in 1885, "alligators were reported to have come up the Arkansas River as far north as Wichita, " but he assured his readers that "they were undoubtedly rare stragglers in Kansas." The *Chicago Citizen* told the Windy City that in 1892 a five-footer was "found near the bank of Rock River, at Janesville, Wis., frozen to death."

Seven years later, a three-footer "was caught in Mile Run Brook, near New Brunswick, N.J.," according to Kellog, "and on August 22, 1901, an alligator 3 feet 9 inches in length was found in the cellar of a house in Jersey City." In 1926, the Garden State was inundated with sauntering saurians, which, as Kellog reported, resulted in "the frightening of New Jersey bathers . . . by alligators of some size." That same year, seven aberrant alligators, from very small to four feet in length, "were captured in the Potomac River near Washington, D. C." Others have been reported from the Pacific Northwest and various locales near the U.S.–Canadian border, where fossils of some of the alligator's ancient and more distant ancestors have been found. Most were probably "pets" that owners loosed when they grew too large or too cantankerous for in-home housing. The truth of the matter, well expressed by Karl Schmidt, is that "The American Alligator is found from the Rio Grande, in Texas, in the streams and bayous of the Gulf coastal plain, throughout Florida, and in the Atlantic coastal plain north to North Carolina. In the Mississippi, it ranges northward as far as the Red River."

While the nineteenth century waned, correct information waxed. By 1897, R. W. Shufeldt could categorically announce, "We may state here that the alligator and the crocodile are distinctly different structurally." He supported this allegation (pardon the pun) by enumerating divergences in the septum, arrangement of the teeth, webbing of the toes, and the skin of the rear leg (fringed in the crocodile, smooth in the alligator) to prove his contention.

The early alligator farms developed as tourist attractions during these last years of the nineteenth century and made a successful business of supplying specimen alligators for a variety of purposes. Karl Schmidt said that "the first farms where alligators were kept, were established primarily to accustom them to captivity and to taking food, preparatory to shipping them to zoological gardens, aquariums and circuses." Turn-of-the-century alligator hunters found the same market. Clifton Johnson wrote in 1906, "There was a ready sale from them in New Orleans to ship to zoos and to whoever [*sic*] had a fancy for owning one of these grotesque quadrupeds."

Raymond Ditmars, among the deans of early twentieth-century alligator studies, summarized the alligator-versus-crocodile question in 1910 by saying, "many regard it as imperative . . . to learn the points distinguishing an 'alligator' from a 'crocodile.' And many have been the answers to the question, prepared in exhaustive fashion that causes the brain to whirl in an endeavor to assimilate the discussion." Then, however, he inventoried all the observable differences noted by earlier scientists. He was followed quickly by Albert Reese in 1915, who recited what had become a virtual litany of distinguishing characteristics.

Schmidt, at the Field Museum of Natural History in Chicago, provided one of the best of the early twentieth-century alligator descriptions in 1922, indicating evolutionary refinements fitting the alligator to its habitat, including closable ears, throat valves, and the like. It was a true wildlife biologist's contribution, applying scientific method to careful observation and largely accurate field data. Inadequacies in available information were acknowledged in the 1920s as professional biologists began to study and manage the nation's natural resources more carefully. Stanley Clisby Arthur called for greater detail in 1928: "a new life history survey should be made, which will very materially add to our sum of knowledge regarding this picturesque inhabitant of our swamps and prairies."

That call was answered by E. A. McIlhenny of Avery Island, Louisiana. In 1934, he wrote *The Alligator's Life History,* a compilation of information based on a lifetime of acute observation and note taking in and around his Iberia Parish home. It has served as an accepted reference and departure point for many alligator biological and behavioral studies undertaken since that time.

These pioneers in wildlife biology—explorers and travelers who left us logs of their journeys; popular writers who entertained and educated two centuries; early naturalists and laboratory scientists who undertook ever-more exacting studies—all contributed to the evolution of both real knowledge and popular opinion generated about alligators from the late Renaissance to the Great Depression. Often their reporting included much more than has been recounted here, encompassing life cycle, reproduction, parenting, and other topics of true scientific, biological, and behavioral interest and value.

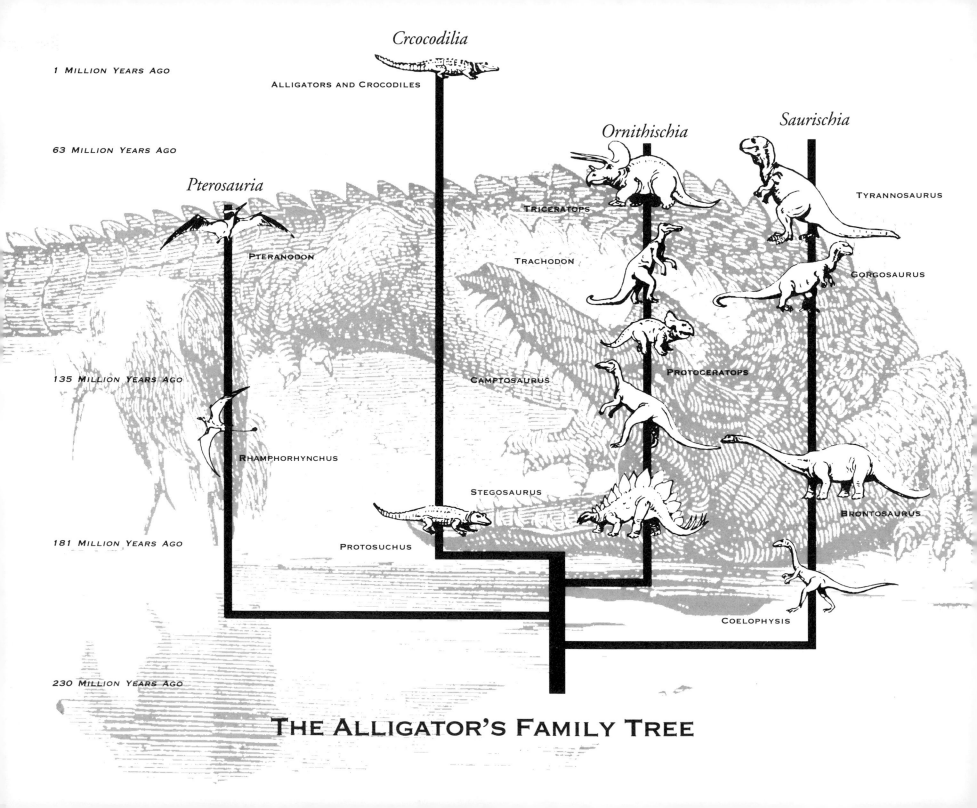

1 MILLION YEARS AGO

63 MILLION YEARS AGO

135 MILLION YEARS AGO

181 MILLION YEARS AGO

230 MILLION YEARS AGO

Crcocodilia

ALLIGATORS AND CROCODILES

Ornithischia

Saurischia

Pterosauria

PTERANODON

TRICERATOPS

TYRANNOSAURUS

TRACHODON

GORGOSAURUS

RHAMPHORHYNCHUS

PROTOCERATOPS

CAMPTOSAURUS

BRONTOSAURUS

STEGOSAURUS

PROTOSUCHUS

COELOPHYSIS

THE ALLIGATOR'S FAMILY TREE

"YOU ARE OLD, FATHER WILLIAM..."

ANCIENT AND CHINESE ALLIGATORS

Modern popular opinion, especially in the South, is fascinated with the great age of alligators, descended from ancestors that walked the earth some 230 million years ago. Diane Ackerman may be stretching the point, but she makes it well by writing, "they've seen the disappearance of the dinosaur and the Neanderthal. They are a hundred times as ancient as human beings." More succinctly, the Baton Rouge Sunday Advocate *reported alligators to be "like the cockroach, another survivor from the age of dinosaurs."*

The alligator, however, is *not* a living dinosaur. It shares with them a common ancestral root, but developed on a separate branch of the family tree. This was not known until modern paleontologists began to study the fossil record. That stony trail was often ignored, and in the mid-nineteenth century, Dr. Buckland said, "fossil remains of the crocodilian family do not deviate sufficiently from living genera to require any description." Some dim idea of its origins, though, were made evident when *Harper's New Monthly Magazine* told its readers in 1855, "The alligator, crawling among the swamps and lagoons, is all that living, is left to us eminently characteristic of these primeval times [of the dinosaurs]." As paleontology developed, so did tentative knowledge of alligator ancestry. By 1897, R. W. Shufeldt could say, "In former ages of the earth's history . . . there were not only a great many more different kinds of these reptiles [crocodilians], but they had a far wider range over the

surface of the globe, and formed a more important figure in its fauna."

Although in 1915, Albert Reese maintained that "The direct ancestors of the Crocodilia . . . are still uncertain," he could also assert, "we have one group of reptiles still living . . . of which the Mesozoic lords of creation need not feel ashamed." He described the fossil alligators of that age: "the fore limbs were much shorter and weaker than the hind limbs, as was often the case with dinosaurs." Later writers, such as biologist Archie Carr, concluded, "Long rear legs indicate that the alligator's ancestors walked upright like many of their dinosaur kin."

At Chicago's Field Museum of Natural History, Karl Schmidt had enough evidence available to him to state in 1922, "the record of their ancestry is rather better known than that of most groups of reptiles. They reached their greatest development toward the close of the great age of

reptiles . . . being contemporaries of the dinosaurs, the flying reptiles and the gigantic sea lizards of the late Cretaceous period . . . the largest fossil forms are estimated at about fifty feet."

Further studies and analysis of additional fossil finds advanced rapidly in the years between the Great Depression and the Vietnam War. This greater understanding led Herbert Zim to state, "Ancestors of all these creatures were the thecodonts, reptiles that lived some 230 million years ago. A few of the thecodonts looked somewhat like modern alligators and crocodiles. . . . The Phytosaurs, a closely related group, were similar in size and shape to the biggest living crocodilians. Some were over 5 meters long." Jack Scott added that phytosaurs were "large flying reptiles . . . that looked like alligators."

During the Cretaceous age, many ancestral forms of the crocodile and a few of the alligator existed, a limited number of which survived. Among the extinct crocodilians, "*Deinosuchus,* the largest of them, had a skull 2 meters long and a skeleton that stretched for nearly fifteen meters," according to Zim.

All fossil alligators may not yet be known. Among those that have been discovered, the oldest that may be a true alligatorine ancestor of the modern alligator is *Albertochampsa langstoni* from the Cretaceous era of about 70 million years ago. As its name suggests, it lived in Alberta, Canada, at a time when the climate of the world was far different from that of today. Bruce Erickson, its discoverer, deduced that "This early alligator lived in swamps and marshes that were also occupied by some of the

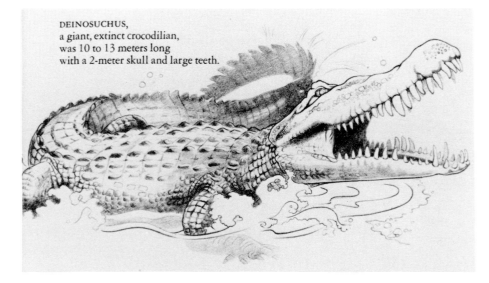

DEINOSUCHUS,
CRETACEOUS AGE
CROCODILIAN.
DRAWING BY JEAN
ZOLLINGER IN
*ALLIGATORS AND
CROCODILES* BY
H. S. ZIM, 1978.

DEINOSUCHUS,
a giant, extinct crocodilian,
was 10 to 13 meters long
with a 2-meter skull and large teeth.

last dinosaurs, but unlike its more celebrated distant cousins, the dinosaurs, it survived extinction."

The name *champsa* for some fossil alligators is apparently taken from an Egyptian word for *crocodile,* which was in turn borrowed from the Ionian Greeks, who had called it that because the crocodile (and consequently the alligator) looked a lot like a hedge lizard, which they called by the same appellation. Appearances can be deceiving; despite the observed resemblance, the alligator is a member of the crocodilian family, and is not a lizard.

Particular alligatorine features of Albertochampsa, distinguishing it from ancestral crocodiles, were its rounded snout, blunt teeth, and the pits in its upper jaw for receiving teeth from the lower—all characteristics used to separate modern alligators from modern crocodiles. It seems to have escaped extinction because of its ability to diversify, evolve, and migrate as northern climates cooled. Its alligator features, blunt snout and crushing teeth, were advantages, allowing it to capture and consume a wider range of prey than some of the crocodilian forms that have left us no progeny.

Albertochampsa is especially important because it helps estabish the American origins of alligators. Erickson, at The Science Museum of Minnesota in St. Paul, has written, "The evidence thus far would then indicate that the earliest development of this reptile was in North America just prior to the time of the break-up of the northern continents . . . subsequent continental drifting isolated groups, which in turn resulted in various evolutionary lines, some of which survive to the present." As the earth cooled,

ancestral alligators moved to the warmer South. "Fossil evidence from [South Carolina] regional rock strata suggests that it existed here some 65 million years ago," Erickson has said.

Wannaganosuchus is a slightly later form, named for the Wannagan Creek Quarry where it was found on the "upper breaks" of the Little Missouri River in North Dakota. It existed there some 60 million years ago, in the company of larger crocodiles and one form—with a long, narrow snout—reminiscent of the fish-eating gharials found today in India, Nepal, and Southeast Asia. Wannaganosuchus bore a stronger resemblance to the modern alligators than any of its known contemporaries, and, like Albertochampsa, had a short, broad skull and long, bulbous rear teeth for crushing its prey.

Howard Snyder poetically described the call of the alligator: "His fantastic, melancholy bellow, so deep and loud that it actually shakes the ground, is a voice from a far distant past, millions of years ago, when reptiles, not men, ruled the earth." Erickson would agree, pointing out that circumstantial evidence suggests that the alligators of 60 million years ago, smaller than the predatory protocrocodiles with which they shared the North Dakota swamps, may have needed this vocal communication to escape the clutches of their fossil cousins and to converse while remaining camouflaged in their murky environment.

By these Paleocene times, alligators had arrived in South America (a long hike from their Canadian homeland) and had even gotten as far as northern Asia. There they evolved into the Chinese alligator (*Alligator sinensis*), the

MAN IN SAURIAN JAWS. WOODCUT FROM *HARPER'S NEW MONTHLY MAGAZINE,* 1855.

only true modern alligator cousin of *Alligator mississippiensis*. As early as 1929, Kellog had recognized this probable American ancestry of all living alligators: "It would appear that the Middle Miocene *Alligator thomsoni* [whose fossilized remains had surfaced in Nebraska] is a direct ancestor of the Chinese alligator." By Eocene times, only 50 million years ago, ancestral alligators were prowling Europe, although they did not survive there. Africa and Australia were abandoned to the crocodiles, as true alligators never seem to have reached those regions.

Martel McNeely, though, had a chauvinistic but mistaken concept of the southern origins and migration pattern of *Alligator mississippiensis*, writing in 1947, "Ages and ages ago, the only alligators in this hemisphere were those living around the mouth of the Mississippi. Then slowly they spread out to Florida, and westward and southward to Mexico, Central and South America." While flattering to local pride, and possibly misinspired by the current scientific name of the U.S. alligator, this theory doesn't seem to hold water. In fact, as early as 1929,

Remington Kellog had reported that fossils of the true *Alligator mississippiensis* from the Pleistocene age of a relatively recent one million years ago had been reported from South Carolina, Florida, and Texas. Primordial Louisiana, on the lower Mississippi, was notably absent from the list.

Erickson has summarized, "The main branch of alligator proliferation was in North America, yet even here only a single species, the American alligator (*Alligator mississippiensis*), survives today." Ackerman has appended, "Today's crocodilians, which have survived with only minor changes since the time of tar pits and thunder lizards, are living relics. . . ." And Will Branan has speculated, "Mayhap one of my antediluvian ancestors served as a choice hors d'oeuvre before his noon-day siesta."

While there are twenty-four different species of crocodiles distributed throughout the globe, there are only two alligators, and they descend from common North American roots. One of these ancestral alligator forms had already crossed the ancient land connection from North America into Asia by the Paleocene age, some 60 million years ago. There it evolved sufficiently from its American beginnings to become a separate species, the Chinese alligator (*Alligator sinensis*). Smaller than its distant U.S. relative, it has a heavier body, shorter tail, and more upturned nose. The Chinese alligator resides in eastern China, chiefly the lower Yangtze River Valley and its tributaries. Like the American alligator, it has been heavily hunted, and is now thought to be extremely rare in the wild.

Alligators have been the basis of myth and folklore in China, just as they have in the United States. Diane Ackerman asserts, "In Chinese, the alligator is called *tulong* or 'earth dragon,' and the etymology strongly suggests that the Chinese dragon began with myths about the alligator." Herbert Zim tells us, "In the 3rd century, the Chinese wrote of a water dragon." It is possible, of course, that medieval European dragon legends were based on stories "leaking" from China via the silk route before direct East-West contacts became common. L. A. S. Williams, however, doubts such a connection, writing, "the theory has been advanced that the Chinese dragon is merely a modified form of the alligator found occasionally to the present day in the Yangtze River, for the emergence of the latter from hibernation sychronises with the coming of spring, when the dragon is believed to be exerting its beneficent influence; it is, however, difficult to trace an analogy between this fabulous animal and any other natural species . . . ."

In fact, a full millennium after the water dragon appeared in Chinese literature, Europeans first heard of the Chinese alligator directly from Marco Polo, who wrote about it upon returning from his epic thirteenth-century Asian voyage, reporting that the Chinese hunted it both for meat and hide. This would indicate that the Chinese were tanning alligators long before the North American variety was discovered by Europeans.

Five hundred years later, eighteenth-century Europeans had discovered the North American alligator and were deeply embroiled in scholarly argument over its

scientific classification. Some Eastern contact had been reinitiated, and the Diderot *Encyclopédie* informed inquiring minds of 1754, "It is told in different reports that the Chinese domesticate the crocodiles [*sic*], that they fatten them in order to eat them; their flesh is white; the Europeans find it unsavory and too musky." Diderot can hardly be blamed for using the word *crocodile,* especially since Europeans had not yet decided that North America's large reptile wasn't one.

Both Americans and Europeans apparently forgot about the Chinese alligator for another century. The first renewed hints at its existence appeared in England only in

1870, and in 1879 a Frenchman named Fauvel, working for the Chinese Customs Service, brought it to wider attention. G. A. Boulenger and other members of the Zoological Society of London were surprised when it "proved to belong to the American genus Alligator."

Fauvel, in fact, realized the connection, gave it the scientific name *Alligator sinensis* (literally, "Chinese alligator"), and obligingly provided a summary of his research into Chinese literature concerning the animal. He sent a stuffed specimen to Paris, where it fascinated European scientists of the 1880s. More Chinese alligators reached Europe very shortly. The German consul in China sent an additional two specimens to Berlin. Yet another pair reached England in 1889, and an Englishman residing in Shanghai presented two live Chinese alligators to the Zoological Society of London in August 1890, where they were promptly put on public exhibition. At about the same time, two more living Chinese alligators reached Frankfurt, Germany. American knowledge was limited to the observations of travelers and the publications emanating from European presses.

Since then, a limited number of Chinese alligators have been brought to the United States. A few rare specimens are shown in zoological parks or at alligator farms. A very small stock is also used in alligator-farming research in the United States. Such a group have been maintained for this purpose by the Louisiana Department of Wildlife and Fisheries at the Rockefeller Wildlife Refuge at Grand Chênier.

FACING PAGE: "CHINESE ALLIGATOR." TINTED LITHOGRAPH FROM AN ARTICLE BY G. A. BOULENGER IN *PROCEEDINGS OF THE SCIENTIFIC MEETINGS OF THE ZOOLOGICAL SOCIETY OF LONDON FOR THE YEAR 1890*.

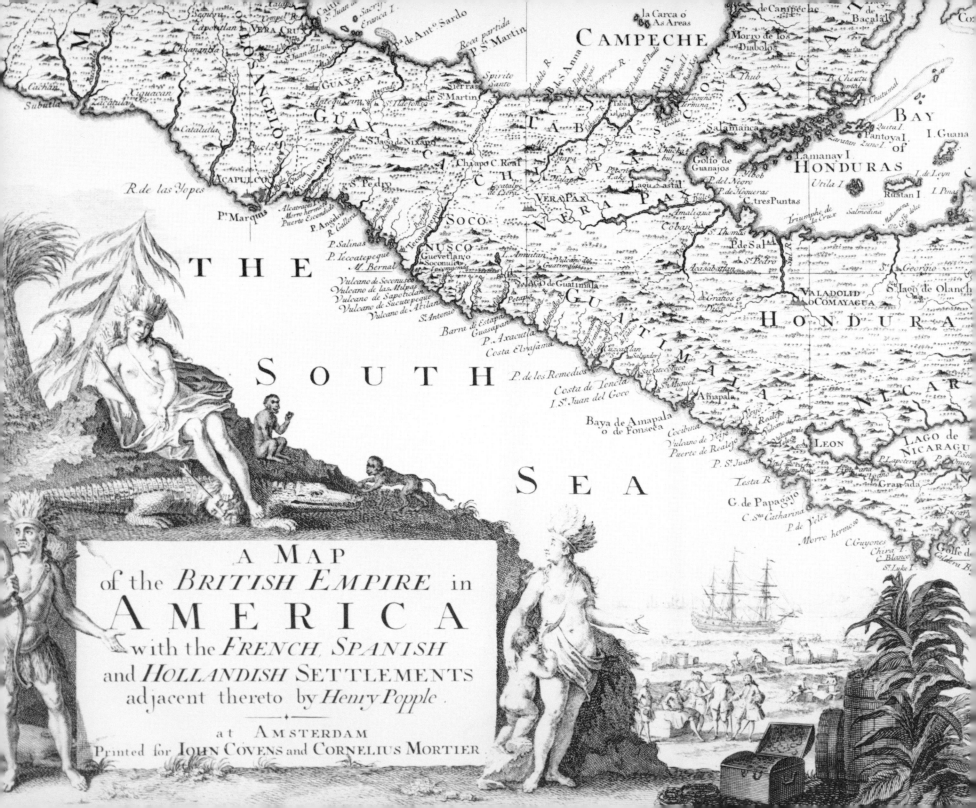

A MAP
of the BRITISH EMPIRE in
AMERICA
with the FRENCH, SPANISH
and HOLLANDISH SETTLEMENTS
adjacent thereto by Henry Popple.

at AMSTERDAM
Printed for IOHN COVENS and CORNELIUS MORTIER

THE GRAY-GREEN BADGE OF COURAGE

SYMBOLIC ALLIGATORS

FACING PAGE: ALLEGORY OF AMERICA. CARTOUCHE FROM A MAP OF THE BRITISH EMPIRE IN AMERICA . . . BY HENRY POPPLE, 1733, PUBLISHED IN AMSTERDAM, CA. 1737.

The alligator has been invested with all sorts of symbolic meanings by various groups of people. Native Americans were the earliest; when European explorers arrived, they found alligator clans among the Alabama, Caddo, Chickasaw, and Creek Indians. The Bayougoula, near Donaldsonville, Louisiana, employed the alligator as their badge or totem. Such symbols were often endowed with supernatural qualities and greatly venerated.

The relationship between Native Americans and alligators did not escape the attention of early European explorers. Their reports led artists throughout Europe to envision handsome Indians living in peaceful Rousseauistic harmony with nature. By the mid-eighteenth century, a feather-crowned Native American beauty queen astride or accompanied by an alligator had established a firm place in European iconography as the allegorical representation of America. This image appeared with great regularity in the engraved cartouches of elaborately printed maps, suites of tapestries depicting the continents, and in sculpture, painting and the decorative arts, persisting until well into the nineteenth century.

This geographic association of the motif of Indian and alligator was adopted even into the design of the seal of the city of New Orleans. There, the alligator beneath a river

god representing the Mississippi, personified the marshy lowlands upon which the city had been built. A 1990 inquiry to city hall failed to produce any real history of the seal, and only a vague analysis of its symbolism. An 1892 account, however, states that "Their [alligators'] omnipresence in the region roundabout caused the first representatives of government of New Orleans to adopt the reptile as the chief figure in the seal of the city. For lack of proper engraving talent in Louisiana, the authorities ordered the seal to be executed in Paris. The French artist cut a couchant *crocodile* basking on a bank, with hills in the background. The alligator is markedly different from his oriental cousin, and New Orleans is 90 miles distant from the nearest hill; hence the seal was inconsistent. Yet it served its official purpose and to this day [1892] is duly attached to the formal municipal acts and contracts of the southern metropolis." Actually, by 1892, the seal with alligator and river god still in use in 1990 was employed already. The Victorian writer must have suffered from poor eyesight, as he or she misdescribed it badly. The hills are on the inner shield with the river god's figure, representing the Mississippi, and are accurate. The river runs through some pretty hilly territory before reaching the flat alluvial delta of Louisiana. Regardless, the city itself seems incapable of divulging who selected the emblem, or when it became the official device of the municipality.

The mysterious gloom of an alligator-inhabited swamp, coupled with the antediluvian appearance of the animal itself, have made the alligator a symbol of the netherworld in both literary and visual imagery. In 1807,

PENDULE AU
NÈGRE. "BLACK"
MANTEL CLOCK
WITH AN ALLEGORY
OF AMERICA BY
GREBERT, PARIS,
CA. 1800.

 THE GRAY-GREEN BADGE OF COURAGE   49

C. C. Robin described such a seemingly mythological scene: "One imagines himself crossing the shadowy Styx with Acheron. Alligators in swarms surround the travelers . . . ." Alleged ferocity and deceitful character (attributes borrowed from the crocodile) contributed to fiendish notions. In 1846, Dr. Bennet Dowler lapsed into Latin, borrowing from the monstrous images of Scylla and Charybdis in the *Odyssey,* to characterize alligators that trickily detoured fish in shallow water into their open mouths: "*Incidit in Scyllam, qui vult vitare Charybdim.*"

Not surprisingly, the U.S. Navy adopted the alligator, and in the nineteenth century named at least two vessels for it. On the eve of the Battle of New Orleans, which ended the War of 1812 in January of 1815, U.S. Commodore Patterson put a gig called the *Alligator* along with five gunboats on guard in Lake Borgne as sentinels to sound the approach of the British as they came inland through the interconnecting system of lakes and passes to the east of New Orleans. Forty-six years later, at the outbreak of the Civil War, Brutus de Villeroi, an enterprising Frenchman, offered his prototype submarine to the U. S. government, just as Robert Fulton once had offered the steamboat to Napoleon. De Villeroi knew what he was doing, having experimented with submarines in Nantes, France, since at least 1835, where he must have entertained the budding imagination of his young fellow townsman Jules Verne. President Lincoln was enthusiastic, had it tested, and the navy ordered one. This first federal submarine was called the *Alligator.* During its construction, de Villeroi had words with the contractor, and left in a huff before the U-boat's completion. The *Alligator*, propelled by a bank of oars, "invaded" Hampton Roads in June of 1862, "but did no more than poke about the bottom." Ultimately, it sank while being towed near Cape Hatteras, and it saw no real active duty during the conflict.

All the supposed evil qualities of the alligator were vested in the forces of federal occupation in the South after the Civil War by the remarkably imaginative illustrator of the cover of "Reconstruction!"—a grand march composed by Charles Young. In two vignettes, he depicted "as it should be" (an angelic choir, complete with wings and harps) and "as it is!" (a glorious scene from hell, replete with monster, serpent, harpies, and winged skull; among the devil's cronies is a prominent alligator). The copyright holder was A. E. Blackmar, Confederate music publisher known for his antinorthern political stance.

Victorian authors availed themselves of a variety of devilish similes, metaphors, and observations. A contributor to *Scribner's Magazine* in 1873 noted, "they [docked steamboats] seem like giant river monsters, crawled out from the ooze to take a little of the sun, even as the alligator does." The *Historical Sketch Book* took visitors on a vicarious tour of the environs of New Orleans in the mid-1880s, advising, "ahead upon the Stygian waters flickers here and there a star. It is the eye of an alligator."

War-torn Europe of the 1940s elicited a noteworthy comment from Will Branan in 1940: "Mr. 'Gator's intentions may be all that they should be, as altruistic as those of Mr. Hitler, but I am still reminded that a certain region is paved with such material." Postwar America began

ALLIGATOR
CIRCUS. SOUVENIR
POSTCARD BY THE
CURT TEICH CO.,
CHICAGO,
CA. 1910.

to consider environmental issues. Anthony Kerrigan was kinder in his 1948 assessment: "Although he may look like the illustration to a chapter on the 'Evils of Sin' or on the 'Allies of the Devil Incarnate' in the gloomy books of the dark ages there is much about him to endear him to the humanitarian and to the nature addict." But, given its heat, humidity, and smell, Mark Robichaux had to admit in 1989, "an alligator farm isn't exactly the Garden of Eden."

Travelers to the South began to expect alligators as part of their tour, and were disappointed when they didn't spot (or shoot) one from mid-nineteenth century steamboats, carriages, and railcars. The alligator became a true symbol of the Gulf Coast region. By century's end, novelties made of stuffed alligators, alligator teeth, and even live "pet" baby alligators had become prized souvenirs for northern visitors. This vogue culminated in Edwardian-era postcards of the early twentieth century. Thousands of such cards were showered on stay-at-home friends and relatives as travelers shared a shudder of Edwardian horror, a good laugh, or a vicarious thrill through an astonishing array of images of alligators singing, dancing, devouring men, or simply basking in incredible numbers and ferocious glory. The remarkable Curt Teich collection at the Lake County Museum in Wauconda, Illinois, houses well over a hundred such historic examples, all created by a single Chicago postcard company for retailing to traveling Yankees in the sunny South.

What with all this attention being paid to the alligator, it is not surprising that southern students reverted to the practice of early Native Americans in their regional totem choosing. As they selected mascots for high schools and colleges, the alligator became a frequent choice.

Best-known of collegiate 'gators is that which embodies the communal identity of the University of Florida at Gainesville. The decision was unofficially made by Austin Miller, who picked an alligator for a symbol when he purchased pennants for the 1908 football season. The alligator was selected because it was native to his state, and, at the time, no other university was using it. The Virginia manufacturer of Miller's pennants didn't know what an alligator looked like, so Miller supplied him with a picture from a nearby library. Later nicknamed "Albert the Alligator," this ivory-tower saurian recently acquired a girlfriend. The coed addition to mascot ranks is called "Alberta," an apparently unwitting reference to Alberta, Canada, home of the alligator's oldest-known fossil ancestor, *Albertochampsa langstoni*.

Live alligators also have come to serve as living symbols of organizations and institutions. "Charlie Bob," a seven-foot alligator that inhabits the tile-lined pool at the center of the Art Deco masterpiece housing the Louisiana State Museum—Shreveport is such a beast. Born (or, more correctly, hatched) about 1960, Charlie moved to the museum about 1964, where he has spent three decades among turtles, trout, some goldfish (they didn't last long, but not because Charlie Bob devoured them), and at least one other alligator. Charlie Bob has been well fed over the years and doesn't even think about eating his poolmates—catching them would be too much like work.

Charlie Bob's most traumatic experiences have been one semiserious bout of ill health and indigestion from swallowing coins that museum visitors have thrown into his pool (not exactly another Trevi Fountain, but it is inviting). Such funds retrieved by museum staffers go toward Charlie Bob's feed bill, which amounts to about $250 annually. At least twice, "he" (Charlie Bob may be a girl 'gator—no one's ever checked) could have filed for workman's compensation for injury on the job. In the first instance, miscreants peppered his tail with steel-tipped darts (which had to be removed long-distance; no one was willing—or foolish enough—to try it up close).

The second occasion was caused by an overaggressive roommate. In 1975, when Charlie Bob, at the length of five feet, was thought to be about fifteen years old, he was sharing his pool with another four-foot 'gator. It was also the occasion of his visit to Dr. Ned Wynn. The museum staff had noted all spring that Charlie had not regained the

appetite that usually flourished after his winter fast. He seemed to be wasting away, while the aggressive 'gator was suffering from no such complaint. Dr. Wynn took a stethoscope to Charlie Bob, made an X ray, gave him a vitamin injection, and sent him home. The cause of Charlie Bob's doldrums seems to have been too much company. The four-footer was seen attacking Charlie Bob's vulnerable tail (the one that had been darted), so it was decided to remove the pugnacious saurian. The smaller 'gator was turned over to Louisiana Wildlife and Fisheries officers to release in the wilds. Once the offender was removed,

"CHARLIE BOB," UNOFFICIAL MASCOT OF THE LOUISIANA STATE MUSEUM, SHREVE-PORT. PEN AND INK SKETCH BY ALAN MOORE, 1983, FOR *THE TIMES*, SHREVEPORT.

Charlie Bob's recovery was dramatic. Heber Long told the press, "The second day he ate enough to sink a battleship."

Over the years, Charlie Bob unintentionally became the institution's ex officio mascot, gave "interviews" to the press, and turned into a genuine local character. Shreveport loved its 'gator. Talented curator Jeanne Mason added the alligator to the museum's education program conducted by volunteers from the Junior League, writing a scenario and even designing costumes. Carolyn Nelson described a typical performance: "Kerry Walsh, dressed as Charlie Bob, the Red-Necked alligator, enchants preschool age children and kindergartners as Allison Wray reads a story about how the real alligator, who [sic] lives in the museum's pond, found his home there. The program concludes with the children making alligator puppets to take home." Ms. Mason, she noted, "once took Charlie Bob on a rare road trip to appear at the Fire Ant Festival in Marshall [Texas]."

Keeping a thirty-year-old live alligator, which by 1990 was seven feet long, in the museum's public access courtyard was recognized as potentially hazardous to the health of those who come near it. Although well fed and docile, the animal could certainly snap at irritating visitors and possibly do serious damage to children straying too far from a protective parent. Removing the alligator would offend the local citizenry, who have taken Charlie Bob to their collective municipal heart. As the 1990s dawned, museum officials were seeking expert advice, along with a solution to their quandary, that would assure that all parties—Charlie Bob, the insurance company, and the city of Shreveport—could live happily ever after.

The most recent mascotship won by an alligator is that of the small town of Ponchatoula, Louisiana. There "Old Hardhide" took up residence in 1972, and lived to the ripe old age of twenty-one in a caged pool at the town's center. The tale of his installation, drawn from Ponchatoula's communal memory, is an interesting one, which is retold in various versions. In general, it goes: A group of children playing along a creek near the Zemurray Gardens was startled when a "log" came to life in the form of an alligator. The local populace was surprised to find an alligator inhabiting that particular creek, and an expedition was mounted by the proprietor of a Dairy Treat business in Hammond. He caught the alligator and displayed it until he went out of business. At that time, the chief of police of Ponchatoula, one of his cronies, found the animal was available. The alligator was transferred to a swimming pool until Ponchatoula could build it a cage. When he came to live in the small city in 1972, the alligator was thought by the powers-that-were to have great potential as a tourist draw, a more or less honorable function that alligators had been fulfilling since the early nineteenth century. Never officially adopted as the municipal mascot, he simply earned the post by on-the-job service. Old Hardhide got one of the finest send-offs that any crocodilian, even the mummified Egyptian ones, has ever received when he died in 1985. Ponchatoula staged an old-fashioned jazz funeral to mark his passing, complete with horse-drawn hearse, a band, and some two thousand "mourners" in the procession. A special casket was constructed to put to rest his thirteen-foot-long, nine-hundred-pound corpse.

Old Hardhide's position was assumed by "Hardhide, Jr."—a ten-footer that lasted until January of 1990. The animal apparently succumbed to a vandal's .22, abetted by a serious freeze, rare in that part of the South. Junior's funeral was not nearly as elaborate as that of his father, according to reporter Karen Didier, who covered the obsequies. Mayor Julian Dufreche described it as a "quiet, private ceremony." Few attended in January, because, as the mayor put it, "We tried to contact his nearest relatives, but apparently they are all in hibernation."

Junior's demise left the town with something of a problem, as the civic-minded alligator functioned as an important tourist attraction. With the Super Bowl being played in nearby New Orleans, they quickly needed a replacement to satisfy visiting football fans. The Alligator Campground in neighborly Hammond kindly loaned them a fourteen-foot specimen to fill in until spring. The mayor gave voice to the municipal master plan: "When the alligators come out of hibernation, we'll notify Hardhide, Jr.'s son that he's next in line for the succession." Ponchatoula, though, got a good deal from the campground, and purchased the stand-in—which became "Hardhide III"—a few months later for one thousand dollars. During the fall of 1990, plans were being made to heat his cage during the coming winter. The mayor, just approaching the end of his first term, feared that a second demise, so soon after that of Hardhide, Jr., might prove to be a political liability.

Although the various Hardhides have never enjoyed official status as the mascot of Ponchatoula, they have certainly earned it. Hardhide III has a bank account, and a previous incumbent was even insured. Hardhide has also developed journalistic talents, authoring the "My Ponchatoula" column (mostly local gossip) that regularly appears in the *Ponchatoula Times*.

These "symbolic" alligators mostly stemmed from the European tradition of an iconography of Indians and alligators that give visual form to the mental concept of New World or America. The alligator lost its continental constituency and became specific to the southern United States when a large immigrant population began to inhabit that region and expropriated the animal from general "American" usage to their own, more regional needs. Other Americans accepted that, since the fairly exotic alligator was not found on, or in most cases even near, their home turf. That southern institutions and municipalities should take on saurian mascots was a simple and logical deployment of usage current in the late nineteenth and early twentieth centuries, extending into our own time. The broad impact of the alligator as the visual symbol of the South, of Florida and of Louisiana is difficult to assess. It has certainly insidiously influenced national thinking, at least on those occasions when the nation contemplates such issues. The concept is now so strong that many Americans are surprised to learn that the alligator was once a sort of ambassador without portfolio, representing the combined continents of our hemisphere.

MANY ARE THE USES OF ADVERSITY

EARLIEST ALLIGATOR APPLICATIONS

Although myth and legend have pitted man against alligator in tales of epic proportion, it is surprising how many and varied are the uses that man has found for this alleged adversary. The earliest Western record of man's utilization of the alligator is that of Marco Polo, who reported that the Chinese hunted them in the thirteenth century. Little is known, however, of ancient Chinese tanning methods. Four hundred years later, French colonists in America were publishing that Native Americans both ate alligators and manufactured useful objects from them. Alligator

'GATOR GREASE MONKEY: ALLIGATOR OIL KEPT EARLY STEAM MACHINERY HUMMING—NOT SQUEAKING. DETAIL FROM *LOW WATER ON THE MISSISSIPPI*, HAND-TINTED LITHOGRAPH BY CURRIER & IVES AFTER F. E. PALMER, NEW YORK, 1868.

BOTTLES FOR
ESSENCE OF
ALLIGATOR?
SÈVRES PORCELAIN
PERFUME BOTTLES,
CA. 1860.

teeth were being worn as medicoreligious charms, to prevent poisoning.

Frank and Ada Graham have said, "American Indians sometimes used the thick gator skins to cover the heads of special drums, which they scratched with sticks to make their tribal music," and S. C. Arthur clarifies that among the Natchez Indians in the eighteenth century "To prepare the alligator skin for its use in this aboriginal jazz band, the skin of the dead reptile was first exposed to the ravages of a colony of ants, so that the softer parts would be eaten away, and the skin was then hung in the sun to dry. The music furnished by this part of the band consisted in [sic] the player scratching the back of the dead 'gator with a stick." The Chitimacha tribe, west of New Orleans, produced some of their most spectacular double-woven baskets in the "alligator's entrails" pattern. Their sophisticated basketry tradition employed native river cane, natural dyes in several colors, and some rare and elaborate curvilinear motifs. "Alligator's entrails" loops its way around such baskets in a sinuous, decorative, elegant Greek-key progression. Indians in other parts of the American South also used alligator motifs in various forms of painted or carved decoration.

Eighteenth-century colonists found an application for alligator in early agribusiness. John J. Audubon has written, "when indigo was made in Louisiana, the oil [rendered from an alligator's tail fat] was used to assuage the overflowing of the boiling juice, by throwing a ladleful into the kettle whenever this was about to take place."

Although Europeans stuffed specimen alligators, they apparently showed little interest before 1800 in tanning hides to produce functional leather. The first recorded attempt, sometime between 1790 and 1810, met with failure; the earliest alligator boots were not waterproof; they leaked. Europeans did, however, adopt various alligator remedies into the colonial pharmacopoeia of folk medicine of the American colonies, perhaps basing their practices on

58 *A Social History of the American Alligator*

those of Native Americans or slaves of African origin who adapted crocodile-inspired beliefs to the new-world alligator.

Colonists, hunters, and frontiersmen often made many of their own accessories when manufactured goods were unavailable or too expensive. Audubon said of a large alligator in the 1820s that he was anxious "to knock off some of its larger teeth, to make powder chargers." This conversion of tooth-to-tool continued, and Timothy Flint observed the utility of the alligator in this regard in 1828: "They have large, ivory teeth, which contain a cavity, sufficiently large to hold a musket charge of powder, for which purpose they are commonly used by sportsmen." A quarter of a century later, they were still at it. *Harper's New Monthly Magazine* in 1855 advised, "The hunters, who have in many instances a taste for rude carving, make beautiful rifle 'powder charges' of the largest." Such implements are regarded today as fine folk art and prize pieces of Americana.

Although indigo had disappeared as a commercial crop at the end of the eighteenth century, the alligator oil formerly used to process it was not abandoned. By the mid-1820s, Audubon reported in a British scientific periodical, alligators "are shot for the sake of their oil, now used for greasing the machinery of steam-engines, and cotton mills." It is tempting to envision early steamboats (that had been plying the Mississippi for about fifteen years when Audubon wrote) and railroads (which were fast being built) traversing the southern landscape in squeakless splendor, thanks to the efficacious alligator.

Through the middle years of the nineteenth century, mounted alligator's teeth were retailed by jewelers as babies' pacifiers. In a shop window of the late 1840s, visiting Englishman Sir Charles Lyell saw "many alligators' teeth polished and white as ivory, and set in silver for infants to wear round their necks to rub against their gums when cutting their teeth, in the same way as they use a coral in England." Native Americans had, of course, been wearing alligator teeth around their necks since time immemorial. In this later case, however, there was something of the primitive belief in the transference of strength from object to man—in this instance from the alligator's powerful jaw to that of the child. It remained common practice through the next decade, and *Harper's New Monthly Magazine* told its national readership, "these alligator teeth are often unconsciously met with in jeweler's stores, handsomely set in silver, as ornaments for infants' necks, and agreeable substances on which the juveniles can try their still toothless but aching gums." One later example is known to have survived in a New Orleans family. Others may be identified as people become more aware of what an alligator's tooth actually looks like.

An even more innovative experimental usage was tried out in the 1840s, although the idea had cropped up earlier in germinal form. The Viscount de Chateaubriand was perhaps the first to indirectly suggest that the aromatic

alligator might be put to good service. In his fictional romance *Atala*, set in French colonial Louisiana and published in 1801, he refers to the "faint odor of ambergris exhaled by the crocodiles [*sic*]." That author may have been drawing on some knowledge of true crocodile usage. From the *Pictorial Museum of Animated Nature*, Victorians learned that Dr. Ruppell had discovered in Africa that "The musk-glands of the animal form a great part of the profit which results from this capture, as the Berberines will give as much as two dollars for them, the unguent being used as a perfume for the hair." Americans took this rank African application at face value and saw potential profit in it, alligator being perhaps less expensive than civet or whale products. In 1842, Dr. John Holbrook reported, "These [musk] glands [under the alligator's jaw] are sometimes preserved and used as a substitute for musk in perfumery." To the best of current knowledge, however, no great antebellum cosmetic fortune was ever built on (or under) the jawbone of an alligator.

During the Civil War, idle soldiers often had a go at carving and whittling when they were off duty. Yankee soldier D. P. Mason wrote to his New Hampshire home from Camp Parapet, at Carrollton (before it was absorbed into New Orleans), in 1863, "when it rains we do not hav [*sic*] nothing to do but lay [*sic*] in our tents & read, write or make rings. . . . thay [*sic*] ar [*sic*] making them of aliegators [*sic*] boon [*sic*, that is, bone]."

Oddly, it was the Civil War itself that brought about the first massive use of alligator leather. A war-deprived South found itself short of shoes and boots, and the alligator was drafted into the service of the Confederate army to provide what a northern blockade of southern ports denied those foot-sore soldiers. The alligator may have bathed those weary feet, as well. The Baton Rouge *Morning Advocate* took an admiring view of the all-providing alligator, reporting, "As the whale is to the Eskimo, so the alligator might have been to the impoverished southerner in the closing days of the war. . . . Besides using the flesh for food and the hide for leather . . . the fat was rendered into lubricating oil . . . and for soap making."

Until this time, however, it is significant that none of the early applications of the alligator involved tanning as it is currently known. The modern vision of the alligator is first and foremost that of the book and movie "monster," and, secondly, that of the luxurious bag or boot. To our southern ancestors, up to the mid-nineteenth century, the alligator was a provider of a variety of at least minimally useful products and a source of materials for novelty fabrication—but only a last resort for leather, adversity being among the mothers of invention.

SILK PURSES FROM SWAMP SOWS' EARS

THE FIRST CENTURY OF ALLIGATOR TANNING

The earliest use of saurian skin appears not to have happened in the United States. Daudin wrote in 1803, "It has even been said that the blacks [in unspecified territory, probably Africa] sometimes make themselves hats, or more especially helmets of it that can resist an axe." This account of black manufacture of crocodilian "armor" was repeated by Baron Cuvier in 1831. By that time, Americans had begun to experiment with alligator tanning, as well.

"Alligator hides have been used for one purpose or another in the United States since about 1800," faithfully reported the U.S. Department of Agriculture in 1929. This had long ago been confirmed by John J. Audubon, who had written in the 1820s, "It was on [the Red] River particularly that thousands of the largest size were killed, when the mania of having either shoes, boots, or saddle-seats, made of their hides lasted. . . . The leather prepared from these skins was handsome and very pliant, exhibiting all the regular lozenges of the scales, and able to receive the highest degree of polish, and finishing."

Audubon was not the first to speak of the large number of alligators taken for their hides when the novelty of alligator leather was introduced about 1800. The resultant decline of the abundant alligator populations of

ALLIGATOR-
UPHOLSTERED
LIT-DE-JOUR, OR
LIBRARY SOFA,
CA. 1870.

THE WAY THAT
DIDN'T WORK:
EIGHTEENTH-
CENTURY TANNING.
DETAIL OF AN
ENGRAVING OF AN
EIGHTEENTH-
CENTURY TANNERY
FROM THE DIDEROT
ENCYCLOPÉDIE,
1771.

the Colonial period was attributed to this cause and was noted by many, including H. M. Brackenridge, who declared in 1814, "The numbers of this animal have lessened of late years from the destruction made by the inhabitants, who value their skins." The vogue continued for a few years longer, as Timothy Flint wrote in 1828: "The skin of the alligator is valuable to the tanner." It was, however, about this time that Audubon remembered, "The discovery that the skins are not sufficiently firm and close-grained, to prevent water or dampness long, put a stop to their general destruction. . . . "

Thus early nineteenth-century sows' ears, in the form of leaky boots, apparently ended the first fashion for alligator footwear before 1830, as B. M. Norman looked back from the vantage point of 1845 to say, "At one period, great numbers were killed for their skins . . . but not proving sufficiently close-grained to keep out the water, the experiment was abandoned." Alligatorless human feet trod through U. S. cities for about another decade, but according

to James D. Nichols and his coauthors, "Commercial harvesting of alligators began in the mid-nineteenth century," and the U.S. Department of Agriculture's expertise revealed that "before 1850, 15-foot long alligators were fairly common in some parts of the South, but shortly afterwards the dictates of fashion resulted in the slaughter of thousands of these animals to supply the demand for shoe material, traveling bags, music rolls, and the like."

Obviously, tanning technology had improved, but Albert Reese found that the new wave of interest quickly subsided, observing, "it was not until about 1855 that these attempts were successful and alligator hide became somewhat fashionable. . . . The demand was short-lived." The spurt of brief popularity was such, however, that an amateur historian could report that "In 1858 . . . a man had killed 400 alligators in three months in Jefferson Parish [Louisiana]. The skins brought 75 cents each." Although the price paid to the hunter was not exorbitant, it was sufficient to encourage enterprising Southerners with a profit motive.

The blockade of southern ports during the Civil War ended the importation of leather to the Confederacy, and the South did not produce enough cowhide to meet the needs of its army and citizenry. Reese noted, "The demand [for alligator leather] . . . was not again felt until the demand for shoe leather during the war between the states revived the business."

Sarah Morgan Dawson was indignant. After shopping until dropping in Baton Rouge on May 21, 1862, this southern belle was finally able to find footwear, but with this result: "Behold my tender feet encased in crocodile [*sic*] skin, patent-leather tipped, low-quarter boy's shoes, No. 2! 'What a fall was there, my country,' from my pretty English glove-kid, to sabots made of some animal closely connected with the hippopotamus!" Although Sarah suffered, and an alligator-shod Confederate army must have been among the world's most elegant, the status quo was not to be maintained. Reese wrote, "At the close of the war the business again failed"; and Karl Schmidt reasoned, "This use came to an end with the war, as the leather is really unsuitable for shoes."

Journalist Maud Ronstrom later took up the story, having reported, "Wenzel Zimmerman the elder . . . is believed to have been the first man to tan an alligator's hide in the Western Hemisphere, and probably the world." Although she exaggerated the worthy Zimmerman's claim, she continued more factually: "When the war was over Mr. Zimmerman established his own tannery on Toulouse Street [in New Orleans], with a capital of $60. . . . Someone brought him a few alligator hides and asked if they could be tanned. Mr. Zimmerman tanned them and sold them to a New York dealer. Mrs. Vanderbilt bought the material and used it to cover a chair, which she liked so well she ordered more alligator skins. Soon a new industry of alligator tanning was born." Martel McNealy said that these agents of Park Avenue popularity were "Shattuck and Binger, dealers in skins in New York," and added that "From that time on the alligator skin started to become more popular until it reached the stage of being considered the world's most luxurious leather." At least one piece of Victorian

ANTEBELLUM FASHION CRAZE: ALLIGATOR UNDER THE HOOP SKIRTS? HAND-COLORED LITHOGRAPHIC FASHION PLATE BY ANAÏS TOUDOUZE, PRINTED BY GERVAL, PARIS, 1855.

furniture has turned up still sporting its alligator upholstery, and others may appear. It does seem, though, that this was probably more of a novelty usage than one of common occurrence.

Frank and Ada Graham attributed part of this postbellum success to postwar economics, arguing, "prosperity spread among a larger portion of Americans, and these people wanted to spend their money on fine things— linen, silver, good clothes—and the elegant leather made from alligator skins." Thus the sow's ear of the southern swamp became a status symbol of the Gilded Age.

The taste for alligator goods quickly became international. "Alligator . . . after the war supported a large export movement, for France had opened a market for boots, trunks, gun cases, wallets and other artifacts made of alligator skins," Thomas E. Dabney wrote, supported by Reese, who said, "about 1869 the demand became greater than ever and has continued unabated." European tanning technology, especially in France and Italy, has dominated international alligator leather production since that time.

This new burst of popularity in Second Empire France was apparently so great that imperial Russia, which looked to French fashion as a model, began avidly to seek Louisiana alligators. The *Winfield News-American* claimed that in 1871 "one man shipped 7000 hides from New Iberia parish [*sic*]," and he continued, "Back in the early [18]80's saddles, for which the Russians were famous, were made out of alligator hides. . . . Alligator hide saddles were the favorite of Russians because the body was not allowed to slip around when riding. . . . Only the hide from the under part of the body was used . . . and all packed in salt preparatory for the long trip to Russia." All this, in a sort of unofficial czarist version of glasnost!

Others rushed to profit. The *Historical Sketch Book* informed visitors to the World's Fair of 1884–1885, "There are not as many alligators in the suburbs of New Orleans as there were before the skins of the mighty saurians became [a] commercial commodity, and hunters went to work to kill them as a profession. . . . " Dr. Hugh M. Smith of the United States Fish Commission estimated that 2,500,000 were taken in Florida alone between 1880 and 1894. Karl Schmidt reported increasing interest in following years, saying, "the leather again became fashionable about 1896, for use in fancy slippers and boots, travelling bags, pocketbooks, music rolls, etc."

Increasing and international interest was, in fact, encouraging the development of a specialized lifestyle as commercial hunting yielded ever-greater financial benefits, although decimating the alligator population. Alligator hunters became "quaint" characters for northern writers to include in the accounts of their exotic southern sojourns at a time when the United States, in the wake of celebrating its centennial in 1876, began to value (or at least regard with nostalgia) rural and pre-Industrial Revolution crafts, trades, and lifestyles. This emerging attitude is espcially seen in nationally distributed magazines of the last quarter of the nineteenth century, such as *Scribner's, Harper's,* and others. On their pages, one finds an early form of reporting that developed into the travel writer's commentary of today. The more peculiar, antique, or primitive their subject matter, the better (especially if the phenomena were Colonial or pre-Revolutionary). All aspects of the alligator trade were fair game for such quasihistorical, quasianthropological journalism.

During this period, alligator exploitation grew rapidly. Dr. Smith reported in 1891 that "The commercial value of the hide has been an important factor in the thinning of its numbers." Reese confirmed this fact, reporting that "In 1899, three firms at Kissimmee [Florida] handled 33,600 hides. After this time the total of hides taken and the average per man diminished greatly." Big business continued, however, with imported crocodilian hides supplementing domestic hunting. Reese determined that "In 1902, the annual output from the tanneries of the United States approximated 280,000 skins, worth about $420,000. Of these about fifty-six per cent. came from Mexico and Central America, twenty-two per cent. from Florida, twenty per cent. from Louisiana, and the remaining two per cent. from the other Gulf States."

The *Brooklyn Eagle* believed that even more hides were being processed, and it stated on June 15, 1902, "Their skins when tanned make excellent leather for the manufacture of such articles as trunks, traveling bags, purses, pocketbooks, and all kinds of . . . novelties. Books are bound with it and it is even utilized for upholstered chairs. . . . " It is evident that as Victoria's reign drew to a close, alligator was very popular with conspicuous consumers. When experimental tanning had begun a century earlier, efforts had resulted in soggy footwear. Improved tanning technology alleviated that problem, and necessity encouraged southerners to resort to alligator leather as a result of Civil War deprivation. French interest in alligator and France's unassailable position as dictator of fashion in nineteenth-century Western society helped make alligator the *dernier cri* from Moscow to Paris to New York as that century ended.

IMITATION ALLIGA-
TOR BOOKBIND-
INGS, CA. 1900–
1950.

ALLIGATOR JOE, MI...

CHAPTER SEVEN

WORKING FOR THE YANKEE DOLLAR
THE ALLIGATOR BECOMES A TOURIST ATTRACTION

"We stared at the far-famed Mississippi, with all our might, as in duty bound, and took it exceedingly ill that the alligators kept under water; but after all, there was such a fog, and so much vapor rising from the flat marshy country through which this giant river rolls, that, if their abodes are in any way comfortable, I could not blame them for remaining at home." This was the gentle complaint lodged by a visitor in early 1834 (when the alligators were probably still winter-dormant) with the editor of the **New York Mirror**. While other visiting firemen were often

disappointed when the alligator was not basking on its appointed log as they passed, such was not the case in the preceding decade when the Marquis de Lafayette ascended the Father of Waters on his last triumphal tour of the United States. He was met by a more than satisfactory welcoming committee, described by his secretary as "Enormous alligators of a sinister appearance and sluggish gait, attached to the floating trunks of trees, [that] menaced the navigator, and seemed to dispute the entrance of the river with him."

The alligator was so well established as an early tourist attraction that by 1839 the Alligator Line ran along the Gulf Coast from Augusta to New Orleans in four days and twenty hours. Thrice weekly departures traveled the route by a combination of steamer, four-horse post carriage, and railcar through prime alligator-viewing territory. An alligator-shaped printer's slug was even devised to attract

 WORKING FOR THE YANKEE DOLLAR 69

the eye to newspaper advertisements that appeared in 1841 for the Prairie Cottage, an "airy and pleasant watering place" in the environs of New Orleans. A decade later, Lady Emmeline Wortley's gastronomic hopes were dashed: "We should have liked to taste alligator much, but, however, failed in doing so: it is said to be pretty good." She was denied her culinary treat because "There are very few, if any, left in the Mississippi; the numbers of steamboats there have crowded them out, and frightened them away."

Some early 'gator gazers may have had no reason for complaint. Alligators have little need for wasted motion, generally economizing on energy whenever possible. By remaining immobile, they do not attract attention to themselves. This is also part of their hunting strategy. Potential prey would steer clear of excess attention-grabbing activity. Alligators have the additional advantage of natural camouflage. Their pale bellies, from underwater vantage points, blend with the patterns of light and clouds of the sky above. Darkish irregular sides and back with patchy pigmentation, combined with a long cigarlike shape, give the upper surface of an alligator the appearance of bark or weathered wood. This, too, helps most saurians deceive potential meals into considering them harmless.

That alligators are the aboriginal woodenheads was immediately clear to sharp-eyed human observers. Brickell noted in 1737 that "they float as if dead, or like a log of wood." The Diderot *Encyclopédie* observed in 1754 that "they let themselves go with the course of the water without making any movement, like a piece of wood which floats in a current." Mark

Catesby in 1771 found the alligator "resembles an old dirty log or tree." Six years later, Jean-Bernard Bossu saw an alligator, but "At first sight we believed it was a big tree that had been cut down." William Bartram wrote in the 1790s, "the head in water resembles, at a distance, a great chunk of wood floating about." Risking plagiarism as usual, Thomas Ashe said in 1808, "the whole head in water appears like a piece of rotten floating wood." Robin, at about the same time, was more descriptive: "Its earthen color, its cracked body and its wrinkled head, give it on the surface of the mire and on the sand bars, the appearance of a tree trunk corroded by the waters."

Dr. John Holbrook wrote in 1842 that alligators were "often mistaken for logs of dead and decaying wood, as well as from their colour as from their perfect immobility." *Harper's New Monthly Magazine* knew that visitors couldn't see the alligators for the trees, and quoted an imaginary conversation with a tourist in 1855: The traveler inquired, "What kind of a looking thing is an alligator?," to which the wily native replied, "Why, something like an old log, sir." The writer of this piece was fooled, as well, and he confessed, "Our attention was also arrested by the apparent phenomenon of a limb of a tree taking upon itself motion, and cautiously moving down the bank of the bayou." Some of the typical visitor's disappointment may have resulted simply from his lack of ability to recognize the well-camouflaged alligator when he saw it, unless, heaven forbid, it walked up and bit him.

The more intrepid were willing to track the reclusive alligator to his lair for a little sport. Mass slaughters and individual encounters by "sportsmen" had been reported regularly since the early nineteenth century. Adam Hodgson wrote from Natchez in 1820, "During the day, many of the party amused themselves by shooting at alligators [from their steamboat]." Potshotting alligators from the decks became so popular in 1828 that Timothy Flint pontificated thus: "The ascent of the steam boat on an alligator stream, at the proper season for them, is a continual discharge of rifles at them." Soldiers on their way to the Texas Revolution in 1835 found alligators to be plentiful and splendid targets for the practice of marksmanship. Young recruit Herman Ehrenberg recalled, "They seemed unaware of our presence, and did not stir from the logs until we began pelting their backs with rifle-shots."

John J. Audubon found alligator hunting to be a suitable entertainment for visitors. He wrote to the Reverend John Bachman in 1837, "We took Harris on an Alligator Hunt on a *fine* Bayou. . . . Harris Killed several. he [*sic*] never had seen any before. . . . We had a fine frolic of this. . . ." In 1855 *Harper's New Monthly Magazine* reported "gentlemen sportsmen," who, according to the correspondent, "year after year, amuse themselves with shooting the reptile . . . ." Even local children on Avery Island in the Reconstruction years following the Civil War engaged in alligator baiting. E. A. McIlhenny remembered, "We, in those days, thought this was sport. . . ."

Regional guidebooks pointed out the best spots to travelers. The *Historical Sketch Book* of 1885 advised, "A favorite sport is alligator hunting . . . there are still enough to furnish the sportsman with plenty of good game. You will have no difficulty in finding as many alligators as you want in the innumerable bayous and lakes just back of Algiers [a community across the river from New Orleans]."

Perhaps the most famous of the late Victorian thrill seekers was the "divine" tragedienne Sarah Bernhardt. Thomas E. Dabney wrote that "on her many visits to New Orleans, [she] always found time, after filling the theatrical engagement, for an alligator hunt. She used to find her sport along Highway 90, about half-way between the Industrial Canal and Chef Menteur [highway]; only then

"SPORT AMONG
THE BAYOU."
WOODCUT BY
KARST IN *DOWN
THE GREAT RIVER*
BY WILLARD
GLAZIER, 1888.

[1890], there was no Highway 90, and over the winding mud road, it took longer to get to the alligator hunting than it now does to drive to Hammond . . . the danger and difficulties offered by the swamps then made alligator hunting a thrill that would long be remembered."

Unfortunately, Willard Glazier had to forego an opportunity to create such memories in 1892, writing, "Had the weather [on Bayou Tunica in the Feliciana Parishes] been more favorable we should either have continued our voyage or accepted Mr. [John J.] Winn's pressing invitation to join him in an alligator hunt—the chief sport of this section of Louisiana."

Cornelia Otis Skinner provided a memorable account of one of Madame Sarah's later forays into the marshes:

there was staged for her the much publicized 'Crocodile Hunt' when she was the guest of Mr. Charles Bell, a millionaire who owned a vast plantation outside of Lake Charles [Louisiana]. . . . Sarah insisted that in such terrain there must be crocodiles (she was unaware that in this country they were alligators) and she requested that a crocodile hunt be organized. As there wasn't a trace of either a crocodile or alligator on the estate, the obliging Mr. Bell sent off telegrams in all directions and managed to get hold of a baby 'gator, which was dumped into one of the lakes. The next morning was chilly and Madame Sarah emerged in a sealskin coat carrying a vast muff. After a bit she tossed coat and muff aside to reveal herself dressed as for an operetta safari with high-heeled shooting boots and a white suede jacket on the lapel of which was pinned a wilting hibiscus blossom. Brandishing a wide-brimmed hat trimmed with pheasant feathers, she shouted dramatically for the "beaters" to bring forth the "pirogues." There being neither "beaters" nor "pirogues," the hunting party had to make do with Mr. Bell, a gardener and a motorboat. They set forth but could not track down the prey. Finally the gardener located the baby 'gator, tied its foot to a line, handed the other end to Madame, and she hauled in her trophy only to find out that the beastie was in a state of hibernation.

Hunting took its toll. In 1915, Albert Reese reported that "Alligator Joe," a local character of indeterminate origin in Palm Beach, Florida, would "For a consideration (by no means a modest one) . . . take out a party of tourists for a day into the Everglades, guaranteeing that he would find an alligator for them to shoot. It was rumored by the natives that an accomplice was always sent ahead to free the alligator at the psychological moment, after the hunters had been paddled by a devious course to the selected spot. . . ." Raymond Ditmars deplored thoughtless sports hunting in the early twentieth century, as well, telling of a party of deer hunters in Georgia: "They had killed three large ones [alligators] and, as a memento of the sport, one of them had removed a section of the hide from the largest animal killed, which was about eight feet long. The guide further explained [to Ditmars] that the section of skin removed from the big brute *was large enough to make into a lady's pocket-book*. This little keepsake for the wife of one of the sportsmen possibly forms an interesting object for recalling reminiscences to the minds of the worthy hunters." Reese

went on to lament that "they have been so ruthlessly destroyed by native hunters for their skins, and by others, for mere wanton sport, that one may travel, perhaps, for days along the rivers of the South without seeing a single 'gator."

The advertising value of the alligator to the tourist industry and to politicians remained high, despite the decline in its numbers. A regular swamp safari was mounted for such purposes in 1937. "The occasion was an alligator hunt staged by Senator S. W. Sweeney of Lake Charles in order that newsreel cameramen and syndicate photographers might take the audiences of a nation on a vicarious dragon hunt. The place was the great marsh of Cameron Parish . . ." reported *The Progress* in mid-November. This was the same area that the Divine Sarah had essayed about forty years earlier.

"ALLIGATOR SHOOTING IN LOUISIANA." WOODCUT BY E. W. KEMBLE IN *HARPER'S WEEKLY*, OCT. 13, 1888.

As late as 1940, state-sponsored tourist publications still touted the "Coastal marshes and inlands of Louisiana" as prime alligator-hunting grounds. By 1980, however, after years of legal protection, outdoors writer Mike Cook told his readers, "A nonresident sports hunting license is $150. Sports hunters, however, must have the permission of the landowner and the use of one of his tags [sanctioned by the Louisiana Wildlife and Fisheries Commission]." Among those who made such arrangements in 1980 was cowboy star Roy Rogers. The Baton Rouge *State-Times* reported, "Rogers said that all his life he'd had a hankering to hunt alligators. He had his sights on a gator he could mount and display along with Trigger and Bullet in his museum back in California." Rogers got his wish. His ten-foot 'gator, dispatched with a pistol near Lafitte, Louisiana, now resides with those famous film companions of Rogers's past in Victorville, California.

While Madame Sarah had been indulging her taste for the exotic, a new form of reptilian tourist attraction had emerged: the alligator farm. The U.S. Department of Agriculture found that "with the increase in the number of winter tourists to the South and West, particularly in Florida and California, added diversions for these people gradually made their appearance, and among those of an exhibitional type were alligator farms." The first seem to have been established about 1880, although this date is uncertain. The number of farms increased relatively slowly, and by the early 1920s there were at least eight of them operating in the United States.

Alligator farms were soon providing the scientific community with easily obtained specimens, and amazing late-Victorian travelers with masses of caged 'gators. Of these early farms, Diane Ackerman revealed, "The St. Augustine [Florida] Alligator Farm is the world's oldest existing alligator farm. It was started in 1893 by George Reddington and Felix Fire, the conductor and fireman on a train that ran from St. Augustine to St. Augustine Beach. As the train wove through the swamps, people would see basking alligators and ask the trainmen to stop so they could watch. Fire and Reddington often had to stop anyway, to remove alligators from the tracks, and one day they decided to gather up some of the animals, put them into a bathhouse on the beach, and charge people a quarter for a look."

The United States had gone car crazy in the early years of the twentieth century, and more and more Americans were jaunting about the countryside on vacations and outings. Hungry for distractions, and often a bit naïve, they could easily be lured into paying "a quarter for a look," particularly if the roadside advertising was sufficiently lurid. With alligators, that wasn't difficult. Exaggerated ferocity, immensity, longevity, and antiquity were the virtues usually touted in such publicity. Gawking ticket holders shuddered with delicious late-Victorian horror at pool banks piled high with basking saurians, and they shared vicarious shivers with friends and neighbors back home by sending them outrageous Edwardian-era postcards of alligator hordes and alligator atrocities.

The U.S. Department of Agriculture analyzed a representative farm, and the inquiry revealed tourism as the major source of revenue, despite revenues from the early function of supplying zoos and laboratories: "the records show that at least half the total income was derived from the gate receipts, a quarter from the sale of manufactured merchandise, a tenth from the sale of live alligators, a tenth from the rental of live alligators, and not more than a twentieth from the sale of hides taken from animals raised in captivity."

Jack Barth and his fellow travelers found that "In the early days of gator farms, visitor entertainment was structured primarily around wrestling matches, often between a Seminole Indian and a feisty alligator. The tourists loved it; the alligators did not . . . alligators have no stamina for a prolonged struggle. They get tired and their necks break. In underwater matches they overexert themselves and drown." Martel McNealy judged that it wasn't for everyone: "That is a highly dangerous sport and should not be practiced by a man with a family and business responsibilities."

A more knowledgeable writer explained, "The power of an alligator's jaw is entirely in its closing muscles. A man can easily hold shut the mouth of a huge alligator with his hands. . . . This trick is also employed by so-called alligator wrestlers at roadside shows." Ackerman investigated further, finding "The secret of alligator wrestlers' ability to put an alligator to sleep or 'hypnotise' it, as they sometimes brag— may be that when you turn an alligator upside down you disorient it; disturb its equilibrium, and upset its eyes' ability to focus. Naturally it lies still, as a human being with extreme vertigo would."

Even model-turned-actress Lauren Hutton was attracted by the delicious appeal of the seeming dangers of alligator wrestling. Among her recollections is this: "When I was a child I watched the Seminole Indians wrestle gators and I remember it was one of the first times I wished I were a boy." Her tomboy instincts resurfaced in 1989, as *Vanity Fair* said, "at a preposterous age for a model," and she tried it during a fashion photography stint. "I don't want anyone thinking I was wrestling a dead alligator," she said. "His jaws weren't tied, and he weighed as much as Schwarzenegger. It was extremely dangerous and I was very scared."

Alligator farms quickly developed other diversions as well, such as alligator slides and alligator feeding time. Florida has triumphed in its array of 'gator spectacles. They include "Snapping Sam" at the St. Augustine Alligator Farm. There, at the alleged age of eighty, he was still on the boards in 1986, when Jack Barth and his companions found him "in blissful semi-coma in his sunny play pit until one of the handlers goads him into opening his massive jaws. The trick is for the handler to pass his arm between those deadly snappers without getting 'banged.' " Barth and company also took in the Gator Jumparoo at Gatorland Zoo in Kissimmee. At this notable roadside attraction, "every day, selected alligators are fed whole chickens by hand or from a cable-and-pulley system (acting as sort of a Swiss style ride for the chicken carcass). Both gators and crocodiles crowd under the morsels and jockey for position. The closest one then rockets up out of the water, sometimes nearly five feet, and locks onto his target with pinpoint

accuracy." At Alligatorland Safari Zoo, also in Kissimmee, they found "the legendary bell-ringing 'Stinker'—worth the price of admission itself."

Shopping was among these additional diversions, supplementing the take at the alligator farm gate. According to the USDA, "Those engaged in alligator farming generally have at least one building for displaying and for selling alligator products . . . it would appear that the trade in such articles was profitable as early as 1890." "Such articles" consisted of alligator teeth, stuffed alligators, picture postcards (featuring an astonishing array of trick photographic images), a variety of leather goods—which included novelty items such as the "souvenir doll 'alligators' wearing top hats and tuxedos, or dressed as doctors, lawyers or professors (complete with pince-nez)" that caught Ackerman's eye—handbags, suitcases, and tanned "specimen" alligator hides. Later proliferations, including the souvenirs manufactured in Hong Kong, are limited only by the imagination. Barth and his traveling companions especially recommended "GATOR MITTS [:] We spotted two different styles of these at several Florida gator farms . . . these mitts grabbed our hearts. Buy both styles and steer your car with them for the rest of the trip. We did."

By far the most famous of these souvenirs was the live baby alligator. They became extremely fashionable with tourists before the turn of the century. There was a good market for wild babies, which, according to Raymond Ditmars, were "sold to curio dealers, thence to tourists from the North who carry them away to endure a slow death from starvation." Reese reported that "In 1890, 8400 alligators were sold to tourists [by dealers in Jacksonville, Florida]." Karl Schmidt wrote that "in 1921, in addition to adult specimens sold to zoological parks, a single farm in Jacksonville, Florida, sold over ten thousand baby alligators." That number may have been overestimated, as by the late 1920s, something like 3,500 per year were being sold by Florida alligator farms. When demand exceeded domestic supply, baby caimans, imported from Mexico or Central America, were palmed off on the unsuspecting, and used to make some of the souvenirs, as well.

Alligators bred poorly on early farms, and their proprietors resorted to purchasing eggs robbed from nests in the wild. Reese explained, "Such eggs may readily be hatched by simply keeping them moist and at a fairly constant temperature. . . . " Recently, one especially enterprising alligator farm near Ponchatoula, Louisiana, even made egg hatching into a tourist attraction. Kate Cohen said in the *Times-Picayune*, "The Kleiberts have controlled the incubation of a number of eggs to ensure the hatching will happen next weekend [mid-August 1990]."

"Pet" alligators have been known since practically time immemorial. Even the biblical Leviathan seemed domesticable. In the Book of Job, one finds this inquiry: "Wilt thou play with him as with a bird[?] . . . "; and in 1806, Thomas Ashe captured a few babies that had "beautiful blue eyes with an expression extremely soft and sensible." He was "determined to rear them up and bring them [home] with me to England."

By the mid-1850s, *Harper's New Monthly Magazine* was aware that "In Louisiana and Florida the alligator is sometimes a pet, and has been, by very little attention, so far civilized and enlightened as to justify the ready belief of its being a harmless inmate of Egyptian dwellings." The journalist was referring to ancient Egyptian religious practices involving the more ferocious Nile crocodile recorded by Herodotus, Strabo, and other ancient writers.

The magazine went on to recount a contemporary occurrence:

A Miss Nel Gary recently went before one of the Recorders of New Orleans, and made oath that one Ernest Dalfin, a neighbor of hers, kept in his yard an alligator of immense size and ferocity; and that, as she was frequently obliged to go through the yard, she considered herself in great bodily fear and danger; wherefore she prayed that her neighbor remove the alligator to some other quarters. On this charge, Dalfin was arrested. When required to plead, he stated that he kept the alligator to guard his premises from intrusion, and that his amphibious guardian was, except when imposed on, as quietly disposed a reptile as ever lived. As for the prosecutor, he contended that she was brazenly inclined, and kept constantly exciting the alligator's ire by tickling him under the short ribs with ten-foot poles, and casting brickbats at his countenance, and on one occasion even went so far as to singe his back with a hot smoothing-iron, since which time his alligatorship swings his tail at her whenever he sees her. On this showing, Ernest was discharged; but Ellen was bound over to keep the peace toward "the pet" and its excellent owner.

WORKING FOR THE YANKEE DOLLAR   77

"ALLIGATOR FARM,
ST. AUGUSTINE."
1925, AND
SEMINOLE
ALLIGATOR
WRESTLER, 1905.
POSTCARD
ILLUSTRATIONS BY
THE CURT TEICH
CO., CHICAGO.

And just as alligator farms were being established, that Victorian trendsetter Sarah Bernhardt got her first 'gator, as related by Cornelia Otis Skinner: "In Louisiana [during her first American tour], Sarah purchased a small alligator whom she named Ali-Gaga. [She also had a monkey called Darwin.] It was a friendly little reptile which manifested a devotion to its owner, following her about in her dressing rooms, her hotel suites, her private [train] car. During meals, it lay docilely at her feet and at night it had a cozy habit of crawling under the covers of her bed. . . . Ali-

Gaga's days were cut short by an early demise due, according to Marie Colombier [an exceedingly jealous and unreliable witness], to a surfeit of champagne."

Souvenir babies had reached the North in such quantity that the Chicago Zoological Park made the following offer to the Louisiana Department of Conservation in 1943: "We have here four or five hundred alligators—animals of all sizes. These have been brought to us by people traveling in the South and if it is the plan of the State of Louisiana to introduce alligators in proper places, I wonder if you could use some of these animals. We would be glad to crate them carefully and deliver them at the express office for shipment wherever you wish." The state, however, declined on the grounds that in the mid-1940s, Louisiana was not suffering from a lack of saurians, some of which were found from time to time in places that weren't so proper.

A few months later, a famous practical joker in Baton Rouge registered this remarkable claim with the clerk of court of East Baton Rouge Parish: "I, Charles Scott Theriot, am the original owner of a talking alligator. . . . I taught him to talk and sing. His best song is 'Casey Jones.' I am now teaching him 'Pistol Packin' Mama.' . . . How I taught him to talk and sing is a mystery to many people." The mystery was so great, Theriot's son remembers, that crowds came to their home for viewings of the nonextant reptile. Theriot would blame silence on the weather, telling disappointed visitors that it was too warm (or too cold) that day, but that the alligator had been talking a mile a minute the day before. While staying at the old Heidelberg Hotel, John Barnum—of circus fame—heard of the miraculous talking alligator from the newspaper, and he called for an appointment to recruit the talented saurian to perform under the big top, frightening its alleged owner into 'fessing up. The irrepressible Theriot, a roofer by trade, who lived in north Baton Rouge, also filed courthouse papers at one time or another on "disappearing paint" and "perpetual motion."

At about the same time that Theriot's alligator was supposed to be chatting and chanting, "Charl" Bazil, also of Baton Rouge, actually hitched up two medium-size

"CHARL" BAZIL AND ALLIGATOR-DRAWN PLOW. PHOTOGRAPH FOR THE *MORNING ADVOCATE*, BATON ROUGE, MARCH 2, 1946.

ADVERTISEMENT FOR LOUIS RUHE'S NEW ORLEANS BIRD STORE. LITHOGRAPH IN *HANSELL'S NEW ORLEANS GUIDE*, 1893.

alligators to a homemade plow and tilled a few furrows in his backyard garden. The local newspaper carried photographs to prove it. Bazil had raised the alligators for eleven years, from the length of ten inches. Alice Cooter described their harnesses: "The yoke Charl uses when he hitches them is made of the top of the back of a chair with dried vines bent for the loops. His harness, made of leather, is put over the mouths and under the necks of the alligators and each harness has different color buttons to identify it. The larger alligator has green buttons on his harness, and the smaller has white ones." These nameless saurians were uncommonly obedient, and, according to Ms. Cooter, would "come when Charl bends over, snaps his fingers, and tells them to. . . . "

Theriot's rare and endangered singing alligator and Bazil's yeoman farmers are, of course, the stuff of which legends are made. Naturally, one arose not about these "pets" but instead about populating the sewers of New York with all those reptiles flushed by vacationing Manhattaners who found when they got home that their new roommates didn't adapt well to apartment living.

Some early alligator farms survived, and a few became true centers of alligator research and breeding. Authorities as early as the 1920s saw tourist interest as gratuitous encouragement to keep some of the thousands of alligator farm residents alive during the years that saw drastic declines in the wild populations of all the southern states. Some of the early farms were indeed densely populated. A federal publication of 1929 stated, "As might be expected, the largest alligator farms in the United States are in Florida, and one of them reports having 12,000 animals on hand, of which about 150 are more than 11 feet in length." Thomas Barbour wrote in 1944, "there are enough in the various so-called alligator farms to repopulate the state [Florida] if there were money available to buy them up and turn them loose." Many of the early alligator farms have now disappeared, and the trade in baby alligators ceased after protective legislation was enacted in the 1960s and 1970s.

Such, however, is the legacy from those pioneering entrepreneurs, promoting tourism and working for the Yankee dollar. Their efforts sealed the alligator's fate as "symbol of the South" to visitors from cooler climes. Promotional language of their advertising, coupled with farfetched claims of guides and other presenters, exaggerated or falsified outright many aspects of alligator behavior to an audience composed of several generations of trusting tourists. Imagery and other souvenirs they distributed, particularly postcards (often featuring laboratory-manipulated trick photography), gave concrete visual form to a great deal of alligator disinformation. Much of this did not serve the true interests of the alligator, and it worked powerfully, especially when spread by word-of-mouth, to contribute to an error-riddled image of the alligator in the minds of the United States public. And, after all, the Yankee dollar was a powerful incentive, and the Yankees were likely to part with more of them if obliging promoters and entrepreneurs gave them what they wanted.

MVSEI
WORMIANI
HISTORIA

LUGD· BATAVORUM
EX OFFICINA ELSEVIRIANA
Acad. Typog. 1655.

CHAPTER EIGHT

LET ME ENTERTAIN YOU
AND WE'LL HAVE A REAL GOOD TIME

THE ALLIGATOR MAKES A PUBLIC SPECTACLE OF ITSELF

Curiosity, repulsion, scientific interests, pageantry, economics, snobbery, and education are among the many motivating factors that have drawn people, over a period of four centuries, to include the alligator in a wide variety of public exhibitions, displays, entertainments, and spectacles. The concept of putting living crocodilians on public exhibition is as old as Ancient Egypt and imperial Rome.

Herodotus, Pliny, Strabo, and other ancient writers told of Egyptian crocodile worship, crocodiles housed in special pools in temple precincts, crocodiles decorated with precious ornaments, crocodiles gilded, and even crocodiles embalmed and mummified. Of those Egyptians not worshiping the crocodile, some became proficient hunters. The first report of "wrestling" came from ancient Rome, where crocodiles and Egyptian handlers were imported for the entertainment of Emperors Augustus and Heliogabale.

This information, whether real or legendary, was available to European savants from the sixteenth and seventeenth centuries onward. It was part of the intellectual baggage carried about in the heads of the well read and well educated, Renaissance Men and early scientists, some of whom strayed not far from alchemy.

CROCODILIANS IN THE BAROQUE CABINET OF CURIOSITIES. ENGRAVED FRONTISPIECE FROM *MUSEUM WORMIANUM*, 1655.

Earliest of the alligator displays in the modern world were the hides and stuffed specimens in cabinets of curiosities. These agglomerations of the rare, the new, and the unusual from the realm of the natural sciences (including two-headed calves) established the learned reputations of early collectors and became a basis for learning for early scientists; inquiring minds wanted to know. By and large, the cabinets of curiosities were private and not easily accessible for public viewing.

The seventeenth century saw the establishment of scientific academies, often under noble or royal patronage, and the enlargement of the menageries or early zoos where living specimens were maintained. These animated cabinets of curiosities were frequently open for viewing for alleged public edification. The menageries and academies persisted and proliferated through the eighteenth century, encouraging the development of additional private, municipal, and national institutions in the subsequent two hundred years.

As curiosities from North America, alligators were included in these menageries whenever they became available. There they often suffered the traumas of climatic change. C. C. Robin noted in 1807, "In effect, those that have been brought to France have hardly been put into hibernation by the cold: they have perished instead of withstanding it." George IV had an alligator at the Tower Menagerie in London in the 1820s, where it remained for about two years.

By the following decade, entrepreneurs had put the zoos on wheels, and alligators lumbered throughout Europe as traveling sideshows. M. F.-E. Guérin wrote in 1834, "One sees from time to time in Europe, small specimens of living alligators among the animals that make up traveling menageries. The mountebanks make use of them to rivet the astonished gaze of the curious. . . ." Even here there are ancient prototypes shown in Egyptian sculpture depicting acrobats tumbling on crocodilian backs. The prototype circus managers were in it for the money, caring little for the creature comforts of their captives and performers.

That such practices continued in the United States is evident from a 1938 comment of the New Orleans *Times-Picayune*: "Saurians caught by [Denny] Massey [professional guide and hunter on Caddo Lake] have appeared in carnival shows and at fairs in many towns within a wide radius of the Caddo Lake section." The 1938 season also saw the Hagenbeck-Wallace Circus touring with more exotic crocodiles, and in the following decade a female performer at the Al-Sirat Grotto Circus appeared with crocodiles in Cleveland in 1948. While alligators may well have been presented in circus menageries during this period, little record is available concerning them. Menagerie attractions were not as well documented as ring acts.

Barnum and Bailey first manifested a known interest in alligators in 1943, when John Barnum attempted to pry Scott Theriot loose from his famed but fictitious singing reptile in Baton Rouge. Forty-five years later, the combined Ringling Bros. and Barnum & Bailey Circus—"The

Greatest Show on Earth"—finally did something about it. On the 1988–1989 tour of the "Blue" unit (the other one is dubbed "Red"), the world-famous circus presented "Tahar, the Moroccan Master," as a featured novelty act. Tahar and a huge alligator even appeared on a poster and the cover of the tour program, and they shared the ring with such attractions as the Lilov Bears, Larry allen Dean and his lions, Carmen Hall and a troupe of African baboons, a "Python Priestess," and the Amabutho Zulu Warriors, while the Flying Morales and other trapeze artists soared overhead. All this was staged in the grand tradition of cirus antics.

Tahar's challenge was great; the program alleged, "the mighty Moroccan Master faces the cold-blooded, primordial power of the largest known alligators in captivity in a terrifying display of strength and courage." As the program described the performance, "with snapping jaws and thrashing tails, the angry reptiles surround him. . . . Never before in the history of *Ringling Bros. and Barnum & Bailey Circus* has Man dared enter the water-filled Chamber of Doom while locked in the creature's lethal embrace. Never before has Man stepped forward to declare himself 'Master' of the Jaws of Death. . . . " Tahar's prowess was unparalleled, as according to official circus rhetoric, "With the force of his presence, he commands them. With the power of his mind, he compels them to do his bidding. Slowly, inexorably, the alligators succumb to his will." Tahar did stick his head into the alligator's open jaws, somewhat in the manner of a lion tamer, as photographs attest. Secondhand eyewitness accounts, though, maintain

that for the most part the alligators acted like alligators— which is to say that the activity level of these cold-blooded reptiles depended on temperature and time of day and could range from downright frisky to something like cinematic slow motion. It was said that among the best parts of the act (and the most action) was herding the reluctant and protesting alligators in and out of the box.

Prior to the Civil War in the United States, the public attitude toward alligators seems to have been that of the curious who patronized the menageries and traveling circuses of Europe, excepting, of course, the natives of the Deep South. Drawing perhaps on the prototype of European sideshows, two balloonists (one of them a Frenchman) made one of the oddest uses of alligators on record. The *New Orleans Bee* announced on February 7, 1858, that high-fliers Smith and Morat would "make their terrific and unsurpassed ascension on the bare backs of two monster alligators (dispensing with the use of the car or other resting place) . . . . After the inflation of the balloon is completed the monstrous alligators (about 11 feet long

each) will be harnessed in their paraphernalia (most beautifully and gorgeously caparisoned) in the presence of the spectators." The follow-up report read: "The aeronauts, alligators and all, descended safely, in some fifteen or twenty minutes after they went up, at the corner of Camp Street and Felicity Road [now in the Lower Garden District]." The flower garden where they came to rest, belonging to one Mary Mallaghan, was put into considerable disarray by these visitors dropping in unexpectedly. The whole thing proved so entertaining (and doubtless so profitable) that the daring duo did it again, about a week later, releasing an alligator by parachute from on high. High was alleged to be five thousand feet. Spectators must have been startled at the apparition. Such "aerial ascensions," as they were termed, were important in the early development of entrepreneurial systems exploiting (and developing audiences for) spectator sports.

After the Civil War, as alligator was becoming a popular leather, living specimens became more and more attractive as civic ornaments. Visitors to New Orleans's first World's Fair in the mid-1880s were regularly directed to the alligator pit at Spanish Fort on the shore of Lake Pontchartrain, where a lethargic batch of large 'gators basked endlessly for their benefit. This installation was typical of alligator displays at United States zoos and parks within a climatic range that the alligators could tolerate. Some advanced zoos, in more northerly climes, even offered heated winter quarters.

European zoos, supported by Victorian scientific organizations, began to compete and collect in earnest, vying for the most unusual or rarest animals. G. A. Boulenger was proud in 1890 that "The society [Zoological Society of London] has now the advantage of exhibiting two living specimens [of the Chinese alligator] in its menagerie. . . . I have heard from my friend Dr. Boettger that two specimens have just been received by the Zoological Gardens of Frankfort-on-the-Main [*sic*]." This gang-of-four were probably the first live Chinese alligators to reach Western civilization (a few stuffed ones had preceded them).

The market for specimen alligators was such that it was among the motivations for the founding of Victorian alligator farms. Alligator hunters participated in the trade as well, trapping live alligators instead of skinning them, to take advantage of ready turn-of-the-century sales. An economic analysis of an alligator farm by the United States Department of Agriculture in 1929 revealed that a tenth of its income was realized "from the rental of live alligators," although for what purposes and on what terms remained unspecified.

By the 1940s, the Chicago Zoo had a surfeit of alligators—several hundred, of all sizes, brought to the Windy City as souvenirs of southern vacations—and offered them for restocking depleted southern habitats. In New Orleans, the Audubon Park Zoo, established on the old World's Fair site, was inundated itself. Over two hundred were donated in one fell swoop when an alligator farm at nearby Michaud was usurped to become the site of a yard to build war-effort Liberty Ships.

THE GREAT BARE BACK ALLIGATOR BALLOON ASCENSION OF 1858. DETAIL OF A DRAWING BY WALTER WADE WELCH, 1989.

FACING PAGE: TAHAR THE MOROCCAN MASTER AND THE JAWS OF DEATH UNDER THE CIRCUS BIG TOP, 1988.

LET ME ENTERTAIN YOU 87

"Included in this donation was old Aleck, who years ago won the eye and admiration of 'Divine Sarah' Bernhardt. This aged reptile, which was presented to the famous actress in the 1890's in the Board of Trade Building, is now 11 feet long and worth almost $1000. . . . [After Sarah declined to take home this, her third-recorded alligator,] Aleck was the pet of the Board of Trade for many years, but he outgrew his pool and was turned over to Theodore Owen, 924 Burgundy Street [in the French Quarter], according to Allen S. Hackett, consulting engineer, who was present when Aleck met 'Divine Sarah.' When Mr. Owen died in 1935 Aleck was sold to Mr. [F. C.] Luthi and taken to his farm [and thence to the zoo]," reported the *Times-Picayune*.

Luthi's gift prospered and grew—to the point that the New Orleans zoo was as overcrowded and overpopulated as Chicago's. The southern zookeepers came up with a unique solution to their problem: barter by the yard. Val Bowman chortled, "alligators are being sold by the yard—like ribbon. . . . The Audubon Zoo had an alligator surplus. . . . Two hundred feet of alligators were swapped for four fine, frisky young ostriches, 30 inches high, and about 90 days old. They are the first ostriches the zoo has had. They were shipped here from Los Angeles, which is the alligators' destination. The other 200 feet of alligators is [sic] also bound for California. . . . Measuring the creatures wasn't exactly as simple as measuring off lace, but it has been done." This may well be the only precedent that sets the value of an ostrich at fifty feet of 'gator.

While the zoos and related spectacles were developing, the old cabinets of curiosities of the early gentlemen collectors underwent their own metamorphoses and entered the public domain, as well, becoming the basis for the emergence of natural-history museums in their embryonic form. These centers of research and collecting quickly put stuffed alligators in their public galleries. In Europe, they were popular international oddities; in the United States, they began to make fabled southern fauna more familiar, more real, and better understood to a nationwide audience.

"The zealous and indefatigable Michaux . . . has given to the Museum of Natural History of Paris a crocodile [sic] that he killed on the banks of the Mississippi," intoned Daudin in 1803. Thomas Jefferson was prepared to underwrite one of Michaux's expeditions and the enterprising Frenchman got over much of North America before official representatives and surveyors of the United States had managed to do so. His "crocodile," however, couldn't have been given to the Muséum d'Histoire naturelle without the intervention of the French Revolution, as a result of which many formerly royal collections were nationalized. In an early fit of sharing the wealth, "Mr. Peale sent a very fine individual [alligator] to the Paris Museum. . . . The specimen above-mentioned, sent to Paris by Mr. Peale, was only five feet in length," reported Cuvier. "Mr. Peale" was no doubt Charles Willson Peale, member of the dynasty of noted Pennsylvania artists, and founder, director, and curator of his own Philadelphia Museum, as well.

The real rarities came a little later. After the U. S. Civil War, "a stuffed specimen [of the Chinese alligator] was forwarded by M. Fauvel to the Paris Museum . . . two others were . . . received in this country [Great Britain], one of which was retained for the British Museum," reported Boulenger. By the 1890s, that venerable institution had an entire roomful of stuffed crocodilians to enflame the British imagination with exotic thought.

In this country, the Smithsonian had just missed a good bet. John Avery's monster, sent at the Smithsonian's request, unfortunately died en route and was buried at sea. By the end of the century, however, any natural-history institution in the country worth its formaldehyde had an alligator or two somewhere in the basement.

Guérin reported in the 1830s that "the druggists [make use of alligators] by preserving the dead in alcohol to make window displays." Although a few alligators may have wound up as apothecary enticements titillating customers in search of various forms of snake oil, this was a limited exploitation of the alligator as public spectacle.

But while Victorian Americans—scientists and public alike—were learning from the study of alligators in zoos and museums, a new use was found for them in the elaborate tableaux and parades of New Orleans Carnival, which developed in its modern form after the initial procession of the Mystick Krewe of Comus in 1857. No one is sure when the alligator rode his first Mardi Gras parade float, but in 1873 one was featured in what may be the all-time scandalous parade. The Comus theme that year was "Missing Links to Darwin's Origin of Species," which proved to be a brilliant satirization of the officials of federal occupation during the Reconstruction era as the meanest,

ugliest, and most repulsive of God's creatures. Each costumed marching squadron was accompanied by a costumed ass with a sign in rather free verse announcing the veiled identities of the contingent. Group Eight were the Amphibia, and among them, it was noted, "While *caimans* wake, with new-born joy elate, and roars the *Walrus*, eager for his mate." Not overexacting in scientific accuracy, this public lampooning on a monumental scale gave vent to white southern frustrations at the time.

The next-known Mardi Gras 'gator arrived about 1878, just in time for the Rex parade. It was a large papier-mâché creation from the French atelier that manufactured them for the New Orleans celebration. Alligators—of European or domestic manufacture—have rolled along

 LET ME ENTERTAIN YOU 89

UNPACKING, IN A COTTON PRESS, THE PAPIER MACHE ANIMALS FROM PARIS, TO BE USED IN TH

Unpacking in a cotton pre... ...from

...CESSION. 1878 – 7³/4 × ...

parade routes ever since. As floats became larger and more elaborate, so did the parading saurians. The greatest of all may well be that created for the recent Bacchus parades by the Blaine Kern Studio. Double-decked, and so long, at 110 feet, that it is jointed in order to turn corners, it is among the largest Carnival/Mardi Gras floats ever built.

The largest architectural alligators must surely be those erected at Florida alligator farms. The apparent intent is advertising that will stop traffic, and it does. Monumental 'gators mark parking lots, and even serve as tunnel entrances, requiring visitors to walk through gaping jaws to get to the varied delights of the farm itself. These overwhelming roadside attractions are mostly on or near "alligator alley," the highway that crosses the southern part of the state through alligator territory.

On the occasion of the centennial of its first World's Fair, New Orleans threw another one in 1984. Naturally, alligators got into the act. They aren't on the city's official seal for nothing, and with a theme like "Rivers of the World: Fresh Water as a Source of Life," the opportunity was not to be missed. Playful alligators cavorted on the fair's "Wonder Wall," and greeted visitors at official gates. Designed and executed by the same talented artists and craftsmen who create them for Mardi Gras floats, the World's Fair alligators delighted hundreds of thousands of visitors and added psychological cement to the growing American concept of Louisiana as the land of the 'gator, particularly in light of the state's pioneering success in wild and farmed alligator management.

SURVIVAL STEW TO SCALLOPINI

THE EDIBLE ALLIGATOR

Among the most interesting phenomena in American dining in the past few years has been the introduction of alligator to the table. At first, this may seem odd, but given the qualities of the product, it is also logical. It has occurred at a time when Americans have become increasingly conscious of the relationship between health and diet, and the alligator is a prime candidate to assist with the first and expand the second. Steve Robbins, president of Preferred Meats in Dallas, has described alligator as a "rising star," and has said, "People want high-protein, low-fat meats, so they are trying something new."

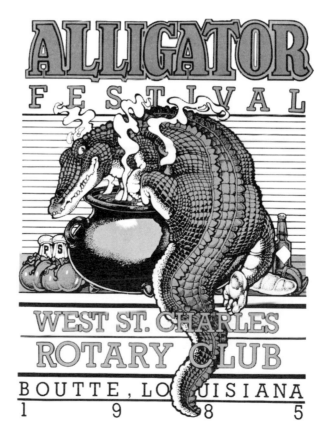

FACING PAGE:
"MODE OF DRYING . . .": SIXTEENTH-CENTURY NATIVE AMERICAN ALLIGATOR CUISINE. ENGRAVING AFTER A DRAWING BY JACQUES LE MOYNE DE MORGUES IN *HISTORIA AMERICAE SIVE NOVI ORBIS*, PART II, 1591.

POSTER, WEST ST. CHARLES ROTARY CLUB ALLIGATOR FESTIVAL, 1985. COMMISSIONED SERIGRAPH BY B. SPENCER FOR THE WEST ST. CHARLES ROTARY CLUB.

Most are surprised to learn that the alligator has been a staple of the North American diet since prehistoric times. When European explorers reached the lands that became the southern states, they found alligator being savored by Native Americans from South Carolina to Louisiana.

"In order to keep these animals longer, they are in the habit of preparing them as follows: they set up in the earth four stout forked stakes; and on these they lay others, so as to form a sort of grating. On this they lay their game [including alligators], and then build a fire underneath, so as to harden them in the smoke. In this process they use a great deal of care to have the drying perfectly performed, to prevent the meat from spoiling"— reads this oldest recorded recipe for American alligator, written down and published by Jacques Le Moyne de Morgues in 1591.

In fact, alligator had long been a regular provision of North American natives within its habitat range when Le Moyne de Morgues discovered the indigenous population of colonial French Florida smoking it at the end of the Renaissance. There, native peoples prepared for winter by gathering in "all sorts of wild animals, fish, and even crocodiles [sic]," which were kept in storehouses after smoking. These emergency rations, "they do not resort to unless in the case of last necessity."

Alligator dishes were also popular among other southern Indians. LePage du Pratz said of a young Indian woman in 1758, "her tribe live along the banks of a lake that is filled with these animals; when the children see the small ones on shore, they chase them down and kill them, then the adults come out of the hut to skin them and then carry them off and make good eating from them."

The taste for alligator was apparently widespread, as LePage du Pratz noted: "besides there are tribes that live in good part from this animal." He was reinforced by de la Coudrenière in 1782: "many savages make it their principal food." A decade later, John Pope determined that it was the tail that Native Americans considered the best eating and that it "yields a very nutritious food." Christian Schultz made the same observation, writing in 1810 that Native Americans "relish the tail part of a young alligator."

Educated Europeans knew that crocodilians could be eaten, for they had learned from Herodotus that "the inhabitants of the territory of Elephantine [in ancient Egypt] eat the crocodile. . . ." and the Book of Job even asked of the Leviathan, "Shall thy companions make a banquet of him?" Furthermore, a quarter of a millennium before Columbus headed for the Caribbean, Marco Polo already had told them that Chinese alligators were hunted

ALLIGATOR TAIL WAS ALWAYS THE FAVORITE. SELECTED FRAMES FROM "BIG ROCK CANDY . . ."—AN EPISODE FROM *POGO* BY WALT KELLY, 1952.

for meat. Thus Le Moyne de Morgues, chronicler of French Florida, was probably not terribly surprised to find them being consumed by Native Americans in the late sixteenth century.

It would be another century and a half before there was a reported European taste test held on New-World shores. In 1753, DuMont de Montigny found that "The flesh of the young is somewhat like that of beef, and may be eaten." Adult alligators, however, he considered too gamy for a sensitive palate. He was in agreement with the Diderot *Encyclopédie*, which announced in 1754 "that the Chinese domesticate the crocodiles [Chinese alligators], that they fatten them in order to eat them; their flesh is white; the Europeans find it unsavory & too musky." Mark Catesby's tongue wasn't tickled by it, either. In 1771 in the Carolinas, he found, "The flesh is delicately white, but has so perfume[d] a taste and smell that I could never relish it with pleasure." Later food critics were to compare alligator to all sorts of meats in taste, and it was a long while before they learned to be careful in the butchering process to avoid the musk glands, which tainted the dishes of these early samplers.

Blacks, of course, had known the joys of crocodile feasts in Africa, where they had eaten both the flesh and the fat, and quickly made the American cousin a part of their diet. In 1792, Pope reported it was such a favorite that "Negroes voraciously englut and gourmandize"; while in 1810, Schultz said that blacks, "never miss an opportunity of securing that delicious morsel [the tail of a young alligator]." In the Carolinas, Baron Cuvier maintained that blacks "kill them with hatchets, and banquet upon the tail."

Dr. J. E. Holbrook found that paralyzed by winter torpor, alligators were easier to gather. Therefore, in 1842, he wrote, "In this state of hibernation [*sic*], many are dug out of their retreats by the slaves, who esteem the tail as an article of food." In the 1840s, a former planter assured Dr. Bennet Dowler "that his slaves were in the habit of eating alligators, which invariably made them sick. All his authority was insufficient to prevent this practice. The sickness was so frequent and so peculiar, that he could readily recognize it without difficulty. He gave emetics for its cure. The suspected substance was always brought up; though the negroes always denied having eaten the same." Exactly a century later, the WPA reported an isolated alligator food custom among blacks: "Some Negroes in the locality [south of Port Sulphur, Louisiana] use the alligator as food, first burying the tails of the younger saurians for several days."

European settlers had settled down to alligator at the table by the 1830s, when M. F.-E. Guérin wrote, "the flesh of the caiman is sometimes eaten, despite the musky odor which is natural to it, and which is not entirely lost in cooking; the tail is the bit that is preferred." John J. Audubon found there were worse alternatives, writing in 1837, "after all, alligator flesh is far from being bad," but that it was not to everyone's liking. "He [a guest named Harris] likes their flesh, too," he chronicled, "but not so Johny [*sic*]. [E]xcepting the latter our *Mess* made a grand Dinner of the 'Tail-end' of one. . . . " Others were not as enthusiastic. Dr. Holbrook found it "tolerable" in 1842, and Dr. Dowler wasn't having any, deferring to the secondhand account of a medical colleague "who once tasted this animal's flesh, [and] informed me that its flavour, in some degree, resembled that of fish, though unpalatable."

The alligator appeared more advantageous from the viewpoint of the deprived. Thomas Dabney noted that "Alligators during the War Between the States furnished food and leather to South Louisianians," and the Baton Rouge *State-Times* has said, "It was plentiful, it was free, and it was there." Alligators even made it into Yankee mess tents. D. P. Mason, a young Union soldier, wrote home to New Hampshire on March 24, 1863, "we had a rairaty [*sic*] for brakfast [*sic*] this morning; it was a piece of aliegator [*sic*]; it tasted like a squirel [*sic*]."

One heard little more of gourmet appearances by the alligator until the Victorian era drew to a close. When butchers discovered the error of their ways in processing the alligator carcass, they began to harvest perfectly palatable meat. Many, including the important early naturalist John James Audubon, thoroughly enjoyed a good alligator meal. Despite their praise, the majority of the population avoided alligator consumption because the poor saurian suffered from an image problem. Seen as a man-eating monster, potential diners were discouraged from eating something they thought might well eat them. American folklore abounded with inaccurate alligator information, often based on equally inaccurate accounts of the Nile crocodile, that had been transferred to the alligator because of family resemblance. Colorful and entertaining to a modern reader,

these stories discouraged many in past ages from trying even the slightest morsel.

As a result, throughout the nineteenth century and well into the twentieth, alligator was eaten by only a few people, living in alligator territory—the swamps and marshes of the southern states, especially Louisiana and Florida. Early tourists—visitors from the North and from European countries—sought it out as an exotic curiosity, something to tell their friends about when they got home. There were even reports of eating alligator eggs. Less-squeamish Edwardians were possibly more willing to experiment. "He cooked the flesh to feed the dogs, though he often fried a portion of the tail for his own use. It tasted like fish, he said, and was very good eating," wrote Clifton Johnson in 1906 about Jake, a professional alligator hunter from St. Bernard Parish.

Raymond Ditmars was puzzled that it was not more favored about 1910, when he said, "it has always seemed strange to me that more use is not made of the flesh of the alligator. This flesh is often said to have too strong a flavor to be palatable; I have eaten it when it had no such rank taste but was decidedly agreeable, being, as might be expected of so amphibious an animal, somewhat like both fish and flesh, yet not exactly like either." Ditmars also identified the two problems that had precluded its popularity: unknowledgeable butchering techniques and the animal's physical appearance and reputation. He recommended, "Perhaps greater care should be taken in skinning an animal that is to be used for food in order that the flesh not be tainted with the musk. It may be a lack of care in preparation that has given rise to the impression that alligator meat is too strong to be pleasant." In those words lies the explanation of the complaints of early samplers; so long as musk glands are not ruptured in the skinning and butchering process, the flesh will not be spoiled by it.

Ditmars also recounted the plot of an interesting practical joke: "It is perhaps, also, the 'idea' of eating a reptile that makes the meat unpopular. A half-grown boy, who was once in the swamps with me, had expressed a great aversion to alligator meat, so the guide, one day, offered him a nicely fried piece of alligator meat, saying it was fish; the meat was eaten with evident relish and the diner was not told until after a second piece had disappeared what he had been eating." Dr. Leslie Glasgow encountered a similar attitudinal situation when his experimental nutria cookbook failed to change the eating habits of south Louisiana in the 1960s. The recipes were delicious, but the locals weren't interested in something native French speakers called a *gros rat* [big rat] and that looked like one, too.

Ditmars saw in alligator eating both nutritional and economic advantages: "It has always seemed strange to me that the poor people of the South should not more often vary the monotony of fat pork and corn bread with alligator steaks." He was also concerned with other health-related aspects of southern alligator consumption, in a day before widespread refrigeration: "Whether the meat could be smoked or salted so that it would keep in a hot climate I do not know; I am not aware of any experiments along this line." Nor was he aware, apparently, that the Native Americans of French Florida had solved that problem well over three centuries earlier; neither could he possibly have known that he was unwittingly predicting the appearance of Gator Jerky on the Florida market in 1990. The brainchild of entrepreneur Bill Burrer, these bite-size bits of cured 'gator were developed as the natural nibbly to accompany Burrer's Growlin' Gator Lager.

S. C. Arthur was concerned with evident waste in 1928: "There is absolutely no use put to about 95 per cent of the living thing that is killed. That there can be use made of the alligator flesh is quite likely." E. A. McIlhenny, unburdened by attitudinal barriers, reported his own experiences in 1934: "The flesh of the tail of the young alligator is excellent, although it is not eaten generally, even by the natives [of Iberia Parish], except a few who are not especially squeamish about their food." McIlhenny came from a family known for its fine gastronomic traditions: They had invented and popularized Tabasco sauce. He appreciatively endorsed alligator: "I have often eaten it fried, roasted, fricasseed, and finely chopped and baked. When properly cooked and seasoned, it is as good flesh as I want to eat, and should be universally used for food." His wide-ranging culinary experiences led him to discern that "Its taste resembles somewhat whale or porpoise meat, having a slight, fishy taste. Resembling, however, in both taste and texture, meat rather than fish."

Wildlife biologist Percy Viosca expanded the repertoire of recipes, remembering that on swamp outings,

"Occasionally tenderloined alligator tail varied our menu." Other outdoorsmen experimented, as well. Harnett Kane reported, "one trapper [near Avery Island] told me that he liked rattlesnake meat and alligator tail but would never touch the mus'rat." Perhaps that should have been a warning to Dr. Glasgow, whose experimental nutria looked like overgrown muskrats!

Alligator (or a close relative confused with it) got back on the military menu during World War II. The New Orleans *Times-Picayune* reported that "The U. S. Navy's seabees here [on an unspecified island] are augmenting their meat rations in an unusual way. . . . Henry T. Christian, ship's cook second class, a native of Florida and an authority on alligator anatomy, prepared the evening meal of the officer's [*sic*] mess. One officer summed up the sentiment of the mess by asserting, 'those succulent saurian steaks were simply superb.' " In later decades, while alligators were under state and federal protection, alligator meat was not available unless, pardon the pun, it was poached. Enterprising outlaw hunters, outdoors writer Mike Cook wrote in 1970, "have managed to sell the tail meat as scallops (after making a mold in the proper shape and stamping it out) and as turtle meat." Edith Duncan, a lifelong resident of Iberia Parish, recalled that unscrupulous restaurateurs in her part of Louisiana also used ground alligator meat to "extend" the then-more-desirable crawfish in some traditional recipes such as bisque (even adding hashed armadillo on occasion). Suspect establishments were to be avoided in the days before alligator eating became popular.

Through 1978, federal restrictions protecting the endangered alligator population prevented the sale of alligator flesh. The situation changed in Louisiana, where alligator management efforts were so successful that the endangered status was lifted in small parts of the state, by the state, as early as 1970, and removed from most of the coastal parishes, through federal action, in 1979.

Among those responsible for a sudden interest in eating alligator at that time was Ernest Liner, of Houma, Louisiana. A dedicated herpetologist by avocation, Liner is respected by professional colleagues in academic and governmental circles. In 1978, he prepared the first draft of *A Herpetological Cookbook: How to Cook Amphibians and Reptiles* for presentation at a confab of three major national herpetological societies taking place in Arizona. Out there in the desert, far from the alligator's watery domain, Liner met with considerable interest. The book contained twenty-five alligator recipes, along with directions for preparing Congo Eel with Cucumbers, Deep-Fried Brandied Amphiuma, and over two hundred more concoctions collected worldwide. Reviewed as "a cookbook for the serious gourmet," it impressed Dr. Kenneth Dodd, amphibian and reptile specialist of the U.S. Wildlife Service's Endangered Species Office. Later in the year, Dodd cited Liner's work when he discussed and recommended the possibility of putting the carcass as well as the hide on the market. Privately published, Liner's book was first printed in an edition of only one thousand copies. Although popular with professional herpetologists, who knew how to order it, it did not appear on the shelves of

Doubleday or other national book distributors, in part because the esoteric ingredients were awfully difficult for the erstwhile domestic chef to obtain.

Acting on federal recommendation, the Louisiana Department of Health and Human Resources, through its office of Health Services and Environmental Quality, quickly issued rules governing alligator butchering that allowed alligator meat processed according to regulations to enter the market legally.

When alligator reached the meat and seafood markets, however, it proved to be a novel and puzzling item to shoppers. Linda Lightfoot explained: "there was little information on what portion of the animal was edible and on the nutritional value of the meat." Only a few specialists knew of Ernest Liner's pioneering publication. The Louisiana Cooperative Extension Service came to the rescue. "It's amazing how good this stuff really is," said Windell Curole, an extension agent in Terrebonne Parish. "We've been trying it out on the staff and everyone's pleased. Alligator has a pinkish color but turns white when it's cooked. It has a texture like chicken and tastes like chicken or frog legs once it's fried in cornmeal. It's a very mild taste."

Just what does alligator taste like? That question has prompted just about as many answers as there are respondents. It is among the many perceptions of *alligator* that have changed over time, according to circumstance, and, in this case, depending on the sensors of tongue and nostril of the individual, as well as his/her point(s) of reference. English traveler Lady Emmeline Stuart Wortley

was disappointed that none was available for her to sample when she journeyed through Louisiana in 1851, because she had heard that "it is said to be pretty good." Scientific opinion began to be recorded when biologist Albert Reese decided that alligator was "somewhat like both fish and flesh, yet not exactly like either." Reese's exact words were unabashedly lifted by Stanley Arthur in 1928. The Baton Rouge *Morning Advocate* vacillated in 1973, describing alligator flavor as "somewhat like a blend of fish and veal." Food science expert Michael Moody called it "bland" in 1982.

Cyrus Tamashiro, promoting the sale of alligator at his market in Hawaii in 1986, said, "Alligator meat is similar to chicken or veal—it has a mild taste." Food critic Tom Fitzmorris opined in New Orleans in 1989, "Its flavor is unique; it has a certain seafoodiness to it, but other aspects suggest fowl or veal. The closest thing I can think of to alligator in taste is turtle meat, but the alligator is lighter." Mike Fagan, president of the Florida Alligator Trappers Association, described alligator flavor as a cross between "the mildness of chicken and the sweetness of lobster." Art Cormier, the nuisance alligator patrol officer for Jefferson Parish, was a bit more down-home in his evaluation that alligator is "like chewy chicken with a hint of fishiness." Charles Lawling, general manager of Messina's at the Riverwalk in New Orleans, provided a wonderful summary in September 1989 when he discerned that alligator is "kind of like beef, but it tastes more like frog leg, which tends to taste something like chicken."

Now that the issue has been thoroughly confused, a

few observations are in order. Everybody's taste buds react a little differently to a new sensation, and sometimes those perceptions are "preconditoned" by mental concepts. This suggests that one take all the opinions expressed above with the proverbial grain of salt. Additionally, the flavor of alligator may depend, in part, upon the area from which the individual specimen comes, and its diet. Alligator feeding primarily on crab may not taste exactly the same as alligator feeding mostly on nutria, and so on. What is clear is that well-butchered alligator is mild in flavor, and as such, it is highly receptive to a wide variety of seasonings and culinary preparations. You'll have to try it and form your own opinion. No one seems to be able to tell anyone else just what alligator tastes like (or doesn't).

Windell A. Curole worked with Jean Picou to develop and distribute recipes, and encouraged restaurants and seafood markets in the Houma, Louisiana, area to handle the new product. In 1979, the extension-service team mounted the first Festival of Alligator Cuisine, which brought attention from restaurateurs and seafood sellers, as well as the general public. In the following twelve months, demands for recipes came from New Hampshire, Washington, Brazil, Santo Domingo, and Guam. Curole estimated that the 1979 season's take would be 16,000 alligators, which would yield 815,000 pounds of edible meat. Sale, however, was restricted to Louisiana only. Harlon Pearce, manager of Battistella's Seafoods, Inc., in New Orleans, complained, "You have to reach the out-of-state market to make it feasible," but he lauded the product, saying, "Once it's sliced into steaks, you can't tell alligator from veal."

Michael Moody and a team of expert food scientists with the Cooperative Extension Service at Louisiana State University in Baton Rouge studied the problem and found an intriguing potential economic advantage to alligator hunters. By comparing the price of raw alligator hide by the pound (instead of by length, which is customary) with the price of meat, they concluded, "Since the dressed weight [of meat] is roughly 60 percent of the total live weight and the skin is roughly 15 percent, the value of the meat may be considerably higher than the skin on larger alligators."

Unfortunately, the enormous increase in skin prices since that 1980 computation kept the prediction from becoming an annual reality (although it did happen at least once in Florida), but meat sales have certainly increased the total value of the take. Meat sales were estimated to have been fifty thousand dollars in 1980, a small beginning that increased tenfold over the following decade.

Moody's team conducted exacting nutritional analysis and determined that alligator is an excellent lean nutritional resource, comparing favorably with other meats. By calorie count alone, it is impressive: Only 232 of those pesky little heat units for a three-and-a-half-ounce serving. In fact, it has less fat content than beef, pork, or chicken, and its protein content is higher than that of pork or beef. Paul Thibodeaux, marine advisory agent for the Louisiana Cooperative Extension Service, observed, "The fat is on the outside, not in the muscle, like beef. You don't want to eat the fat off an alligator, anyway. It's pretty rank stuff."

The year 1980 also saw the first rash of alligator

cookbooks that followed in the wake of Ernie Liner's 1978 issue. *The Daily Iberian* included an alligator section in its special supplement on "Cajun Creole Cookery" at the time of the annual Sugar Cane Festival and Fair. Tom and Barbara Malik helped themselves liberally from Liner's book in preparing *Gator,* which they billed as "Louisiana's First Specially Prepared Alligator Cookbook" when it appeared in Morgan City, Louisiana, with twenty-three recipes. The West St. Charles Rotary Club put out the *1980 Alligator Festival Cookbook* in conjunction with its annual celebration in Boutte and featured just over sixty alligator preparations in it. The International Alligator Festival in Franklin, Louisiana, not to be outdone, published *Gator Gourmet* two years later topping the 'gator recipe race with two hundred plus entries. In comparison, *The Alligator Cookbook* from the National Alligator Association in Orlando, Florida, with some seventy offerings, looked a bit paltry by comparison. Virtually all of these drew heavily on Liner's original compilation.

All of the interest generated at festivals and other events piqued the curiosity of more adventurous eaters and brought about a demand for alligator at southern eateries. Founded by the Alciatore family in 1840, Antoine's is New Orleans's oldest restaurant and reportedly the first to add alligator to its regular menu. Food critic Tom Fitzmorris evaluated the first dish as follows: "The *potage* alligator at Antoine's is a superb soup and is hearty enough to serve as a luncheon entrée. It is thick and chunky—almost a stew, really—and is abetted by sherry, a good shot of pepper and a dark roux." It has remained popular and was featured at a function of the Wyvern Club held at the restaurant in the fall of 1990, a full decade after its introduction.

Other restaurateurs "realized that the 'gator's [*sic*] long deadly tails were full of tasty meat. Slowly, alligators started making special appearances," said journalist Michelle Nicolosi. Tommy Wong of Trey Yuen Cuisine of China in Mandeville, Louisiana, reports, "When we first started serving it [about 1980], it was a novelty sort of thing. People would order it and laugh. Now they order it because they like it, and they tell other people about it." Thus alligator reentered Chinese cuisine, where it had been at home for at least a millennium.

During those early years of alligator-meat marketing, many of the curious tried cooking it at home, too. In addition to all the alligator cookbooks (often hard to find, and printed only in small quantities), Curole and Picou made their new recipes available, moving the age-old saurian from marsh to microwave technology. They declaimed, "Alligator meat is versatile and can be served in a variety of dishes . . . alligator should prove to be a delightful change for any of your favorite meat recipes." Their offerings included Fried Alligator (in regular and Italian versions), Alligator Dip, Smothered Alligator, Alligator Balls, Microwaved Alligator, and 'Gator Sauce Piquant. With alligator introduced to traditional Louisiana cookery, alligator cook-offs even became a feature of the alligator festivals staged in the early 1980s as curiosity was piqued and the race for new recipes was renewed.

The most entertaining (literally) of all, however, is the "Official Song (number 43 in your hymnal)" of the Hot

Jazz and Alligator Gumbo Society, an organization of jazz enthusiasts in Fort Lauderdale, Florida. The main lyrical ingredients are "the juice from two ripe 'gators . . . twenty pecks of peppers . . . lots of Irish spuds . . . a couple of gallons of gin . . . the ears, a nose, [and] a couple of yards of tail." According to HAGS chef and Lerrikin Will Connelly, "This savory concoction remains unessayed by the membership because we have never been able to accumulate two whole gallons of gin at one and the same time (somehow it disappears quickly, possibly due to evaporation. Or possibly not)."

By 1984, alligator was on the road. In that year, it was

Antoine's Alligator Soup

2 1/4 lbs. alligator meat, cut in small pieces
1 large onion, finely chopped
4 bunches green onions, finely chopped
4 to 5 "toes" of garlic, finely chopped
1/2 oz. parsley, finely chopped
2 1/4 oz. butter, melted (for sauté)
1 lemon, sliced
3 bay leaves
thyme (to taste or your preference)
6 oz. sherry wine
1 oz. Worchestershire sauce (original recipe calls for "Lea & Perrin" sauce)
16 oz. tomato juice
1/2 gallon beef stock
Salt and pepper (to taste)
Caramel coloring (to your preference)
3 to 4 oz. brown roux (flour and oil)

Fry alligator meat in butter, set aside. Sauté all finely chopped vegetables in pan drippings, remove vegetables and make brown roux next, then add beef stock and caramel coloring to the roux. Season to taste with salt and pepper, Worchestershire sauce, tomato juice and sherry wine, lemon and bay leaves. Place the vegetables and meat into the gravy and simmer for two hours or until meat is tender.

Yield: approximately 1 gallon

first carried by the Tamashiro Market in Honolulu. Prices began to rise, as well. From $2.99 per pound in 1982, they had risen to $5.00 for "quality cuts." The limited Florida alligator harvest of 1984 brought hunters and trappers more for the meat ($40,000) than for the hides ($25,000), just as Michael Moody had predicted. By 1986, the Louisiana Department of Wildlife and Fisheries was conducting experiments at the Russell Sage Wildlife Refuge on Marsh Island to see whether "it is profitable for alligator hunters to sell their catch whole to companies that use both the hide and the meat," according to agent Johnny Tarver. In fact, it was. Now hunters often sell to a whole alligator processor rather than undertake the laborious procedure of skinning their catch. Prompting the experiments was the over 170,000 pounds of alligator from Louisiana alone consumed by the domestic and international markets. Meat was being shipped to France, Italy, Japan, and Singapore.

French writer Jacqueline Denuzière reports that English sales began at this time. "Jim Moran," she says, "a young British fish dealer specializing in exotic imports, attended a lecture in New Orleans in September 1986 on the art of cooking seafood and hit upon the concept of importing Louisiana alligator meat into England." It went over well, and by the end of 1987, Harrods and several London restaurants figured among Moran's regular clients.

New products were also being developed. In New Orleans, the Marciante brothers became the first wholesalers of alligator sausage in the state, at the behest of David Barreca of the Olde N'Awlins Cookery, who first tasted some they were selling at the annual Italian Open

Golf Tournament. Barreca purchased 1,500 pounds of the spicy stuff to sell at the New Orleans Jazz and Heritage Festival. That put the Marciantes into the alligator business in a big way, and they've been supplying restaurants and seafood markets ever since. It led to the creation of such sophisticated restaurant fare as boned chicken breast stuffed with alligator sausage and slathered with crab sauce. Alligator had entered the hallowed kitchens of haute cuisine. Prices rose commensurately; in Hawaii, tenderloin was being retailed at as much as $10.95 per pound in 1988, where the Honolulu paper published recipes from a chef in Baton Rouge for such delicacies as Alligator Primavera, Alligator Stuffing and Alligator Scallopini.

The entire Louisiana meat crop in 1988 was 600,000 pounds and had a value of $2.1 million. Of that total, $650,000 came from farmed alligator, with the remainder derived from the sale of wild carcasses. *Cooks* magazine celebrated by publishing an alligator butchering chart in its April 1989 issue. In an unprecedented philanthropic gesture, Art Cormier began to cook up his catch of "nuisance" 'gators from swimming pools and car washes to feed the homeless on an occasional basis. There was even a persistent rumor that a Mainland Chinese trade delegation inquired about quantity purchases to feed the students at Beijing University, but they went home disappointed after discovering that there was not enough available on the U.S. market. Remember that the Chinese had been eating it for centuries—and that the students revolted.

With the wave of national interest in Cajun cuisine, some of the newly recognized superchefs from Louisiana

began to prepare and present alligator dishes in the late 1980s. Paul Prudhomme, premier among the bunch, contributed an alligator sauce piquante to the range of local dishes. John Folse shared his knowledge of alligator sausage after returning from preparing a triumphal state dinner in the Soviet Union. Randy Guste, proprietor of Antoine's, made known the secrets of that establishment's famous alligator soup. The Wong brothers at Trey Yuen sent the author one of their justifiably famous Chinese alligator creations. Andrea Appuzzo adopted the alligator into his well-known classical Italian fare. Marcelle Bienvenue published her creations in the *Times-Picayune*. Tom Fitzmorris adapted an old New Orleans favorite and

FOOD BOOTH WAITING LINE AT THE ALLIGATOR FESTIVAL, BOUTTE, LOUISIANA.

released a recipe for alligator grillades. Justin Wilson began his PBS series on Louisiana cooking and prepared an occasional alligator dish, while the graphic designers who prepared the titles for the show used a filmed alligator among the "establishing shots" at the beginning of each segment, just to be sure viewers knew they were looking at Louisiana.

The British also were becoming more gourmet-minded. Madame Denuzière says that Joanne Gravier, "young chef at the French restaurant Chemies [in London], prepares alligator meat sautéd, then deglazed in a sauce of fruits and garlic; at Manzi's, the famous London seafood restaurant, they cook about 10 kilograms [over 20 pounds] of Louisiana alligator meat each week." However, Madame Denuzière noted regretfully in 1989 that to the best of her knowledge, "no Parisian chef had yet seized on the idea of this specialty." Someone in France must have tried it, though, if one is to believe the list of destinations reported in 1986 for exported alligator. French jazz great Claude Luter says that he sampled it at a restaurant in Switzerland.

By 1989, however, alligator had gained considerable popularity in New York in some of the more sophisticated restaurants. For example, Marvin Paige, the owner of Claire, started serving alligator meat to his customers in early 1989. Readily available from alligator farms in Florida and Louisiana, "the dish was partly popular because it was high in nutrients and low in cholesterol," reported Paige. About five percent of all of his customers now order alligator tail, which is comparable in price to a high-grade beef cut, such as prime rib or filet mignon.

Like any other foodstuff, best results in the preparation of alligator are obtained when the cook has a little background information with which to work. Cardinal rules for succulent saurian include:

1. **Know your butcher** if you obtain homegrown alligator. Be sure he/she knows to avoid the musk glands. You will not have this problem if you acquire commercially processed alligator.

2. **Avoid fat**, as it often imparts a musky or rank taste to alligator. The best alligator will be well trimmed of fat and well cleaned of any blood. Well-butchered alligator should be of a remarkably even overall color—neither marbled nor veined.

3. **Learn the cuts** before you buy. Most important among them are:

Tail meat. This is generally almost white in color (and remains white in cooking). It is the most popular; most recipes call for it, and it is generally the most widely available.

Filets. These are located on either side of the backbone within the tail of the alligator. They are the filet mignon or Canadian bacon of the saurian world—the best eating, and also the most expensive. Beware of boned alligator from other parts of the carcass being billed as filet.

Jowls. These are those puffy cheeks that make the 'gator seem to grin. Pinker than tail meat, they are considered just as good by many chefs. Some prefer them.

Leg. Consisting of the muscles of both front and back limbs, this is the stringiest and also the darkest or reddest portion. Best used in long-cooking preparations such as étouffé, soup, or sauce piquante.

Flank. From the area of the rib cage, it is sparse on an alligator, generally whitish in color, and not much used. Ribs may be barbecued.

4. **Know the age** of your 'gator before it goes into the pan. Would you prefer a scrawny old rooster, or a spring chicken? The same applies to alligators. Younger ones (up to six feet or so) are more tender than superannuated specimens.

5. **Tenderize your 'gator** before cooking. This can be done with marinades or by pounding with a meat hammer, just as you might treat a flank steak of beef.

6. **Please don't overcook** your alligator. If you do, it will become rubbery. Actually, there are two methods of achieving table-ready 'gator of (almost) melt-in-your-mouth consistency. Quick cooking of thin pieces over high heat will result in moist, almost flaky dishes. Slow cooking will take the 'gator past the rubbery stage, just as long cooking can convert tough stew meat to fork-tender dining pleasure.

7. **Use your imagination** in trying new seasonings and new recipes. Alligator gourmet cooking is still in its infancy. You, too, can contribute to culinary history.

If you come up with something really wonderful, send me the recipe for the next edition at P.O. Box 2448, New Orleans, LA 70176. I'm serious!.

An interesting postscript to the edible alligator is its equally edible egg. Baron Cuvier generalized in 1831 that "Their eggs [those of all crocodilians] are good eating, though they have a strong smell of musk, and are in great estimation in all the countries inhabited by these animals." In 1910, Ditmars had heard that "The eggs are eaten in many portions of the South. . . . Never having eaten an alligator egg, I cannot speak from personal experience of its flavor." Ditmars's experience was primarily in Georgia and Florida, where there was also a substantial nest-robbing business so as to provide alligator farms with eggs to incubate and hatch to supply the tourist trade with babies. Alligator-egg eating seems not to have been widespread. E. A. McIlhenny, writing of his experiences extending back to the 1870s and 1880s, remembered in 1934, "I have never known alligator eggs to be used by humans for food, although there is no reason why they should not be as palatable as turtle eggs."

"ALLIGATOR JOE" SUCKING EGGS. POSTCARD BY THE CURT TEICH CO., CHICAGO, CA. 1905.

Alligator Farm, Florida.

CHAPTER TEN

ALL THAT JAZZ

THE ALLIGATOR TAKES A SENTIMENTAL JOURNEY FROM SONG TO SILVER SCREEN

The song-and-dance alligator has entertained, moralized, educated, and terrified American audiences for several centuries. Alligators first burst into song long before permanent colonies were founded by European powers in America. The Seneca Indian culture included a traditional alligator song (it was recorded in New York in 1936), and music for ceremonial alligator dances was once current among the Creek, Seminole, and Iroquois nations. The Natchez even made an early percussion instrument from the alligator's cured hide.

In 1815, New Orleanians entertained a contingent of Kentuckians who had come to participate in the Battle of New Orleans. Samuel Woodworth's popular ditty "The Hunters of Kentucky" was sung in their honor to an audience comprised largely of keelboatmen. After the first rendition, they replied with their own parody, referring to British General Packenham (whom they had roundly trounced on the battlefield at Chalmette): "No matter what his force is / We'll show him that Kentucky boys / Are alligator horses." They did. The defunct British officer went home from the battle pickled in a barrel, just as many local specimen alligators had gone to Europe before him.

However, it took the invention of jazz at the end of the nineteenth century to popularize the alligator in American music. Early offerings included novelty numbers such as "Alligaitor [*sic*] Bait," published in New York in 1912, and Rudolph Ganz's "Alligator's Promenade." About

SEE YA LATER, ALLIGATOR: LOGO OF THE HOT JAZZ AND ALLIGATOR GUMBO SOCIETY. DESIGNED BY K. O. ECKLAND (AKA WHOOPEE ZECK-ENDORFF AND/OR INGOMAR GASSPIPE).

FACING PAGE: EARLY ALLIGATOR RECORDING ARTISTS: KING OLIVER AND THE CREOLE JAZZ BAND. PROMO-TIONAL PHOTO-GRAPH, CA. 1923.

"THE PRIVATE LESSON." POST-CARD ILLUSTRATION BY THE CURT TEICH CO., CHICAGO, © 1893, PRINTED CA. 1910.

1922, pioneering jazz musician King Oliver recorded "Alligator Crawl" by Thomas Waller, Andy Razaf, and Joe Davis. Fats Waller also released it on the Bluebird label. King Oliver and his Creole Jazz Band recorded "Alligator Hop" for both Century and Genette Records. The Genette version appeared in 1923. Originally called "Alligator Flop," the composition was attributed to Oliver and clarinetist Alphonse Picou. And, as the 1920s roared to a close, Parlophone released "Alligator Blues," and a rerecording of "Alligator Crawl" appeared on the Okeh label, both performed by the legendary Louis Armstrong.

All that jazz naturally inspired novelty dances for flappers to flap to, and gave rise to some interesting slang. Black musicians are said to have called white colleagues who "borrowed" their musical ideas "low-down alligators." That phrase is perpetuated by a contemporary white ensemble, who took it as their group name, operating out of Cornell University in Ithaca, New York, as the "Low Down Alligator Jass Band." There was also a particular style of playing the trombone (the slide instrument, as opposed to the valve variety) that required the early jazz trombonist to sit at the back of the bandwagon to give free reign to his instrument. This was described as "tailgating," and the perpetrators were known as " 'gaters." The musicians'

phrase "See you later, 'gater" was misconstrued into the ever-popular "See ya later, alligator."

Though not musical, the alligator has given us another entertaining phrase, in a political vein. Writing about the wit of Louisiana politicians, Dr. Ed Haas said of a state governor, "Responding to charges of corruption, Richard Lèche once exclaimed, 'I deny the allegations and I defy the alligator.' "

Alligators themselves have been said to possess musical talents. Poetic authors such as Howard Snyder have inquired, "who can ever forget the hollow, reverberant bellow of a big bull 'gator as he trumpets his love call among the cypress stumps . . . a voice from a far distant past, millions of years ago, when reptiles, not men, ruled the earth." And biologist Archie Carr says, "it is a song 200 million years old." In 1943 in Baton Rouge, Charles Theriot fraudulently claimed to have actually taught an alligator to sing "Casey Jones." Alligators, of course, are not alone among the living crocodilians to "bellow." As early as 1855, an American journalist speculated, "what must have been the feelings of the ancient people of the Nile, when, in the quiet hours of an Oriental night, they heard their great god waking up from the waters of that still unexplored river, and sending his gigantic voice vibrating through the vaults of their temples, or whispering in soft murmurs among their groves of palm."

Diane Ackerman found that the alligator's preferred one-note samba is B-flat. Louis Guillette told her, "You see, back in 1944 they had a big alligator named Oscar living in a tub in a lab [at the American Museum of Natural History in New York], and he seemed to respond when they strummed steel rods at certain intervals . . . one night when an orchestra was using the museum auditorium they asked a French-horn player to help them out with an experiment . . . whenever he hit B-flat Oscar went wild with bellowing. Then they tried a cello and the same thing happened. The instrument didn't matter—just the right pitch." This doglike sing-along response prompted Ackerman to ask, "Has no composer, I wonder, written a composition in B-flat for alligator and orchestra?"

One speculates as well about the possible relationship of the museum's singing saurian to Oscar of the Okefenokee. Andrew H. Malcolm and Roger Straus III report him as wandering the grounds of a visitor center in their book *U.S. 1*. Reputed to be about eighty years old, lengthy tourist-attraction Oscar tips the scales at over 650 pounds, and might be either uncle or nephew of the New York resident and possible namesake.

The well-tempered alligator caused quite an uproar in suburban Detroit in the 1950s. There, George Campbell, a naturalist, kept at his home what he alleged to be the second-largest collection of living crocodilians in the world. They were residing in the suburbs with the Campbells in defiance of (and secrecy from) municipal ordinance. Clandestinely maintained, the collection was nearly found out when Mrs. Campbell entertained her sewing group and "the ladies all plugged in their portable sewing machines, and suddenly thirty male crocodilians began to bellow from the basement. One of the machines must have hit a B-flat." According to Ms. Ackerman, Mrs. Campbell was "non-plussed, but quickly collected herself, explained that the plumbing had been acting up for days, and told them to pay it no mind."

The advent of rock' n' roll in that same decade inspired a new crop of alligator songs and dances. "See You Later, Alligator," with words and music by Robert Guidry, became extremely popular. Johnny Horton's rendition of "The Battle of New Orleans," a sort of country-rock ballad, attributed the American victory at Chalmette in part to an alligator aimed in reverse, powdered up as a cannon. An outraged A. L. Mogford smashed copies of the recording of this worldwide hit at a shop in Southern Rhodesia. Hauled before a judge for his vandalism, Mogford described the song as "the most subtle and dangerous form of communist propaganda that is designed to worsen Anglo-American relations." The judge's sentence, passed in July 1960, forced Mogford to pay for the damaged merchandise. "The alligator," a novelty dance, came along a few years later. It was performed by doing push-up–style motions on the floor. And finally, "funk" music of the late 1970s and early 1980s contributed "Alligator Woman."

In Chicago, contemporary musicians and their works are handled by Alligator Records & Artist Management, Inc., while in Atlanta you get "blues, booze & Cajun food" at Blind Willie's, where a guitar-strumming alligator serves as the establishment's logo. Alligators, of course, invaded the blues just as they did other musical forms. Screaming Jay Hawkins put ultimate faith in "Alligator Wine" by writing, "You'll be a slave forever" to that potent beverage. Lyricist Victoria Spivey anthropomorphized her saurians

when she versified, "The old alligator was teaching his babies to do the Georgia Grind."

The alligator lent both exoticism and verisimilitude to literature of the Romantic and mid-Victorian eras, which often featured escapism to remote, unspoiled places. In Chateaubriand's *Atala*, a French best-seller of 1801 that went through many subsequent editions, the coming of the southern night is invoked: "The spirit of the breezes shakes out his blue tresses, embalmed with the perfume of the pines, and one inhales the faint odor of ambergris exhaled by the crocodiles [*sic*] bedded beneath the tamarinds of the river. . . ."

Chateaubriand further says of the lower Mississippi: "grace is always united with magnificence in scenes from nature: while the central current tugged cadavers of pines and oaks toward the sea, on the lateral currents along the riverbanks one sees floating islands of *pistias* and waterlilies, their yellow blossoms rising up like little nautical pennants, climbing upstream. Green snakes, blue herons, pink flamingoes, young crocodiles [*sic*] climb aboard, passengers on these ships of flowers, and the colony, furling its sails of gold to the wind, runs aground, asleep in some bay sequestered away from the river." And Atala, a beautiful young Indian maiden suffering the pangs of a Romeo and Juliet–like love affair, declaims rhetorically, "Unhappy was the womb of thy mother, oh Atala! Why don't you throw yourself to the crocodiles [*sic*] of the Spring?" Chateaubriand continues, "At that very moment, as the setting of the sun was eminent, the crocodiles [*sic*] began their roaring. . . ."

Napoleon, like Chateaubriand, had never been to the banks of the Mississippi, and he didn't known that "pink flamingoes" belonged in Florida [roseate spoonbills and scarlet ibis are found on the lower reaches of the Father of Waters]. And neither did he know that the local crocodilian was really an alligator, as Daudin didn't publish his findings until two years after *Atala* had appeared. Regardless, Napoleon liked the book so well that after dinner at the Château de Malmaison, he regularly had his adopted niece, Queen Hortense, read a chapter aloud to the ruminating Bonapartes and their guests. Permeated with a Rousseauistic vision of unspoiled man living in harmony with nature, it charmed later generations of Frenchmen as well, contributing to the opinions and impressions that tireless armchair travelers formed of the South as the land of milk and honey and "crocodiles."

Mid-Victorian analysts found a basis for some of this idyllic imagery in the Bible. *Harper's New Monthly Magazine* told subscribers in 1855 that "its elongated, Chinese-looking eyes are so really beautiful, that they called forth from Job one of the most striking figures that can be found in Eastern imagery. Speaking of them he says, 'they are like the eyelids of the morning' . . . [and even] the severely truthful naturalist [Dr. Bennet] Dowler, declares them as worthy the attention of poets as are the eyes of the famed gazelles."

In fact, the American poet Col. James R. Creecy already had put the alligator to good rhyming use as an element of local color in this bit of versifying from 1829: "Have you ever been in New Orleans? If not you'd better go / It's a nation of a queer place; day and night a show / . . . / Ships, arks, steamboats, robbers, pirates, alligators / Assassins, gamblers, drunkards and cotton speculators . . . ." While this sort of writing made the city out to be even more colorful than it actually was, it titillated readers as the Victorian era was dawning. At the height of the Gilded Age, Mark Twain found the alligators an amusing problem. In one of his tall tales, he reported the Mississippi to be so thickly infested with them that dredge boats were needed to clear out the alligator shoals. Something rather like that had actually happened when the alligator-covered prehistoric logjam of the Red River, a tributary of the Mississippi, was cleared for navigation.

Romancing the 'gator continued for the rest of the century. Americans became interested in folk culture and the quaintly expressed truths embedded in folktales. Joel Chandler Harris created *Nights with Uncle Remus*, and the edition of 1883 featured two anthropomorphized alligator stories. "Why the Alligator's Back is Rough" recounts the adventures of a saurian in a brushfire. "How the Bear Nursed the Little Alligator" tells how baby bear is nabbed for breakfast by an adult alligator that converts him instead into a babysitter for its brood; baby bear dines on his charges, but fools the parent alligator into thinking none were missing by showing it the remaining hatchlings twice before escaping.

In 1896, Margaret Avery Johnston recalled "Trouble, Trouble, Brer Alligator," as it had been told by her childhood nurse on Avery Island. Like the Uncle Remus stories, it was written in thick dialect. In this tale, the

protagonist, Brer Rabbit, is in the habit of digging up alligator nests and leaving the eggs exposed to die and spoil. This is resented by Mr. Alligator, who remains on the lookout for Brer Rabbit and revenge. Brer Rabbit went exploring around Deer Island during a drought. Deer hunters set the marsh on fire to drive their quarry; Brer Rabbit gets caught between fire, the hunter's dogs, and a wide bayou. Mr. Alligator, seeing an opportunity for revenge, refuses Brer Rabbit a ride to safety on the other side, reminding him of his destructive ways, and saying that the rabbit can be eaten by the dogs, burn in the fire, or drown as he pleases. Brer Rabbit bargains by promising to stop destroying alligator nests and to give Mr. Alligator all

"HOW THE BEAR NURSED THE LITTLE ALLIGATOR." LINE DRAWING BY CHURCH IN *NIGHTS WITH UNCLE REMUS* BY JOEL CHANDLER HARRIS, 1883.

of his own children (presumably to eat). Mr. Alligator takes Brer Rabbit on his back but changes his mind halfway across the bayou, preferring revenge. Mr. Alligator begins to sink into the water; Brer Rabbit fears drowning as his feet get wet. Brer Rabbit complains, and the alligator tells him to climb onto his neck. Brer Rabbit moves, but the cruel alligator continues to sink slowly as he swims toward the far bank, all the while forgetting how far Brer Rabbit can jump. Before the dim-witted alligator figures things out, Brer Rabbit leaps to security on the far bank and beats a safe retreat home.

Diane Ackerman reminds readers that the most famous saurian of literature is not an alligator but, rather, a crocodile: "By far the best-known crocodilian is the one in 'Peter Pan.' As most of us remember, Barrie's crocodile has swallowed a clock, so 'the way you got the time on the island was to find the crocodile, and then stay near him till the clock struck.' Of course, he had also swallowed Captain Hook's severed arm and, as Hook lamented, 'followed me ever since, from sea to sea and from land to land, licking its lips for the rest of me.'" (Note: Neither crocodiles nor alligators have true lips.)

These Victorian and Edwardian classics firmly established the alligator in children's literature, where it has occupied an important place ever since. They also created the fully anthropomorphized alligator, and by investing it with human thought, feelings, and foibles, they altered our perception of the alligator as a natural phenomenon. It should be noted that although the timing may be entirely coincidental, these works were published just as tourist-attraction alligator farms were being established and began selling large quantities of "cute" baby alligators as pets to visitors.

In his novel *V*, set in the mid-1950s, author Thomas Pynchon picks up on the abandoned pet theme, but he makes out that a Manhattan department store had furnished them:

Geronimo stopped singing and told Profane how it was. Did he remember the alligators? Last year, or maybe the year before, kids all over Nueva York bought these little alligators for pets. Macy's was selling them for fifty cents, every child, it seemed, had to have one. But soon the children grew bored with them. Some set them loose in the streets, but most flushed them down the toilets. And these had grown and reproduced, had fed off rats and sewage, so that now they moved big, blind and albino, all over the sewer system. Down there, God knew how many there were. Some had turned cannibal because in their neighborhood the rats had all been eaten, or had fled in terror.

Pynchon then devotes a full and colorful chapter to Profane's short-lived career as an officer of the sewer department's alligator patrol. Pynchon did touch upon one true aspect of alligators (and most other animals), the occasional unusual color phase found in nature. While alligators do not turn white from living in sewers, they do turn white from genetic reasons. The most unusual are leucistic alligators. Leucism is a state of partial albinism. Leucistic alligators have normal dark eyes but pure white hides due to a total lack of skin pigmentation. They look rather like white patent leather on the hoof. Albino alligators are also known. Like albinos in other species, these aberrant saurians show a change in eye color, in their case to a pale gold. In the albinoid form, the patterns of skin pigmentation are retained, but in a very light yellowish off-white on a white background. It has been speculated that twentieth-century fencing of alligator territory by landowners has not allowed breeding populations to move about as before. The unintentional results may have been a limited gene pool and inbreeding, more conducive to the development of such mutations.

A. C. Crispin's *V* of 1984, a work of science fiction completely unrelated to Pynchon's earlier book, concerns the invasion of earth by reptilian extraterrestrial beings and uses alligator imagery quite differently. In Crispin's book, a character named Caleb Taylor says, "I asked him if he could pay the paperboy, and he whipped a roll out of his pants you could choke an alligator with."

In the 1970s, there was a flowering of literary alligators to entertain and enlighten the preschool set. "An a Story," from the *Sesame Street ABC Story Book* of 1974 features a remarkably anthropomorphized saurian in a leading role.

Diane de Groate's *Alligator's Toothache*, written in 1977, is a wordless scenario, told in pictures, for the benefit of illiterate toddlers. It cleverly defuses the terrors of dentistry by depicting a suffering alligator, painlessly cured, who celebrates with a party. James Stevenson's *No Need for Monty* appeared a decade later. Monty the alligator is doing school-bus duty, ferrying the other animal children across a

river on his back. Some animal parents consider this mode of transport a little outdated, and conduct several experiments to find a better way. They can't. On the final page, after Monty has been put back into service, the grateful parents comment, "Monty is a truly trustworthy alligator!," "Most Reliable!," and "Irreplaceable!"

Among the best of the crop is Thacher Hurd's *Mama Don't Allow* of 1984. In it, an enthusiastic but noisy

FINAL ILLUSTRA-TION FROM *NO NEED FOR MONTY*. REPRODUCED FROM *NO NEED FOR MONTY*, WRITTEN AND ILLUSTRATED BY JAMES STEVENSON.

saxophonist offends all but the alligators, who invite him to play at the Alligator Ball aboard a steamboat. Dinner is to follow, featuring "something tender, something juicy," which turns out to be swamp band soup. Asked to play a final encore, the musicians put heart, soul, and prayer into a lullaby that sends the alligators into a sound sleep, allowing the musicians to escape from menu to safety.

These charming fantasies, along with many others, were probably considered "environmentally correct" at a time when the alligator was darting on and off the endangered-species lists. Most, however, denature the

alligator and endow it with so many cute and cuddly characteristics that its true identity as a carnivorous large predator is also defused. Some of this may be due to the physical appearance of the alligator itself, especially the arrangement nature has given to its lower mandible and jowl. Edward King observed as early as 1875, "The wrinkle underneath his lower jaw gave him a good-humored look, and he seemed actually to smile as the bullets hissed around him." In 1940, Will Branan found that "The expression on his face is quite benign, albeit a bit mysterious, as if he were an off-spring of the Sphinx and Mona Lisa, saying, 'Why are you afraid, my good fellow, I am not very hungry to-day. . . .'" Diane Ackerman noted as recently as 1988, "Alligators, because their massive jaws curve upward, appear to be laughing even when they're in repose. They seem caught in a great big private chuckle."

The process of anthropomorphizing the alligator had been so thoroughly completed by the mid-1960s that at that time Frank and Ada Graham noted, "Now millions of people were finding them transformed in their favorite comic strips into characters as loveable as the family puppy." In some cases, notably *No Need for Monty* among those cited here, the writing could be considered irresponsible. Countless children have been dangerously misinformed, and should one try with wild alligators any of the stunts presented in such texts, he or she might well be eaten. Additionally, their adult conceptions of *alligator* will always be tainted by ideas gleaned from such publications. Thacher Hurd, however, personally regards the alligator as "the most terrifying animal in the world." His healthy respect for them permeates his work, and he presents the alligator in a fanciful but much more realistic light for a young audience.

Shelley Katz erred in the opposite direction. Death, destruction, natural disaster, stereotyping and exaggeration sell well. Katz employed them all, and set the stage for the 1977 novel *Alligator*, exploiting the image of the antediluvian monster, with this prologue:

> They tell grim tales of him along the Florida Everglades. . . . Whites in the small towns that border the swamps have hunted him for years. They have tried to kill him with axes, shotguns, and hooks. They say he has suffered hours of agony from the wounds they have inflicted; many times he has been close to death at their hands. Huge chunks of flesh have been torn from his leathery sides, and his monstrous dragonlike head is riddled with the lead of their shotguns and the steel of their rifles. But still he has survived. He has survived because, in some mysterious way, the people want him to. He is a legend. And there are very few legends left.

William F. Buckley, Jr., has a novelized Ché Guevara cleverly parting company with an agent of U.S. Intelligence by saying, "*Hasta luego, caiman*" on several occasions. The literal translation, "See you later, alligator," served as the title for his 1985 book. Two years later Carl Hiaasen published *Tourist Season*, the particularly imaginative story of a cracked newspaper reporter, a drug-addicted former Miami Dolphin, and a crazed bingo-rich Seminole bent on environmental terrorism to drive out tourists and retirees so that Florida and its Everglades may evolve backward to a

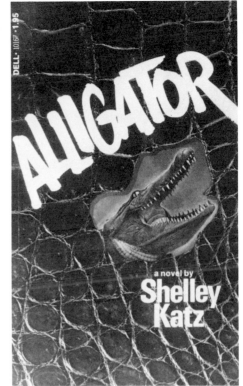

pristine ecological condition. Alligator mentions abound, but among the oddest is this description of a murder weapon from the opening pages: "Nobody could have guessed what actually had killed Sparky Harper. It was supple and green and exactly five and one-quarter inches long. Dr. Allen found it lodged in the trachea. At first he thought it was a large chunk of food, but it wasn't. It was a toy rubber alligator. It had cost seventy-nine cents at a tourist shop along the Tamiami Trail. The price tag was still glued to its corrugated tail. B. D. 'Sparky' Harper, the

BACK AND FRONT COVERS OF *ALLIGATOR* BY SHELLEY KATZ.

president of the most powerful chamber of commerce in all Florida, had choked to death on a rubber alligator."

The snobbery of alligator as status symbol was utilized by William Diehl in *Thai Horse* of 1989. A visiting military officer is characterized as "An arrogant little man impressed with his own importance, carrying an alligator briefcase and a little stack of files." And an incompetent United States Embassy employee, bringing from a jungle-bound South American jail a newly released political prisoner who wants to bathe in the caiman-infested river they are following, imagines the worst: " 'That's all I need,' he muttered to himself. 'Where's Hatcher?' 'Oh, I'm dreadfully sorry, sir, an alligator ate him.' "

These, of course, represent only a sampling of the many books for children and adults that have used alligators as leading characters, supporting players, scenery, and so on. They are a good cross section of the various attitudes of diverse authors, and the images, sometimes true but more often false, that have been implanted in the minds of the reading public.

At the end of the nineteenth century, new technology developed by Raff and Gammon, first marketed in 1896 under the Edison name, allowed the alligator to be translated from printed page to silver screen. Called the Vitascope, their invention was the first successful commercial projector for a motion-picture theater.

The only films available at that time consisted of short continuous loops, with running times often less than a minute, that previously had been viewed by one customer at a time in hand-cranked nickelodeon machines in penny arcades. It took film directors and producers a little while to discover that they could now make much longer movies, complete with plots and character development, that might be even several reels in length. Some of their earliest efforts were filmed in the South, which offered a conducive climate and exotic scenery. Only later did they discover the perpetual sunshine of southern California, where they could also escape the ravages of the southern mosquito.

Among the earliest films to feature alligators was *Wild Oranges* of 1924, directed by King Vidor and based on the novel by Joseph Hergesheimer. It was partially filmed at Belle Chasse, not far from New Orleans, although the action allegedly takes place in Georgia (sometimes Louisiana looks more like Georgia than Georgia does). In one scene, the heroine, Millie, is borne into the swamp by the vile Nicholas, where she was "threatened by rapacious alligators." Unfortunately, the film did not survive; one is unable to review the performances turned in by the alligators.

In the fall of 1937, newsreel cameramen were treated to an alligator hunt in Cameron Parish so that they might "take the audiences of a nation on a vicarious dragon hunt." Although sensationalized in presentation, this seems to have been the first quasidocumentary look at the alligator from the safety of a theater seat. Among the great early documentaries, of course, was Robert Flaherty's *Louisiana Story* of 1948. Called "the father of the documentary," Flaherty was already famous for such films as *Nanook of the North.*

Sponsored by Standard Oil of New Jersey, *Louisiana Story* was designed to show petroleum technology coexisting harmoniously with a traditional Cajun lifestyle. As the *Variety* reviewer put it, "Filmed entirely in the bayou country of Louisiana, the picture tells of the Cajun (Acadian) boy and his parents, who live by hunting and fishing in the alligator-infested swamps and streams, and of the oil-drilling crew that brings its huge derrick to sink a well. . . . There are no real heroes or villains (unless the terrifying alligators could be considered the latter). . . . There are exciting incidents as the youngster paddles his tiny boat through the lonely swamps with his pet raccoon and is almost killed by the savage 'gator, until he finally captures and slays it in a spine-chilling struggle."

Composer Virgil Thomson's score, played by Eugene Ormandy and the Philadelphia Orchestra, included "The Alligator and the Coon" to enrich this sequence, and it won the only Pulitzer Prize ever given for movie music. The later progeny of this genre of film encompasses many true documentary and nature films such as those produced by Jacques-Yves Cousteau and the National Geographic Society.

Passing from the sublime back to the ridiculous, we next encounter alligators in *Swamp Women* of 1955, cogently summarized as "Heavy-handed nonsense of four female convicts escaping jail, chasing after buried loot." The professional reviewer at the time found the alligators to be among "routine hardships" that also included rattlesnakes.

The star of the next offering was not a living alligator but, rather, a piece of luggage. In the 1957 British release *An Alligator Named Daisy,* the cast included Diana Dors, Stanley Holloway, and Margaret Rutherford. Leonard

FACING PAGE: MURDER-BY-ALLIGATOR. COVER ILLUSTRATION BY GEORGE CORSILLO FOR THE NOVEL *TOURIST SEASON* BY CARL HIAASEN, 1987.

PROMOTIONAL
STILL FROM *THE
ALLIGATOR
PEOPLE,* 1959.

FACING PAGE:
007 AMONG THE
ALLIGATORS:
POSTER FOR *LIVE
AND LET DIE,*
1973; AND
SUCCULENT
MORSEL: POSTER
FOR *GATOR BAIT,*
1973.

Maltin opined, "Dors reveals pleasing comic talent in fabricated account of salesman who mistakenly picks up someone else's alligator suitcase, leading to complications." Another alligator accoutrement "starred" in Alfred Hitchcock's *Rear Window* of 1954. The pocketbook in question became a key clue and piece of evidence in the tale of homicide filmed by an all-star cast under Hitchcock's usual four-star directorial aplomb.

The Alligator People of 1959 introduced serious science fiction to the film and alligator mix. It starred Beverly Garland (that queen of the B movies, who had first encountered alligators in *Swamp Women*). Michael Weldon and Charles Beesley synopsized the film by saying, "Beverly Garland finds her missing husband at the home of a doctor. The poor man has horrible scaly skin and after another operation turns into an upright alligator (with pants on and no tail)! The unlikely alligator man (designed by the man who made the Fly) is one of the more outrageous screen monsters."

The *Variety* reviewer further clarified the plot, writing, "Near the mansion is a hideaway clinic where a physician is trying to discover an antidote to a serum he has developed. The serum, extracted from alligators, permits humans to regrow damaged body parts just as some reptiles do. An unforeseen after-effect—the reason the husband so treated fled from his wife—is that the humans gradually acquire the physical characteristics of alligators. . . . The cure backfires and he is transformed into a real human alligator. In grief and terror

MADE-FOR-THE-
MOVIES: FOUR-
TEEN-FOOT LATEX,
FOAM, AND STEEL
MECHANICAL
ALLIGATOR.

he flees to the swamp and dies in quicksand while his hysterical wife watches helplessly."

Gator Bait, an unfortunate release of 1973, was the product of Sebastian films, and it seems to have featured most of the Sebastian family in one role or another. It came out at the same time as *Live and Let Die,* eighth in the series of James Bond thrillers. Staring Roger Moore, the latter was partially filmed in and around New Orleans and on the north shore of Lake Pontchartrain.

One of its most spectacular stunts didn't turn out too well. Bond is seen running across a body of water by leaping from alligator to alligator. The living raft was created for the scene at an alligator and crocodile farm in Jamaica, using eighty-six crocodilians with weighted feet and wired jaws, but the beasts were insufficiently immobilized. In fact, they had been starved into action by a three-month fast prior to filming. The stand-in stunt man slipped, was bitten, and

A Social History of the American Alligator

was patched up, rather like the sequence in the completed movie.

When real alligators don't, or won't, cooperate, Hollywood resorts to special effects. As Frank and Ada Graham explained, "The alligator does not look or behave in a way that is scary enough for some moviemakers. In the past they have constructed artificial alligators, just as other moviemakers have turned out artificial sharks or gorillas." Some of these performing fakes were unconvincing. W. T. Neill, a Florida-based alligator expert, has not been deceived, discerning that "as the sham reptiles float down upon their supposed victim, their upper jaws pop open to reveal white teeth in a mouth painted bright scarlet." It is, we know, the *lower* jaw of the alligator that moves, despite ancient myths to the contrary, and the interior of the mouth is a dull white-to-pink, not bright red.

One of these simulated saurians, named "Ramone," starred in *Alligator* of 1980. Thirty-six-foot-long Ramone lived in a sewer, and even attacked a sewer worker named (believe it or not) Ed Norton, before being conquered. Weldon and Beesley reviewed it as "a giant-monster film that's as good or better than the best of the '50s film[s] it resembles." Other fake 'gators contribute greatly to the terrors of 1987's *Sister, Sister* and made-for-television's *Three on a Match* of the same year. It's actually the same fake that appears in both. Filmed in Louisiana, they feature a fourteen-foot highly realistic but foreshortened (for photographic effect) rubber alligator built over a light steel frame, operated from underneath by a pair of scuba divers. It was manufactured in Hong Kong as part of a fleet of

eighteen for the filming of an Asian epic. Its seventeen siblings perished in the effort. The sole survivor was brought to the States for the production of *Sister, Sister* and stayed around, even appearing in an exhibition on filmmaking at the Louisiana State Museum.

Television audiences have been regaled with much the same fare. In addition to news footage documenting alligator hunts since 1974, the major networks have served up fictionalized 'gators in prime-time series such as a 1984 episode of *The Fall Guy.*

All of these Hollywood glamour 'gators (with exceptions of the suitcase and the handbag) appeared in horror films or in villainous roles. Hollywood is in the business of selling movie tickets, and tickets are sold by cinematic creations that are bigger and fiercer than life. To achieve these ends, Hollywood is just as guilty (if not more so) of exaggerating, stereotyping, and sensationalizing alligators as it is of doing the same thing to various innocent people (notably minority and ethnic groups), to achieve cinematographic effect that often sacrifices the daily reality of life to the economic reality of the box office.

The image projected by Hollywood of the alligator as horrible man-eating monster has not been an asset to the rather placid reptile's reputation. The movie 'gator hasn't yet been admitted to the Screen Actors Guild and is seldom paid a living wage (although fake 'gators rent high to film companies). In fact, the alligator has more than enough celluloid grounds to sue for defamation of character.

SUE THE BASTARDS!

THE ALLIGATOR'S DAY(S) IN COURT

The alligator's legal history is a long and complex affair, varying from state to state within its entire natural range and complicated from time to time by the intervention of state governments outside its range or the federal government itself, to say nothing of international regulations that have been imposed upon it.

As a case study, the situation in Louisiana serves well. There the legal embroilments of the alligator go back to the nineteenth century, and the most spectacular twentieth-century complications occurred there, resulting from conflicts between

an excellent alligator-management program and conservation interests from other areas, producing the "alligator wars" of the 1960s and 1970s. The torturous route of legislation, conservation, political embroglios, and actions by the well-intended but misinformed have produced a surprisingly fascinating story.

In Louisiana, the court system had first taken note of the alligator (in a class-action as opposed to individual cases) in the second half of the nineteenth century. Individual parishes of the coastal region had independently outlawed the alligator, often placing a bounty on it as a nuisance animal, sometimes for the ill-considered protection of the fur industry. Trappers were under the mistaken impression that alligators ate so many muskrats that their livelihood was endangered. This fur-trapper controversy raged until well into the twentieth century.

Home rule among the parishes was still endemic in 1908, but in that year it was nudged toward alligator

U. S. POSTAGE STAMP COMMEMO- RATING ENDAN- GERED SPECIES— ISSUED IN 1971 DURING THE "ALLIGATOR WARS."

FACING PAGE: LEGAL PROCEDURE: OBLIGATORY USE OF TAGS ISSUED BY THE LOUISIANA DEPARTMENT OF WILDLIFE AND FISHERIES ON ALLIGATOR TAILS.

conservation. R. W. Shufeldt had made the dire prediction two decades earlier that "the crocodiles and their near kin are marked as a declining group, and they will eventually be exterminated completely." Thus Act 37 of 1908 authorized "Police Juries of each Parish to enact such laws and fix such penalties for the violation of same as they deem necessary to prohibit the killing and destruction of alligators."

Fur trappers lost additional support when scientists such as Albert Reese began to point out that alligator populations had declined by as much as 80 percent between 1880 and 1900, and that the resultant increase in cane rats posed a serious threat to the sugar crop, while overabundant muskrats were weakening levees with their burrows. In 1915, Reese proselytized, "Legislation to forbid the killing

of alligators less than five feet in length has been suggested and should be passed, since animals of less size have almost no commercial value for leather." Later conservationists would recommend protecting the larger breeding animals instead.

E. A. McIlhenny related that from 1912 to 1916, alligator hunting was prohibited on state-operated wildlife refuges covering 174,000 acres. In 1916, it was decided to remove excess alligators and just over one hundred men were licensed to do so, taking over 88,000 animals. McIlhenny deduced that protective measures had been successful, concluding, "This is illustrative of how rapidly alligators will increase if left alone."

Isolated incidents of legal protection were not common, and Raymond Ditmars pointed out in 1920 that over much of its southern range the alligator was becoming a rare inhabitant, due to pressures from sports hunters, hide hunters, egg robbers, and trappers of baby alligators for the expanding tourist trade.

The state of Louisiana saw some economic advantage in this wholesale alligator commerce, and it began to impose a severance tax (probably in 1916) on skins handled by pelt dealers. Stanley C. Arthur discovered that in 1925, tax was collected on 21,885 belly skins passing through the hands of raw-pelt dealers, probably because the drought of 1924-1925 lowered water levels and made alligators easy prey.

Louisiana law regarding all nongame quadruped trapping was amended and codified by Act 80 of 1926. A general open season, "extending from November 20th to February 5th," was instituted. Possession of live animals was prohibited throughout the entire year. Skins or pelts could be possessed only during the open season (except by dealers). Animals could not be trapped within ten feet of their known dwelling places, and their nests or lairs were protected from destruction. Young animals, "whose pelt, skin or hide has no regular market value," could not be taken at all.

The law of 1926 continued with provisions for mandatory licensing of trappers and dealers, requiring them to report their take, tag hides, keep detailed shipment records, tag shipments, and pay license fees and severance taxes. These taxes were to be paid to the state's Department of Conservation (forerunner of the Louisiana Wildlife and Fisheries Commission), where they were to be "devoted to the policing, conserving, replenishing and upbuilding" of populations and to "scientific researches into the life habits . . . through technically trained officers and employees and, when practicable, give full publicity to such biological findings."

Except during the legal season, the alligator retained its outlaw status, however. The "outlaws" consisted of all the alligators in the fourteen coastal parishes, which could be "destroyed at will," but excluded the alligators found in the remaining fifty inland parishes. The open season, fine for fur trappers, was not much good to alligator hunters, because it started just as alligators were beginning to cease feeding and retire for the winter, ending just as the alligators were about to consider resurfacing after the short coastal cold season. That "destroyed at will" allowance for the parishes with the greatest alligator populations neatly

sidestepped what otherwise might have posed a serious problem to hunters. That clause had the additional effect of practically nullifying any real protection the law might have extended to the dwindling number of 'gators. The practical result, as Stanley Arthur said in 1928, was "Gator hunting is carried on in this state from the first of March to the first of October."

It is also notable that the 1926 law taxed hides regardless of length, and did not preclude the taking of very small alligators, as Reese had recommended. Arthur was outraged. In 1928, he proclaimed, "the 'gator is doomed to certain extinction—and soon—as the demands for trade now call for the very small skins as well as the larger ones and, to hasten this saurian's departure from our fauna, the State of Louisiana has 'outlawed' it, and it can be taken at any time and in any manner and by anybody in any of our coastal parishes—and is . . . it seems that some sort of prompt legislation will be needed for its protection if this animal is to be preserved . . . the minimum for alligators to be taken and for skins to be sold should be 4 feet at least . . . ." Knowing of those "scientific researches into the life habits" to be supported by the severance tax, Arthur demanded one.

Arthur was quickly followed by the United States Department of Agriculture, which noted in 1929 that drainage projects and reclamation of alligator habitat for agricultural purposes, as well as uncontrolled hunting, had brought about the population decrease. The federal agency was more hopeful for the future than Arthur, citing protected refuge areas, including the Okefenokee, the

Everglades, and, in Louisiana, the Rainey, Rockefeller, and state game refuges that "probably will never be reclaimed," as retreats in which the alligator would not be exterminated. According to the USDA, these refuges were apparently all that would keep the alligator going. The report also stated that based on a survey, "only Florida and Louisiana have imposed either local legal restrictions or taxes on the capture of alligators."

Florida was a bit more progressive than Louisiana. By 1927, alligators were protected in some counties by local laws. Generally, these made hunting illegal between early March and late October, during the alligator's breeding season and greatest period of growth. But Floridians were not entirely satisfied with this arrangement, as was noted in 1931: "Until the exact status of the alligator is determined, the remnant of his kind should be protected. At the present, of the nine states in which it is found, Florida is the only state to offer any direct protection, and that only in a few counties." Florida's protection, however, was really not as extensive as might have been implied. In 1929, Remington Kellog named only eleven counties in Florida that closed the alligator season, with dates varying as local regulation changed from county to county, but generally extending from spring through fall, with winter months open to hunting. The state of Florida did not tax alligator hides at that time, although Louisiana was doing so.

E. A. McIlhenny voiced his concern in 1934 by indicting the country at large: "That the alligator has already been exterminated over a large portion of its former habitat is a fact, and one that civilization should not be proud of . . . it is extremely doubtful if they ever again will be an attractive feature of our waterways." McIlhenny himself closed five thousand acres of his Avery Island domain to alligator hunting, but he said, "it will require ten years more of protection before they [young alligators] will be sufficiently large. . . . Let us hope this protection can be given to them." Unfortunately, minor revision of Louisiana state law in that same year did nothing further to promote alligator conservation. McIlhenny lamented in 1938, "The hide hunters who have all but exterminated them for the few dollars their skins brought, have robbed us of one of our most interesting wildlife features, the last representative of the great age of reptiles . . . ."

During World War II, a north Louisiana initiative came in 1943, on rather surprising patriotic grounds. The Baton Rouge *Sunday Advocate* reported, "These men [a group of Shreveporters] . . . declare he [the alligator] is a great friend of man and is now playing an important part in the war effort through destruction of predatory reptiles which destroy edible fish." The predators preyed upon by the 'gator included turtles, snakes, and the voracious garfish. Louisianians were indebted because "These three are his main diet and he saves many thousands of other fish for the sportsmen and commercial fishermen."

The idea that an alligator was a conservationist in disguise may have been novel to the general public but had been known by wildlife experts for some time. The concept of the alligator as a cleaner of the environment had hit the popular press in 1855 when *Harper's New Monthly Magazine* said, "it is his mission, in the order of Providence,

 SUE THE BASTARDS! 127

to assist in the destruction of those millions of fishes that come out of the sea, in the annual overflow of the rivers, which might otherwise die, and by their decay breed pestilence throughout the land." This was a rather advanced view for 1855, written at a time before the Corps of Engineers had channeled most of the Mississippi, which, like the Nile, was still subject to annual flood. The alligator's value as a predator of the voracious gar also had been noted by Stanley Arthur (1928) and E. A. McIlhenny, "the sage of Avery Island," in 1934.

Anthony Kerrigan revoiced the Shreveport argument in postwar 1948 when he wrote, "the alligator preys on his primeval cousins, the very gar pikes themselves; he devours fish-destroying turtles; he makes water-holes beneficial to cattle in the dry seasons; and he gives of himself in generous quantity for the finest in ladies' handbags, shoes and belts." Dr. Leslie Glasgow amplified this view, and even proposed the alligator as a friend of the trapper, when he was quoted in 1956 as saying, "By devouring nongame fish like gar, he clears the water for game fish. And when the water dries up in the marshes, thousands of fish and muskrats find haven in the deep holes dug by 'gators."

Like commentary issued from Mike Kirkland (1957), Richard Yancey (1959), and Percy Viosca (1960), who also pointed out an economic advantage: "By thinning out surpluses of muskrats, nutria and other fur-bearers, especially by weeding out sick and undernourished mammals and birds before epidemics can spread, they tend to minimize the alternate periods of superabundance and scarcity which make investments in wetland resources such

a hazardous undertaking." Biologist Archie Carr wrote in 1967, "Like a Noah in reverse, the alligator provides a place where a few aquatic creatures of every kind can survive until the water returns," additionally itemizing that alligator droppings fertilize the water, alligator channels through the landscape slow the process of marsh takeover of open waters, and that the spoil banks of alligator holes and their old nests provide elevated nesting sites for other creatures such as turtles, and terrain for plants that don't grow with their feet in the water. Bruce Erickson indicates that fossil remains far to the north suggest that alligators eating gar is not a new situation. Millions of years ago, it appears likely that ancient crocodilians were hot after ancient gar for lunch, dinner, and between-meal snacks.

This ecological approach is an interesting reversal of the old trapper controversy in the coastal parishes. As late as 1965, however, feelings were still strong. The *Times-Picayune* editorialized, "This setting of 'gator against gar has aroused mixed feelings in the past among muskrat trappers, livestock raisers, hunting-dog owners and others whose own losses to the alligator have not been inconsiderable." Fortunately for the alligator, gunpowder was diverted from hunters to soldiers during the war years, and according to Thomas Barbour, "the scarcity and the high cost of ammunition [in July, 1944] are giving the animals a welcome respite."

By 1946, Maximilian Rinow, a manufacturer of alligator goods in New Orleans, himself had taken a conservative stance, imploring, "Let's get laws passed to conserve this valuable Louisiana product that stands as the

No. 1 quality in its class in the entire world." By January 1947, McNealy reported that "It has been suggested, therefore, that a commission of experts from the Bureau of Wildlife and Fisheries of the Louisiana Conservation Department make a study of the matter in cooperation with representatives of the alligator [hunters] and of the hide industries, and then recommend to the State Legislature measures in the interests of both." Apparently, the suggestion fell on deaf ears. It was pointed out that "Mexico and most of the Central and South American countries now [1947] have legal protection for their alligator [*sic;* caiman] skin business. A Mexican law severely punishes anybody who kills an alligator [*sic*] less than four feet in length."

The trapper controversy reared its ugly head again in 1947, when "Harry Reno, veteran wildlife enforcement agent, and a darn good alligator hunter . . . [found] seven muskrats and two baby otters in an alligator he recently skinned . . . as protection for the valuable fur bearer, Louisiana, a number of years ago, outlawed the alligator in all the coastal parishes . . . ." There were ambiguities in that law, however, such as one found by the *Roosevelt Review:* "Headlight hunting is against the law in Louisiana, and yet since alligators are considered outlaws in the coastal parishes, the law says also that outlaws can be killed at any time by any means." Richard Yancey agreed, writing in 1959, "This has led to some confusion, according to agents

SUE THE BASTARDS! 129

of the [Louisiana Wildlife and Fisheries] Commission's Enforcement Division, all of which has worked to the detriment of the alligator industry."

The law came under closer scrutiny in 1948: "Since the adoption of a resolution by the Louisiana Wildlife Federation at its last convention favoring a close season on alligators in Louisiana, there has [*sic*] been numerous questions as to the present laws on the statute books pertaining to alligators." A look into the matter revealed that the only significant change since 1926 had been a slight increase in the severance taxes.

Florida was moving faster. Anthony Kerrigan found that "the State of Florida . . . protects alligators up to four feet in length. . . . A number of Florida counties also prohibit the taking of alligators entirely, and all counties must observe closed [*sic*] season during the alligator's mating months of March, April, and May. Baby alligators may not now be shipped in interstate commerce." But the problem lay, in Florida at least, not with the law but with the general perception of the animal, since "Nearly every alligator that is killed in Florida is killed upon sight, law or no law, because to the average person they are known only as hideous beasts, cold-blooded killers and of no practical value."

In Louisiana, alligators propagated so successfully in protected areas under federal jurisdiction that, according to the National Wildlife Service in 1948, harvesting "on the Delta [Plaquemines Parish] and Sabine [Cameron Parish] refuges, as well as others, is necessary and desirable to maintain a balance of wildlife." Edgar Poe noted in 1949,

"As the yearly kill of the big reptiles [nationally] dropped to less than 50,000 there was considerable apprehension that the alligator would become an extinct species. Subsequently with the establishment of the refuges, the alligator population began to climb in Louisiana, Florida, Georgia and other places." By that time, "the number of alligators in the Sabine refuge was increased to such a point that the wildlife service is permitting licensed hunters to kill about 1500 a year."

Such reports, pertaining only to the very small portion of alligator habitat under protection, led many to believe the plight of the alligator had ended. Louisiana recodified its state laws in 1950. The revised statutes concerning alligators legislated more stringent licensing of trappers and dealers and more elaborate documentation and reporting procedures, but gave no significant increase in legal protection. The alligator even retained its "outlaw" status in specified parishes. New provisions called for breeders to be licensed in order to capture breeding stock and prohibited the taking or sale of alligators for human consumption.

Little changed until the late 1950s. Alligators suffered from an image problem in Louisiana just as they did in Florida, which led wildlife biologist Dr. L. L. Glasgow at LSU to say in 1956, "There's no basis for the thoughtless killing of alligators . . . but people kill them anyway." Dr. Glasgow's encouragement, along with the findings of graduate students studying under his direction, coupled with the recommendations of other professionals, led the state's Wildlife and Fisheries Commission to exercise some of the powers vested in that body. James Nichols and his coauthors have recorded that "In 1958, the Louisiana Wildlife and Fisheries Commission initiated an intensive alligator research program. . . . The Commission also effected various management procedures which included strict harvest controls, restocking, and increased law enforcement efforts against poaching. These management efforts resulted in dramatic increases in the alligator population. . . . "

In 1959, though, before new management could produce results, Maximilian Rinow expressed renewed concern. Richard Yancey reported, "He would like to see the harvest of alligators more properly regulated in order to insure a sustained yield for the future." Yancey, a respected wildlife biologist, recommended, "To provide adequate safeguards it would appear that this could be most readily done by additional legislation. A five or six foot size limit instead of a two foot limit as it is now would provide an opportunity for the females to reproduce. Protection from mid-June to the end of August would also give them an opportunity to bring off young during the summer months."

Statewide, it had become illegal "to take or possess the eggs of alligators . . . in any Parish," and "Orleans Parish says you cannot catch any size alligator there at any time for any purpose," according to Ezra Adams. "In 1960 Louisiana prohibited the killing of alligators over five feet long in an attempt to save the animals that were large enough to produce eggs and young," Frank and Ada Graham have reported. In fact, Louisiana joined four other alligator-producing states that year "to regulate the harvest of

alligators by implementing a 5 foot size limit and a 60 day spring season," as A. W. Cooper, Jr., told the Wyvern Club in New Orleans. Three years later, the in-state alligator season was completely closed. During the decade, "protective legislation was enacted by all states within the animal's range." This respite offered to the alligator varied from state to state and frequently was not well enforced.

The Louisiana measure was certainly helpful but not entirely effective. Outdoors writer Mike Cook explained: "Game outlaws continued to work and deplete the population. Good game enforcement didn't mean much because the outlaws were, for the most part, given a mild slap on the wrist in court and freed to go about their business . . . the game outlaws have, for the past several years [during the 1960s], been able to get around selling 'gator hides in the state. They simply take or ship them to a dealer in Texas who then ships them back [legally] into Louisiana." Florida's Senator Smathers concurred, telling the U.S. Senate, "by far the greatest threat is the poacher who pursues the alligator into his few remaining refuges, including Everglades National Park." In fact, according to J. D. Scott, "By 1961, the alligator population had dwindled so alarmingly that Florida was forced to move to eliminate the hunting season. . . . But the profit was so tempting that poachers ignored the law . . . even stealing them from alligator farms."

Louisiana followed suit when "the state closed the alligator season in 1963 and banned all legalized trapping," wrote herpetologists Harold Dundee and Douglas Rossman. By that time, 'gator-napping had reached

Louisiana. C. C. McClung raised a hue and cry when 155 were taken from his Laplace reptile farm. This occurred just days after McClung had sold seven large replacement 'gators to Arthur Jones for his reptile farm at Slidell, which had also suffered thievery. Jones later transferred to Florida and became internationally prominent for his Nautilus gym equipment. Terry English explained to newspaper readers this opening salvo in the ensuing 'gator wars: "They can be skinned and sold on the black market or to dealers who could resell them to reptile farms in other states." Business had to be temporarily suspended at two Florida farms until they could be restocked after poachers' raids. Even the internationally known Ross Allen wasn't immune. "Thieves even stole the breeding stock," he told Archie Carr. To discourage such traffic, the state "made it a crime to kill any alligator. Soon every southern state had laws against killing them," reported the Grahams. Actually, the Louisiana alligator trade had been entirely prohibited. Cook wrote that it was "illegal to buy or sell Louisiana alligators—dead or alive."

The state entered the poaching war wholeheartedly. The Baton Rouge *State-Times* reported from the combat zone that "Sweeping the skies with planes and churning through bayous in high-powered boats, Louisiana's game wardens are waging a blitzkreig on alligator poachers. Wildlife agents are using the most modern pursuit equipment. The marshes are abuzz with walkie-talkies and two-way radios. And state judges are cracking down with jail terms of up to six months and stiff fines."

"Old Joe," a semiantique, semidomesticated eleven-foot alligator at Wakulla Springs, Florida, became the symbol and rallying point of the fray. The Grahams reported that his death in 1966—shot by poachers or miscreants—"brought angry comments in newspapers and on television programs all across the country. The National Audubon Society offered a reward of five thousand dollars for the capture of his killers." The dramatic outcome of this incident, combined with a great deal of additional evidence, was that the alligator was placed on the federal list of rare and endangered species. As a result, said the Baton Rouge *Morning Advocate*, "All states granted the gator total protection and most backed-up their restrictions with vigorous law enforcement programs." The alligator wars were truly underway.

At about the same time, according to Cooper, "The Southeast Association of Game and Fish Commissioners organized an Alligator Committee to coordinate activities regarding the research and management of the reptile. The American Alligator Council was later formed [as was the Louisiana Fur and Alligator Advisory Council], composed of representatives of state agencies, conservation organizations, and concerned individuals. Later the group was joined by those interested in alligator farming and representatives of the reptile products industry." Cooper further intoned to his Wyvern brotherhood, "All participants agreed that illegal hunting was a serious threat to the alligator and that effective legislative measures should be adopted to plug loop holes in existing laws."

One of the biggest problems was that poachers were still practicing interstate sleight of saurian. Or, in Cooper's words, "Alligators taken illegally in Louisiana, for instance, could be shipped to another state and although that state was also closed to alligator hunting, it was impossible to prove the origin of the skins."

The alligator wars took on a James Bond–like cloak-and-dagger turn as agents went undercover. In June 1966, Louisiana Wildlife and Fisheries sleuths Merle Hebert and Russell Landry confiscated over one thousand "hot" hides in Abbeville. By this time, Dr. Glasgow had left the ivory tower at LSU and become director of the Louisiana Wildlife and Fisheries Commission. From the commission's offices at 400 Royal Street in the middle of the New Orleans French Quarter, Dr. Glasgow, Jack Edson [assumed name of an undercover agent], and a photographer actually staked out a hide dealer barely across the street, and seized over 450 hides (more than 300 of which were shorter than five feet) within less than a block from headquarters. That case, however, was never prosecuted, despite Dr. Glasgow's efforts.

Mike Cook wrote, "[Gerald P.] Aurillo, the man originally charged with the case [within the Orleans Parish district attorney's office], told Edson that it had been taken out of his hands . . . and given to [William R.] Alford [Jr.]. Alford said he had orders from the 'main office' to nolle prosse the charges. Charles Ward, first district attorney, told Edson the order to nolle prosse came directly from District Attorney Jim Garrison. And Garrison wasn't available to explain his reasons for the action." Score one for the poachers.

In 1967, biologist Archie Carr found that an old federal law of 1906 might be modified to help. The move was "to amend the Lacey Act—which forbids taking certain illegally caught game across state lines—to include a ban on transporting alligator hides." Senator Smathers from Florida did just that. He introduced the amendment into the U.S. Senate, "which would make it a violation to transport and ship in interstate or foreign commerce alligators or alligator hides taken in violation of federal or state law," wrote Cook.

The deadly serious comic opera that constituted the alligator wars took on new and unexpected dimensions. For the 1968 holiday season, a Cincinnati, Ohio, department store advertised alligator goods as ideal Christmas presents. This may have been a fashion statement of the 1960s, but it was a tactical error on the part of the store. The Ohio Audubon Societies were incensed and banded together to stop it, using the slogan "Give an alligator his hide for

"ENVIRONMEN-TALLY CORRECT" SUBSTITUTES: "REPTILIAN PRINTED CALF" SHOES.

Christmas." They won, in a big way. The store's embarrassed buyer alleged she would never order another alligator handbag, and the National Audubon Society took up the flag, turning a local campaign into a national battle.

That organization launched a four-part program: (1) to provide public education that would discourage purchasing products made from a protected species; (2) to promote legislation banning alligator-product sales in large markets; (3) to promote amendment of the Lacey Act as Senator Smathers had proposed; and (4) to imprison those who received hides from the poachers.

Save-the-'gator legislation was reintroduced to Congress by Representative E. A. Garmatz of Maryland. Its notable co-sponsors were from North Carolina, Minnesota, Michigan, and Washington, none of which were large alligator-producing states. This was a "safe" bill for them, as alligator poaching had become a national issue, but did not constitute a homegrown nemesis for any of the five. Thus the Lacey Act was amended, with the intended result. The remaining southeastern states, which had not enacted their own alligator legislation, promptly did so. By the end of 1969, "it was illegal to hunt alligators anywhere in the United States," recited Cooper to the Wyverns.

Peter Brazaitis, assistant curator of animals at New York's Central Park Zoo, explained to Diane Ackerman the increasingly complex situation that escalated the alligator wars to global scale: "By the end of the nineteen-sixties, it was clear that many species of crocodilians were on the verge of extinction . . . the Convention on International Trade in Endangered Species was formed, as part of the United Nations. . . . Each of the countries that signed CITES became an enforcement agency. . . . If a species was protected in Brazil, its importation into the United States or any other CITES country was automatically prohibited. And this is the way it remains today."

Under pressure from all over the United States, Congress went the additional mile and passed the Endangered Species Conservation Act of 1969. It included U.S. adherence to CITES regulations and added other animals to the list, as well. Unfortunately for the alligator, this federal legislation dealt only with interstate and international situations. As the magazine *Audubon* explained, "the federal government could not prevent the [individual] state from hunting a nonmigratory species." Since alligators do not journey seasonally, the new law came into play only when they were packed up for involuntary interstate or international travel. Poaching continued at an unprecedented rate by those willing to risk it for the profits it brought.

By this time, Dr. Glasgow had left Louisiana to become assistant secretary of the Interior in Washington, D. C. There he was instrumental in convincing the boss to support good game-management practices and enforce wildlife laws. The Baton Rouge *Sunday Advocate* reported, "Interior Secretary Walter Hickel says that an additional $100,000 will be sent to the Everglades. But conservationists suggest that the most effective measure might be stronger penalties and, especially, stronger enforcement of laws against possession of illegally taken hides."

The Audubon Society was trying to reach the same goals, but its lobbying tactics weren't always terribly subtle. During his tenure as Assistant Secretary of the Interior, Dr. Glasgow told his son that he spent half his time on the hill undoing the damage to the conservation effort done by the Audubon Society's overaggressive and often antagonistic methods, which offended lawmakers. Glasgow felt that a quiet educational approach worked far better than accusation, preaching, and doomsaying.

Back home in the Bayou State, things had taken a peculiar turn. By 1970, the alligators that had received increasing protection for over a decade (since 1958) had rapidly proliferated despite poaching. Nichols and his colleagues reported that "In 1970, the Louisiana state legislature established the framework for an open alligator season. . . . Preliminary results indicate that the 1972 harvest had no detrimental effect on the Cameron Parish alligator population." Any interstate or international trade in hides, however, was now carefully policed, and governed by the provisions of the amended Lacey Act and the new Endangered Species Conservation Act. Some critics, not understanding the population explosion that had taken place among Louisiana's 'gators, regretted that these federal laws couldn't prohibit in-state hunting.

New York City now entered the fracas. A municipal ordinance was introduced to prohibit sale of alligator products in the Big Apple. Called the Mason-Smith Act and intended to discourage poaching, its provisions also, and possibly inadvertently, covered objects made from legally hunted hides. The proposition was supported by virtually all the national conservation organizations. It passed. As the Grahams exulted, "The country's largest market for hides had been closed to poachers and hide dealers."

The same writers regretted that "there are people in every state who are willing to break the law if they can make money. A network of poachers and dealers in illegal hides soon sprang up. These gangs killed gators in the swamps and marshes and shipped the hides in unmarked trucks to factories in Georgia, New Jersey and New York. There the hides were tanned and otherwise prepared, and smuggled aboard ships to markets in France, Japan and other countries." Several cases were tried in Louisiana under Louisiana House Bill 798, signed into law by Governor John McKeithen in July 1969. One multiple offender got five years.

The most exciting of the cases involved a wild cross-country chase that took agents in pursuit of illegal hides from a New Orleans motel parking lot up the East Coast. In Georgia, they almost lost the smugglers. When they recovered the trail, they feared that the hides might have been ditched. When cats at a gas station pounced at the smuggler's vehicle, however, they were sure the malodorous evidence was still inside. The chase ended at a New Jersey tannery, where the agents closed in, arresting transporters and tanners alike. Another offender in Louisiana was fined $1,500 and given a six-month sentence, meted out in federal court. The sentence was suspended, but only because of the intervention of the U.S. Attorney's office, which also recommended against the $10,000 maximum fine the judge would have liked to have imposed.

When you're up to your ass in alligators its hard to remember that your original goal was to drain the swamp.

POSTER CELEBRAT-
ING RECOVERY OF
THE ALLIGATOR
POPULATION.

That convicted but unjailed lawbreaker was connected to a much larger operation centered in Georgia. There a federal raid arrested a father and son team with interstate and international connections. Confiscated records led back to individual poachers or clandestine transporters in several states, including Louisiana. *Audubon* maintained that "Two years of persistent investigation, moreover, had identified [the business owner] as a prime figure in a network of 460 poachers and dealers, who between 1967 and 1971, killed and brought to market 127,000 alligators worth an estimated $4,000,000." After pleading guilty to all counts on charges that might have brought life imprisonment and a $600,000 fine, "the father was given only a six-month jail term and five years on probation. The son was sentenced to just 60 days—to be served after his father is freed, so the family business will not suffer." *Audubon* thought the verdict stank: "The sentence smells like a naked, rotting alligator carcass left in the swamps . . . ." The magazine called the decision "an astounding act of judicial charity" that "dealt a crippling blow to the enforcement of America's wildlife protection laws."

The experimental alligator season in Louisiana in 1972 came in for its share of harsh words, as well. *Audubon* conceded that "Years of research had convinced state authorities that the alligator population in some parts of southern Louisiana was again high enough to warrant an experimental hunting season," but it also maintained that Louisiana "defied public and official opinion across the country by declaring an open season on alligators . . . within a week [of announcing the intent to open a season] the alligator poachers were back in business in the coastal parishes, once again given a legal outlet for their bloody wares . . . the worst effect of the Louisiana alligator season will be the reopening of channels through which poachers across the South can market their stolen hides, including thousands believed to be [*sic*] held in storage since passage of the Endangered Species Act."

However, *Audubon* didn't bother to credit the special hide-dressing instructions (leaving a specified paw or flap of skin attached to identify the year of the catch) or tagging procedures introduced by Louisiana to prevent illegally taken hides (untagged, and/or without the appropriate flap) from entering the market. National and international attention was paid to that season, with the result that "after 1972's fall experimental alligator season in portions of Cameron Parish the whole world knew that Louisiana was again 'gator hunting, but legally," according to New Orleans TV personality Frank Davis.

The state reacted in the following manner, as Cooper told the Wyverns: "In view of the alligator's large numbers, effective existing laws, and increasing population in many areas of their range, the Louisiana Wild Life [*sic*] & Fisheries Department [*sic*] has recommended to the United States Department of the Interior that alligators be removed from the endangered species list. They state that while alligators remain on the list the general public is misinformed as to the true status of the alligator and [it] encourages the enactment of unwarranted, largely ineffective legislation for their protection. The endangered species list also loses much of its significance by including a species as abundant as the alligator. Another reason for reclassifying the alligator is that legislation pending in Congress would place all species listed on the endangered list under federal control."

The state was indirectly supported by the IUCN. Nichols and his colleagues reported that "The dramatic recovery of the American alligator has been noted by the IUCN Crocodile Specialists Group which transferred the alligator from the 'critically endangered' category to 'recovered' in 1971." *Audubon*, however, responded, "Other Southeastern states and the Bureau of Sports Fisheries and Wildlife [of the U.S. Dept. of the Interior] have decried the Louisiana move as premature. So does the National Audubon Society."

Thus the alligator wars entered a peculiar phase, with a state government attempting dignified negotiation with a

federal agency and simultaneously having to wrangle with an obstreperous but well meaning national organization. The results weren't always dignified, and they weren't always pretty. The *Audubon* viewpoint and national opinion were reinforced by tardy (and from Louisiana's angle, ill-timed) legislation of that year, as explained by J. D. Scott: "In 1972, Florida finally passed laws that levied fines of $5,000 and five years in prison for persons capturing or killing any size alligator."

In a "kill 'em with kindness" move, Louisiana answered the Audubon Society's call in a manner reminiscent of the Chicago Zoo in the 1940s—by offering its embarrassment of reptile riches to other states for restocking purposes. The national press categorically ignored this logical and generous move. The Baton Rouge *Morning Advocate* did tell the story: "The task was and remains a relatively simple one. There were too many alligators in Cameron Parish. The problem was what to do with them. The public heard only that the state wanted to harvest and that the Bureau opposed. . . . The public was not informed if any negotiations took place to move excess gators to wildlife refuges and other suitable areas where populations have not recovered. . . . Louisiana did supply alligators to Missippi [*sic*] and Arkansas for those states' restocking programs."

The state's offer embarrassed the National Audubon Society, to which Louisiana rather magnanimously "gave" two thousand alligators on the hoof (and still in the marsh). After Mississippi and Arkansas agreed to accept them, as Scott said, "because landowners and timber companies in

those states had asked for the reptiles to help control an overpopulation of beavers that were [*sic*] harming forest lands," Audubon Society personnel began the arduous work of rounding 'em up and moving 'em out. It took over three years to complete. As *Audubon* slantedly and rather petulantly put it, "Reasons for the massive transplant this year [1975] of 1,000 of the officially endangered reptiles . . . can be traced to September 1972, when the Louisiana Wildlife and Fisheries Commission authorized the killing of up to 4,000 alligators in the Gulf Coast marshes of Cameron Parish." Louisiana, of course, went right ahead with its plans for future controlled hunts, based on successful management results of the controversial 1972 experiment, expanding to a triparish area in 1973.

Louisiana also continued to give away alligators. Fifty from the state were turned loose by the National Wildlife Service in 1979 on the Tennessee River in the Wheeler Wildlife Refuge in northern Alabama. They were brought in, as they had been in Mississippi and Arkansas, according to refuge manager Tom Atkeson, "in an attempt to thin a troublesome beaver population and as part of an experiment in expanding the range of the endangered species." There they also quickly became embroiled in politics. Bob Dunnavant wrote in the Baton Rouge *State-Times* that U.S. Rep. Ronnie Flippo (D-Ala.) was "incensed that the National Wildlife Service would introduce a new species into his congressional district without studying the potential impact on the area." His concern was that the alligators, on protected lands, "would multiply and become a menace to swimmers, fishermen, and others enjoying the region's creeks, lakes and rivers." The following spring, federal employees were badgered into retrieving as many as possible for retransplant back to Louisiana.

The "pending legislation" that Cooper told the Wyverns Louisiana found objectionable was the Federal Endangered Species Act of 1973. Reaction was strong. The Louisiana Wildlife and Fisheries Commission, proud of its successful work to propagate the 'gator within the state, took the stance that "The alligator is back in great numbers and keeping it on the list of endangered species makes a farce of the whole program of designating certain species of wildlife as endangered." The commission charged that "Having the alligator in the same category with the whooping crane and other truly endangered species is poor management," recorded the Baton Rouge *State-Times.*

When such opinion was overruled and the Federal Endangered Species Act became law, the alligator was no longer subject to home rule. Plans for the 1974 controlled hunt had to be canceled, despite an alligator surplus. The governor at that time was Edwin Edwards. He went to Washington with the state's cause. And he got a response, reported by the Baton Rouge *State-Times:* "The [U.S.] Fish and Wildlife Service will study the status of the American alligator in 10 states at the request of Gov. Edwin Edwards. Edwards wants alligators removed from the list of endangered species since they have become so numerous in Louisiana in the past seven years." The gubernatorial effort was too late to salvage the 1974 season, but it was successful. As Ted O'Neil reported, "By 1975 the federal government had delisted Cameron, Calcasieu and Vermilion parishes."

The Louisiana idea and model were spreading, as other areas began to rebuild their alligator populations, despite the Audubon Society's continued resistance. In reality, the state's concept caught on with professional game-management officials. The Grahams said, "Biologists on the [Florida] game commission would like to start a sustained yield program like the one in Louisiana, but there is strong opposition from many of Florida's conservationists." The Audubon Society fought back. Peter Pritchard, their Florida spokesman, claimed, "A legal hide market is harmful because it will encourage poachers." And *Audubon* frankly didn't believe the Louisiana alligator-management success, rather lamely offering, "Most alligator people will tell you that it's impossible for so many animals to be born in such a short time, so what probably happened is that the shy animals felt safer in the open once people had stopped hunting them, and all of a sudden the swamps seem packed with alligators." *Audubon* editors didn't seem to realize that time had not been so short; Louisiana's alligators (if not the nation's) had been professionally managed for seventeen years—since 1958.

Louisiana seasons were held in 1975, 1976, and 1977. That initial effort of 1972 remained the celebrated test case, however. A biologist told Frank Davis, "Louisiana is setting the example for the rest of the nation to follow. It is hard to convince the eco-freaks that conservation has a meaning different than preservation, but I think if anything ever helps to get the point across, this alligator harvest issue will do it."

Davis personally accompanied a contingent of writers

that had come to investigate: "When the season ended and the scribes packed up and headed for the airplanes and home, the potential of writing about 'gator extinction in Louisiana was gone . . . the harvest of last season [1972] did wonders to support biologic management principles." A survey of the hunt area showed an increase from 90,000 alligators (1972) to 120,000 (1973). The 33 percent rise backed Davis's opinion, and supported the program initiated by the Louisiana Department of Wildlife and Fisheries.

Attitudes began to change in the later 1970s in the face of the Louisiana success story. The Grahams reported that "Many Americans believe that the alligator is a product to be managed wisely for business profits. . . . If its hide is not used for leather, people will either destroy it because it is a nuisance, or fill in the swamps and marshes to make money from the land in some other way. Their slogan is: 'Buy a bag and save a gator.' " That's a far cry from Cincinnati at the height of the 'gator wars. The worldwide mind-set of many, however, still perceived the alligator as a defenseless victim. Jean Mazel, popular commercial author and lecturer in France, let the prevailing bias show in the phrasing of his 1979 commentary: "Instituted not long ago, the 'great alligator slaughter,' fixed in principle for the beginning of September, each year, has seen the calm waters of the bayous dyed with blood and the Atchafalaya [Basin] resound with the crack of arms of war. Fortunately, the drama only lasts two weeks, and as of yet, not every year, because the world market in crocodile [*sic*] skin and the [U.S.] office of export licenses also have their piece to say."

New York remained in Mazel's camp and had not relented. As the 1970s closed, alligator could not be sold there. CITES regulations prevented alligators legally taken in Louisiana from being shipped internationally because they were still ranked as endangered in other parts of the South. The Grahams noted, "The biggest market for those hides is a factory in Texas that manufactures cowboy boots. . . . " The triparish Louisiana hunt, scheduled for 1978, was actually canceled because of this situation. Without the foreign market, Louisiana alligator hides were hardly worth the taking.

Alligators continued to increase throughout the whole South. They became so numerous in both Florida and Louisiana that in areas where man encroached on alligator territory, the animals began to show up in unlikely spots: golf courses, car washes, swimming pools, and carports, to name a few. Wildlife biologist Ted Joanen told the Baton Rouge *State-Times*, "we had more gators than we know what to do with, and there was no way we could keep up with the complaints. The Lake Charles [Louisiana] airport had to shut down once because they had alligators on the landing strip." This was about the time that posters lampooning the situation appeared with the slogan "When you're up to your ass in alligators, it's hard to remember the original goal was to drain the swamp."

State and local governments were forced to face this new legal issue by working out nuisance codes that governed the fate of errant alligators. Alligator nuisance officers were appointed to remove the innocent offenders, and they were generally obliged to release smaller individuals in distant natural-habitat areas, and to destroy truly dangerous animals. The nuisance patrol had its close scrapes. The *Times-Picayune* recounted such an incident when, as the officer crossed the Mississippi River, "the gator got revenge. After tying up the [ten-foot] alligator and loading it into the back of the van, [Art] Cormier decided to run an errand . . . before returning . . . to release the animal. On the return trip . . . he suddenly heard a deafening banging sound in the rear of his van. The alligator had gotten partly loose and was lashing its tail about. Because he had already started up the bridge, there was nothing Cormier could do but keep driving—and wince as the alligator knocked out one of the windows of his van." In some cases, officers were allowed to take the hides of larger animals either in lieu of pay for their services or to be sold to benefit wildlife programs.

By 1979, with federal permission, a regulated season had been established and expanded to twelve of the fourteen coastal parishes in Louisiana. In that year as well, legal provision was made for the hygienic processing and marketing of alligator meat. However, Louisianians were still in the trenches fighting the alligator wars. In the spring, experts and officials from the Louisiana Wildlife and Fisheries Commission went to the front in San José, Costa Rica, where the International Trade Convention on Wild Flora and Fauna was meeting. Their goal was to convince that body to remove the alligator from internationally regulated endangered species lists, thus restoring the international market. As the Baton Rouge *State-Times* presented the case, "Since most alligator products—such as shoes and pocketbooks—are made and sold in other countries, the elimination of overseas markets creates a glut of hides in the United States markets." After all, that factory in Texas could make and sell only so many boots.

The Louisiana request, according to United States Congressman John Breaux, who also traveled to Costa Rica, was simply to take the alligator from Appendix 1 (all international trade prohibited) and place it in Appendix 2 (trading allowed under controlled circumstances). Breaux argued that "One of the purposes of placing an animal on the endangered species list is to get it off again." Louisiana had done that very well, even though faced by great opposition. Optimistically, Breaux said, "We have a great potential for Louisiana becoming the alligator capital of the world if our proposal is adopted." Some United States and international officials, however, were fearful that lifting the ban on alligator would inadvertently reinitiate a clandestine trade in other, endangered crocodilians. Fortunately, Louisiana prevailed.

Word came in late August—dramatically just before the opening of the 1979 Louisiana alligator season—that the wish had been granted. For all intents and purposes, except for a few later and minor skirmishes, the alligator wars were over. A victorious Louisiana could finally reap the benefits of what game-management wisdom had sown within the state twenty-one years before. Two years later, Julia McSherry assessed, "Louisiana gator management is probably one of the world's most

TRIUMPH AS THE "ALLIGATOR WARS" END IN 1979. DETAIL OF PEN-AND-INK SKETCH BY CHUCK SILER, 1990.

SUE THE BASTARDS! 141

successful wildlife management stories . . . through technical papers published by [Louisiana Department of Wildlife and Fisheries] biologists, Louisiana's program has served as a model for other crocodilian management programs around the world . . . . The alligator is important for commercial value of the hides and meat. But it is perhaps even more important because its sustained yield gives landowners incentive to protect their land[,] thereby preserving remaining wetland habitats so critical to many bird and wildlife species."

In a celebratory postscript to the alligator wars, the Louisiana State Legislature passed Act 572, signed by the governor on July 14, 1983, "to provide a state crustacean and to provide a state reptile . . . ." The crustacean of choice was, of course, the crawfish. The act continued, "The official state reptile shall be the alligator. Its use on official documents of the state and with the insignia of the state is hereby authorized." The alligator had graduated: From matriculating into the legal system as a turn-of-the-century outlaw, it had been promoted to the ranks of the pelican and other symbols of Louisiana's official totem pole.

Florida waited a decade after the Louisiana experimental season of 1972 to try one of its own. The

Baton Rouge *State-Times* noted that while the Sunshine State "does not have a formal alligator hunting season, [it] is holding a brief hunt Sept. 4–24 . . . near Gainesville." Two years later, Texas was "negotiating for a similar arrangement" to the legal Louisiana hunt, according to Jack Scott, and Florida was "trying an experimental three-week, state-directed hunt, with 20 hunters selected by lottery, hunting just three lakes, and with only 300 alligators to be taken." The belated Florida experiment was studied by the state's biologists "to determine if a legal hunt is logical for the future." At that time—in 1984—alligators were still federally ranked as "endangered" in Alabama, Mississippi, North Carolina, and the inland portions of both South Carolina and Texas. Their status had been lowered to "threatened" in coastal regions of Georgia, South Carolina, and Texas, and the whole of Florida.

Florida's biologists did determine that the population had recovered to such an extent that a carefully limited hunt, based on the Louisiana concept that the alligator is a naturally self-renewing resource when harvested in moderation, was workable. The Florida version of alligator reaping was reinstituted in 1988.

Over the period of a century, these legal entanglements primarily concerned the trapper (whose economic livelihood depended at least in part on the alligator), hide dealers and tanners (for the same reasons), the scientist (who studied, managed, and conserved it), the lawmakers—legislative and judicial (who worked within political and legal parameters to impose and enforce alligator law), police and other enforcement officials (who dealt with the "alligator wars" in the trenches), designers, fabricators, distributors, and retailers (who depended on the creation, manufacture, and sale of finished products), and the conservation-minded citizen (through organizational membership and independent thought and action). This is a surprisingly long list. The actions, public statements, and rallying cries of the more vocal brought a great deal of national and international attention to the alligator in the 1960s and 1970s. A deeper respect for a remarkable phenomenon of nature, and a national consciousness of the alligator and the problems it faced were engendered. The American public could feel righteous about its national stand as once again the collective perception of its southern saurian altered.

CHAPTER TWELVE

BY THE DAWN'S EARLY LIGHT

THE AMERICAN ALLIGATOR HUNT

The commercial alligator hunt has evolved over two centuries, from the gathering of animals for their oil in the later eighteenth century through the uncontrolled slaughter for leather of the later nineteenth century to the carefully regulated harvest of the later twentieth century. It has become a recognized element in a traditional lifestyle centering on the natural southern abundance of fur, fish, and saurians that is often identified with Cajuns and Isleños of south Louisiana. The hunt is part routine, part ritual, and part danger, with unpredictable moments of drama and excitement. It often provides the hunter a significant portion of his annual income.

Based on sound management principles, the hunt is carefully controlled to assure the future of the alligator as a renewable natural resource that will provide a sustained and substantial yield. Louisiana, which reinstituted legal alligator hunting in 1972, has had more experience in legislating, directing, and patrolling an alligator season than any other state. The geography of its coastal marshes is also somewhat different from that of the alligator territory of Florida, which only recently reopened an alligator season. Description of the modern hunt and its regulation in the following paragraphs is based on the Louisiana model.

Quotas are established for each parcel of land for which hunting licenses are issued, based on land type and alligator-population surveys. Hunting rights belong to the landowner or his authorized agents or lessees. Each landowner, authorized agent, or lessee is given a quantity of

FACING PAGE: ALLIGATOR HUNTER AND GUEST PHOTOGRAPHER THREADING A TRAINASSE IN PIROGUE.

portion. Changing the shape and location annually and announcing them only on the eve of the season assure that the year the hide was taken can be ascertained and prevent illegally taken hides from previous years from being clandestinely slipped onto the market. All trappers and dealers must be licensed and must maintain careful records, which they are obliged to provide, according to an established schedule, to the agents of the state's Wildlife and Fisheries Commission.

Only the ventral or belly skin of the alligator is useful for leather production, including the underskin of throat, chin, and legs. The ridged "hornback," or dorsal skin, damages tanning equipment and, even if tanned by hand, makes up into a spiky, ridged product that has few applications.

Other parts of the alligator are harvested, requiring a "parts license" and "parts tags." These include skulls, heads, and teeth, which can be made into souvenirs and jewelry. Alligator meat, to be sold for human consumption, must be processed within hours of the catch, and in licensed, inspected, hygienic facilities conforming to official regulations.

The earliest methods of hunting were varied. In a time before the hide was valued, damage to an alligator's skin was not a consideration as it is today. The most ancient hunts are those recorded in Egypt, where the quarry was a crocodile. Herodotus's account of Egyptian hunting, as published in the *Pictorial Museum of Animated Nature,* is almost a preview of the contemporary alligator hunt. It was "managed by means of a hook, baited with the chine of a

individually numbered tags corresponding to the quota, which must be affixed to each hide taken, and each tag must be logged by its number along with other information such as size and sex of the animal. Tags are self-closing; they cannot be removed and transferred to another hide after first use, which prevents a hunter from discarding a smaller in-season hide for a larger postseason trophy. The tag remains with the hide until it is manufactured into salable goods, which often takes place in Europe or the Orient.

Just before each alligator hunting season begins (usually only forty-eight hours in advance, for security purposes), special hide-dressing instructions are issued to each tag holder, requiring that a specifically shaped and located flap of back skin be left attached to the usable belly pig, while the attention of the monster was aroused by the cries of a living pig, which the fishers had with them on the shore . . . meeting the baited hook [the crocodile] instantly seized and swallowed it, and was then dragged ashore."

The Book of Job warned against certain procedures for dealing with the Leviathan that might well have been construed as advice to Native Americans: "The arrow cannot make him flee: slingstones with him are turned into stubble. . . . Darts are counted as stubble: he laugheth at the shaking of a spear. . . ." Apparently, the indigenous population figured out for themselves that such methods wouldn't work, as accounts of their alligator pursuits include no slingshots and are not dependent on bows and arrows entirely.

The earliest description of the American Indian alligator hunt was provided by Le Moyne de Morgues, who published his account of French Florida in 1591: "They put up, near a river, a little hut full of cracks and holes, and in this they station a watchman, so that he can see the crocodiles [*sic*] . . . the watchman calls the rest of the watch, who are in readiness [when the alligator approaches the hut]; and taking a portion, ten or twelve feet long, of the trunk of a tree, they go out to find the monster, who is crawling along with his mouth wide open . . . and with the greatest quickness they push the pole, small end first, as deep as possible down his throat, so that the roughness and irregularity of the bark may hold it from being got out again. Then they turn the crocodile [*sic*] over on his back, and with clubs and arrows pound and pierce his belly, which is softer. . . ." This log-ramming technique is also seen in a detail of the earliest view of the city of New Orleans, painted in 1726.

Another Indian hunting account, detailing a different technique, is that of Father du Ru, who accompanied the Iberville expedition of 1700. After sighting a large alligator in the Mississippi, "A Bayougoula, who was following us, threw himself into the water and enticed the crocodile [*sic*] to a swim. He gently passed a hand under its throat, seized its back with the other hand, pressed it against his chest, and brought it in this manner to the foot of a tree where he killed it; he only suffered a few scratches."

Other versions—particularly of early blacks, who may have known African crocodile hunting, include variations on this swimming-for-the-alligator method. In one of these, recorded by Christian Schultz in 1810, "They first prepare a piece of hard wood about six or nine inches in length, which is sharpened and barbed at one end, and has likewise a shoulder, to prevent it entering too far. A strong cord is then fastened to the middle, one end of which is held by two or three on shore; while another takes the stick and swims out toward the alligator, frequently dashing the water with a dead fowl, by way of lure . . . at the moment he has extended his jaws to seize upon the prey, the negro thrusts his stick and fowl into his mouth; when the alligator, by closing up his jaws, runs the two points of the barbed stick through them up to the shoulder of the pin, and being thereby rendered unable to open them again, he is . . . drawn to the shore. . . ."

"PONCHO" DUHÉ TAGS AN ALLIGATOR'S TAIL, LAKE MAUREPAS. PHOTOGRAPH FROM THE *TIMES-PICAYUNE*, NEW ORLEANS, SEPTEMBER 10, 1989.

KILLING
CRCODILES:
SIXTEENTH-
CENTURY NATIVE
AMERICAN ALLIGA-
TOR HUNTING.
ENGRAVING AFTER
A DRAWING BY
JACQUES LE MOYNE
DE MORGUES IN
*HISTORIA
AMERICAE SIVE
NOVI ORBIS*, PART
II, PUBLISHED BY
THEODORÈ DE BRY,
FRANKFURT, 1591.

FACING PAGE:
EIGHTEENTH-
CENTURY ALLIGA-
TOR HUNTER.
DETAIL FROM *VIEW
OF NEW ORLEANS*,
WATERCOLOR BY AN
UNIDENTIFIED
ARTIST, 1726.

The Indians, too, had additional methods. In one eighteenth-century version by William Byrd of Virginia, East Coast Indians rode them like horses, and "holding the Ends [of a bit-like stick in the alligator's mouth] with their two hands, hinder them from diving by keeping their mouths open, and when they are almost Spent, they will make to the shoar [*sic*], where their riders knock them on the Head. . . ."

Europeans came equipped with more sophisticated technology. Their first thought was to use firearms in the pursuit of alligators. But it didn't always work. The Diderot *Encyclopédie* recounted in 1754 that "The skin of the back

resists the shot of a musket with a double load; but it can be wounded in the belly & especially in the eyes." Apparently musket balls frequently glanced from the scaly backs of alligators, and a popular legend arose that they were invulnerable to gunshot, except when it was discharged directly in the eyes. This is perhaps why DuMont de Montigny advised in 1753, "The best way to catch one is by the eyes, if it is in the water. If on land, it is easy to beat it." As late as the 1820s, even Audubon observed, "they are quite difficult to kill, if not properly shot."

If shooting didn't work, settlers were perfectly willing to try other means. Schultz reported an early trapping method in 1810: "[they] make a kind of triangular trap out of a large crotch of a tree . . . an ordinary black bottle is filled with as much air as can possibly be conveyed into it through a quill inserted in the cork. . . . A long line is then tied to the bottle (which passes over the trap), and it is thrown as high and as far out in the river as possible. . . . The alligator makes after it with all imaginable haste, and as often as he attempts to seize it he disappoints himself, by emitting so strong a blast of air that it sends the light bottle continually beyond his reach. He pursues his object . . . until he is drawn into the snare." Some methods, however, didn't work. In the Carolinas, the Frenchman Bosc tried out a variety of snares set at the entrances of alligator dens, but to no avail. Baron Cuvier reported that "every morning he [Bosc] found his snares broken, and the crocodiles [sic] had come out and re-entered safe and sound."

Alligators also were netted. During the late summer, when they congregated in deeper parts of shallow drying lakes that were evaporating in the heat, Audubon said, "The alligators are caught frequently in nets by fishermen; they then come without struggle to the shore, and are killed by blows on the head, given with axes."

Seasons could make a difference. Audubon told that in autumn, as alligators became lethargic in cooler weather, blacks "put all danger aside by separating at one blow, with an axe, the tail from the body." The tail was then rendered for its oil. According to Dr. John Holbrook, writing in 1842, food gatherers waiting until later in the year had an easier time of it: "On the approach of winter, these animals seek out holes in the earth, where they remain torpid until spring. . . . In this state of hibernation [sic; although alligators become lethargic in cold weather, they do not truly hibernate], many are dug out of their retreats by slaves. . . ."

The seemingly prescient biblical Leviathan provided a prototype for some of the many ways that were tried in the early days of alligator commercial hunting. The Book of Job relates, "Canst thou draw out Leviathan with an hook, or his tongue with a cord which thou lettest down? . . . Canst thou put an hook into his nose, or bore his jaw through with a thorn? . . . Canst thou fill his skin with barbed irons, or his head with fish spears? . . . Lay thy hand upon him, remember the battle, do no more."

It was from the Carolinas that Cuvier drew an early description of the method employed today in alligator trapping, saying, "They can . . . be taken . . . with small living quadrupeds, or birds, attached to a thick hook, and fastened to a tree by means of an iron chain." This sort of

FACING PAGE: ALLIGATOR TRAP AT POINTE-AUX-CHÊNES.

trapping by fishing was apparently widely known by 1842 when Dr. Holbrook wrote, "The alligator takes the hook readily enough, when baited with flesh, but it requires strong tackle, such as is used in shark-fishing, to secure them, so great is the strength of an adult animal."

Baited hooks seem to have been abandoned when high-powered firearms became available. As Raymond Ditmars said, "the old theory that the reptile's plated skin is proof against a bullet, no longer holds good. A ball from a modern rifle or a good revolver, will easily penetrate the tough hide of an alligator and produce a mortal wound." In the early 1880s, the Winfield *News-American* later reported, "The hunts always took place at night. Torches were used to shine in the eyes of the unsuspecting alligator. When shot the victim sank to the bottom of the lake or bayou and not until a boat food [boatful] was killed were the bodies located. The hunters would retrace their path and locate the bodies with a long pole. The job of loading them in to [*sic*] a skip [skiff] was no small job and required skill." By this time, of course, alligators had become commercially valuable for their hides. Vast numbers were taken for that purpose during the final decades of the nineteenth century and were sold to dealers operating from coastal cities and major ports. In Louisiana, such markets developed in Lake Charles, Abbeville, New Iberia, Morgan City, Houma, and New Orleans.

Refinements were added to the shine-and-shoot technique. E. A. McIlhenny recalled that in 1883, hunters near Avery Island worked in pairs and used a lard-burning bull's-eye lamp:

The alligator being blinded by the light could not see the boat . . . when the boat was near enough, usually not more than six or eight feet from the alligator, the top of its head would be blown off with the concentrated load from the shotgun. The man who did the shooting would . . . take up a short heavy pole to which was attached, on each side of one end, a sharpened [heavy iron] hook . . . which he would put under the alligator and draw it to the boat, or if the alligator had sunk, he would feel along the bottom with the pole until it was located, get one of the hooks under the body, and with a quick jerk drive it into the skin, pulling the alligator to the surface . . . the man in the bow would catch it by the nose and if it was not too large . . . would slide it over the side of the boat. . . . If the alligator was too large, it was pulled on the bank, a small rope tied to a front leg . . . and it was left to be retrieved in the morning . . . a cut was made across the back, immediately behind the hind legs and through the vertebrae with a sharp hand axe or hatchet. This cut was made in order to keep the alligator from thrashing about, as they often do for some time after being shot through the brain; for a large alligator in its dying struggles is not a very safe companion in a small boat.

Emile Billot told Annie Miller of such an incident that occurred on a night hunt during the Great Depression. The Billots had landed a nine-foot 'gator and were shooting at another when "it seemed as though all Hades broke loose in the bottom of the boat. We didn't need lights to know what had happened. Our 'dead' gator had revived. Dora [Mrs. Billot] plunged over the bow, I went out backward over the

NINETEENTH-CENTURY AX HUNTING FOR ALLIGATORS. PHOTOGRAPH, CA. 1895.

stern. As we swam for shore we could hear the alligator giving the boat a terrific pounding and hoped he'd leave it in good enough shape to get us home. . . . After a few minutes, he crawled over the side and we heard him no more. . . . Luckily, all he'd done was rip loose the seats."

McIlhenny also described the proper Victorian dressing procedure:

In the morning the alligators were skinned by making a cut from the underside of the chin along both sides of the lower jaw, then around the head below the eyes to the heavy bony plates of the neck, then down each side following the edge of the bony plates of the back to where these plates end a short distance back of the hind legs. The cut then extended along the upper edge of the tail to its end. The cut having been completed . . . the two men immediately started the work of skinning, and as they always kept a whetstone suspended from their belts with which they kept the skinning knives sharp, this work progressed very rapidly. When the skin was taken off it was at once thickly covered with salt on the flesh side, and then rolled up, beginning from the head to the tail, the sides being turned in as the rolling proceeded. These skins were then packed in the hole [sic] of the boat or in a special part of the camp.

Some unknowledgeable people apparently thought that alligator scales were like those of a fish, fixed at the front and movable at the back. The French publication, *Histoire naturelle*, therefore offered this sage observation to alligator hunters in 1883: "it does not work, in order to wound a crocodilian[,] to shoot it from back-to-front, as if the scales were overlapping, but instead, [shoot it] in the joints of the bands [between the scales] which present only skin . . . ." This, of course, was of little use to commercial hunters because it would mar the valuable hide. Besides, they had already perfected their blast-the-head technology.

Just before the turn of the century, a new way of taking alligators in the spongy coastal marshes became popular. Instead of nighttime expeditions, daytime outings were planned. First, the wet prairie was burned. Hunters walked the burned area in pairs, with poles twelve to eighteen feet long that were armed with single heavy iron hooks at one end, and short shovels. When they located an occupied alligator "hole" within the burn, the hunter would probe it for the underwater entrance to the alligator's den. If the pole didn't encounter the alligator at the den entrance, its underground tunnel would be tracked, and a small opening would be dug into it from dry ground above. Then probing was renewed. If the den tunnel was exceptionally long, or had multiple branches, several dig-and-probe trials might be made before the alligator was finally tracked to its lair.

According to McIlhenny, once contact was established, "The pole was moved backward and forward until the alligator became enraged, and grabbed the end of it in its mouth . . . the hunter with a quick tug would fasten the iron hook . . . in the alligator's throat . . . and draw it to the entrance that the pole went into. As soon as the alligator's head came above the water, a quick cut from a hand axe

"PONCHO" DUHÉ DISPATCHING AN ALLIGATOR, LAKE MAUREPAS. PHOTOGRAPH FROM *TIMES-PICAYUNE,* NEW ORLEANS, SEPTEMBER 10, 1989.

HUNTER POLING FOR ALLIGATOR. PHOTOGRAPH FROM THE *ROOSEVELT REVIEW,* OCTOBER 1947.

through the brain put an end to its life. . . . Sometimes they hooked on to a very large, powerful alligator that could not be pulled from its den, and occasionally a hunter would lose his pole, as the alligator would be so strong he would twist the pole out of the hunter's hand and pull it down into the den."

These poled alligators were skinned on the spot; only the hides were brought back from such marsh-tramping expeditions. Over a dozen could be secured in a day's march. Carcasses were left as carrion unless some portions were carried away as human food.

A professional hunter took Clifton Johnson along on such a marsh tramp about 1905. "Jake," the hunter, called his 'gators after he "ran his pole half its length into the muddy cavity to let the inmate know that something was going on. Then he bent over, and holding his nose between his thumb and finger grunted with a peculiar guttural in imitation of the voice of an old alligator. . . . Jake watched the water intently, repeating the grunting at intervals. There was a slight movement at the surface, and he made a sudden grab and out came a little alligator a foot long. He grunted again and secured another little fellow, and pretty soon a third. Then the ground quivered faintly and the long pole trembled. 'That's the big one—the mother,' whispered Jake, and resumed his vocal gymnastics. In a few moments there was just the least ruffling of the water, and before I could discern the cause, Jake had plunged in both hands and was pulling forth a seven-foot monster firmly gripped by its jaws . . . the beast rolled over into the slue, and with a vigorous splash . . . in a twinkling was back in its hole. Jake

was mad, and he made some remarks more vigorous than elegant. . . . This time he imitated the cries of the little alligators. The monster responded to this appeal to its maternal instinct, and Jake caught it in the same way as before. . . . "

All this excitement was almost too much for Johnson, as were the primitive conditions, and he concluded, "Any very intimate acquaintance with the moss-pickers and alligator-hunters entails some hardships. Food, shelter, and traveling are all poor, and you never know just what unusual discomforts you may encounter . . . the enterprise is more picturesque than agreeable, unless you have a fancy for roughing it."

Calling, however, was a very real part of alligator lore. Alligators will respond, whether from protective parental instinct, juvenile curiosity, or other unknown reasons. Among the earliest datable accounts of alligator calling is that of E. A. McIlhenny, who remembered of his childhood in the 1870s and 1880s, "we always took great pleasure and not a little excitement in seeing how many 'gators we could call around us during our swim [probably in Bayou Petite Anse]. We would attract them by imitating the barks and cries of dogs and by making loud popping noises with our lips, as these sounds seemed to arouse the 'gators' curiosity, and they would come swimming to us from all directions." Albert Reese, who investigated alligators in the Everglades and the Okefenokee, wrote in 1915, "In younger animals the voice is, of course, less deep and in very young individuals it is a squeak or grunt, easily imitated by hunters for the purpose of luring the animals from their hiding places." After probing an alligator's den to see whether anyone was at home, Stanley Arthur said in 1928, the hunter "calls the reptile by imitating its sucking cry of '*umph, umph, umph.*' As a rule the 'gator responds and crawls out of its hole. . . . "

A few years later, Harold Smith visited the Luthi alligator farm in 1939, where he noted that "one of the caretakers, who is quite proficient at imitating their calls, assembles them for their one daily meal." Thomas Barbour described the technique in 1944: "The call is made by holding your nose and croaking rather like a frog. The sound is indescribable but is not at all difficult to imitate." Three years later, the *Roosevelt Review* advised an incredulous readership, "You've heard of duck calls, hog calls and such, and the gator call is somewhat along those lines except that it sounds like a gator." Biologist Ted O'Neil summed it up as "a throaty croak."

Alligators become habituated to being called, and react in a rather Pavlovian fashion, particularly in places such as the Luthi farm or the McElroy Swamp (near Lake Pontchartrain) where they have enjoyed protection and are not hunted. Back in the McElroy, the author was taught to call alligators by Dr. Robert Potts in the late 1960s. While the procedure sounds like the proverbial snipe hunt, it actually worked. First, one hits the water with a stick, allegedly to get the alligators' attention. Then the caller makes a deep booming noise from the back of the throat, through the sinuses, with the mouth closed. It sounds like something halfway between an aggressive bullfrog and a cow in distress. Routinely, it got alligators of up to seven feet in length to leave their swamp pools and clamber up on the roadbed, where they fully anticipated being fed chicken necks or hot dogs on the end of a bamboo switch. Nothing makes quite the same impression as an alligator calmly advancing on you without fear, mouth open, on a gravel road with deep swamp on either side, in expectation of its dinner.

Today's swamp-tour guides often take advantage of this knowledge and call alligators boatside, thrilling astonished tourists. C. C. Lockwood wrote of "Alligator Annie" Miller and the alligators of Lake Hatch, which he found "the friendliest by far" of those he had encountered: "Annie floats into the lake calling 'Ba-a-a-by, Ba-a-a-by,' and sure enough, the 'gator comes right up to Annie, delighting her passengers." In 1982, the author had the pleasure of accompanying a party that included Michel Crepeau, French Minister of the Environment, on such a tour with Ms. Miller. On that occasion, she assembled four alligators (one of which was black, an unusual color phase) that simultaneously circled the open excursion boat while she stick-fed them from the stern. The visiting French official had to be warned not to dangle his hand in the water during the saurian lunch hour.

New technology contributed to hunting success. Albert Reese knew of a "more progressive" individual who "had as a torch an acetylene lamp, attached to his hat, with the tube for the gas extending down his back to the generator in his pocket." And by 1915, the ax for dispatching probed and poled alligators was being displaced by the .22.

Reese also recommended rapid and careful hide dressing, for economic if no other reasons: "The skin should be removed soon after death as, in warm climates, putrefaction sets in very early and the value of the skin is depreciated." The rolled, salted skin "must be kept in a dry cool place." In addition, "Great care must be taken not to cut the hide since small cuts that are not noticeable in the raw skin may be so conspicuous in the dressed skin as to render it of much less value."

The economic impact of the alligator became even more apparent by the mid-1920s. S. C. Arthur observed that it "has long been an important article of our commerce and has given many thousands of our people of the lowlands an occupation and a livelihood in hunting the giant saurian for its skin." Its ecological impact was also being studied, especially as the decline in the alligator population became widely evident. Some legislation was passed requiring licensing of hunters and dealers, tagging of hides, and payment of severance taxes on alligator skins, but until well after World War II the law offered little protection to the alligator itself. Shine-a-'gator and pole-a-'gator hunting proceeded as before as the commercial demand increased. Stanley Arthur found that experienced hunters preferred pole-a-'gator as "the only proper method, as commercial-sized alligators can be secured in this manner, while in shooting at night all sizes, particularly small ones, of not much commercial value, are killed." But Arthur was also depressed: "Skins from 4 to 8 feet are considered best by the hide buyers and smaller or larger ones were not wanted a few years ago, but today [1928] the demand appears to be for any size skin a dealer can get."

During the early 1930s, the number of alligator hunters increased as a result of prevalent economic conditions. Annie Miller investigated a case in point: "The Billots, who live on Waterproof Plantation near Houma, Louisiana, say their adventures with alligators began in earnest during the Depression. . . . 'In those days,' recalls Emile, 'jobs were few and far between; but there was an abundance of alligators and fur-bearing animals, and a man had no reason to go hungry. Like many of the bayou folk, we eked out a living with our traps and guns.' " *The Progress* concluded as early as 1937, "the depression drove to the uncomfortable and strenuous occupation of alligator hunting, men who hunted both for hides and meat."

Some justified hunting 'gators as a way of protecting the more valuable fur-bearers. Ralph Graves summarized their argument for the *National Geographic* in April 1930: "The alligator has been given a bad name by the fur trappers of Louisiana, among whom there is a saying that 'every 'gator killed means the salvation of from 10 to 100 muskrats.' But it is not solely for the muskrat's sake that these creatures are hunted relentlessly in the coastal parishes; their pelts [*sic*] are much sought after by manufacturers of ladies' slippers and purses. More than 36,000 alligator skins have been shipped from the State in a single year."

New forms of technology began to contribute to the demise of the alligator and the efficacy of the hunter. The "marsh buggy," concocted in its original form by adding caterpillar treads to an elevated Model T or Model A, and the increasing availability of the outboard motor, added large and distant tracts of alligator territory to the hunter's range. In 1934, E. A. McIlhenny felt that this did not bode well: "Because of the extensive hunting of these creatures for their skins, and the ease, due to internal combustion engines, with which skin-hunters can reach the most distant and secluded sections, it is extremely doubtful if an alligator will be allowed to live long enough to attain maximum size." *The Progress* added in 1937, "The buggy has made possible hunting in the farthest reaches of the marsh, beyond sight of any elevation of any dry land. . . ."

And the hunters were getting cagier. The hide pricing system in effect was such that length was not rewarded. McIlhenny found hunters to be particularly enterprising in the face of this adversity: "The hunter is paid no more for a twelve foot skin than for a seven foot skin. . . . It is

FACING PAGE: SEVEN-FOOT ALLIGATOR FAVORED IN THE 1920S AND 1930S. PHOTOGRAPH BY E. L. WISHERD FOR AN ARTICLE BY RALPH GRAVES IN NATIONAL GEOGRAPHIC, APRIL 1930.

generally the practice of the alligator hunter, in order to get the most from a large skin, to cut it diagonally in two. . . . If a hunter kills a twelve foot alligator he cuts the skin so as to get two seven foot pieces . . . and the buyer pays full price for two seven foot skins. . . . During 1933 a hunter on Marsh Island killed a fifteen foot alligator, the skin of which he cut in such a manner that he got two seven foot and one six foot pieces of hide."

A few of the more daring began to give up poles and lights altogether in their quest for alligators, developing a 'gator-wrestling method of securing their quarry. McIlhenny knew such a Cajun daredevil named Alpha LeBlanc: "unless the alligator was an unusually large one, Alpha would never condescend to use the pole. . . . He would go in to the hole quietly, feeling with his feet and hands until he located the alligator, and would then slowly slip his hand along the alligator's body until he came to its head, and getting his hand under its head, would feel along until he located the nose, then grasping it by the nose, would pull it to him and out of the hole, with a series of quick jerks." The victim was then dispatched, utilizing the by-then-traditional ax-a-'gator treatment. McIlhenny appended, "Alpha has caught hundreds of alligators in this manner, and has never been bitten."

Martel McNealy described a Jefferson Parish variant of this method in the mid-1940s, "used by only the courageous soul who goes out in daylight and trails an alligator for a fight to the death." After calling the alligator from its hole, the hunter followed this procedure.

The daring sportsman does the job with his hands and, in so doing, literally takes his own life in his hands. The alligator does not open its eyes or mouth the first second after coming out of the water. This gives the hunter his chance. In this brief moment the hunter leaps forward, grabs the animal by the jaws with one hand to keep the mouth shut [alligators have very strong gripping muscles in their jaws but very weak ones to open them] and hits it in the back of the head with the hatchet in the other hand. Sometimes . . . the blow so stuns the alligator that it can be killed without a struggle. But the alligator is a terrifically strong animal—[and] sometimes revives quickly and rushes in to the attack. Then the skill and courage of the hunter is [*sic*] really put to the test. Mr. [Wilfred] Berthelot [Jr.] told of one authentic case where two men fought with a very large alligator for more than an hour before they were finally able to kill it. The men had to know and anticipate what the alligator would do next, both to save their own lives, and to land the fatal blow.

The biblical hook came back into vogue to catch the "blinkers." These were alligators that had been "shined" and shot at night but had escaped because the marksman had missed or they had been only slightly wounded. Once burned, twice shy; such 'gators simply sank whenever a light was sighted. When a "blinker" was encountered that was not "poleable," McIlhenny said, the hunter "kills a bird or catches a fish and baits with it a very strong hook, to which he attaches a one-fourth inch [diameter] rope eight or ten feet in length. This rope is firmly tied to a tree growing on the bank or to a strong stake driven into the earth. It is then looped up and the bait hung about one foot above the water from a forked limb stuck in the bank."

The alligator, lunging for the elevated bait, would swallow it hook and all. It was then easy for the hunter to use the rope to draw the hooked 'gator within easy range of the .22. This "hook-a-blinker" method spread in popularity and is now the most widely used by commercial hunters of the wild alligator, unless local law specifies employment of some other means. The 'gator's ability to leap for its prey from open water has even been utilized as a tourist attraction at feeding time on at least one alligator farm in Florida.

During the late 1930s and through World War II, alligator hunting declined; waning popularity was generally attributed to the decrease in the number of alligators because of overhunting. Some men, however, continued the practice. A few hunted for alligator "farms" that entertained tourists and supplied specimens to the scientific communities of zoos and laboratories. A WPA guidebook appearing in 1941 explained, "while much less abundant than formerly, alligators are still sufficiently numerous to be hunted for the curio and leather-novelty trade." The guide added, "In the summer months the trappers of this marshland area [south of Port Sulphur] catch alligators, selling the hides to the dealers who purchase the winter catch of furs."

The *Roosevelt Review* looked back at the 1940-1941 season and said, "because alligator trapping is rather a hazardous occupation, the yearly take varies, depending largely on the conditions of the market. During the 1940–

41 season, for example, when alligator skins brought low prices, total production in Louisiana was only 2,928 'gators."

Prices rose in the postwar economic boom. The *Roosevelt Review* noted this trend: "Last season [1946], when alligator skins brought an average of $1.40 per foot, largest price in recent years, production reached 33,409, largest take in recent years."

Public notice of alligator hunting was reduced to infrequent newspaper or magazine articles for the remainder of the 1940s and through the 1950s. The small number of professional hunters continued as before, their exotic occupational hazards occasionally described by journalists in glowingly vicarious terms, emphasizing the dangers and narrow escapes they sometimes endured.

The size of the annual catch also ebbed, bottoming out in Louisiana at 10,300 for the 1955–1956 season, according to Richard Yancey, but suddenly jumping to 28,600 in 1957–1958. The unusual reason for this dramatic change was recorded by Yancey: "the storm-driven tidewaters of Hurricane 'Audrey' swept many thousands of alligators from the Refuge areas of southwest Louisiana [where they had been protected] on to [*sic*] adjacent private lands to the north . . . most survived only to be taken shortly thereafter by hunters. Reports were received that one pair of hunters made several thousand dollars during a three-week period after 'Audrey' near one of the Refuges. This storm was the only apparent reason for the increase in harvest for 1957–1958."

Poachers were the most frequent alligator hunters for the next fifteen years. Serious alligator-management studies and first limited and then closed seasons were initiated by coastal states, beginning in 1958.

With legal protection, alligators made a steady comeback over the next decade, but legal hunting was not reinitiated—in the interests of good game management—until 1972, and then just in Louisiana, where only 1,337 hides were taken. A series of carefully controlled and widely publicized experimental seasons were held, leading to the current alligator hunting situation that prevails today. The first of these expanded "great" seasons in the coastal marshes was that of 1979. It has been followed by annual repeated successes.

The current alligator hunt has social as well as economic overtones. The thirty-day Louisiana season begins in early September, well after alligator breeding time. Hospitable hunters often use the opportunity to invite friends and family for house parties at their camps. Good food and good company reign in anticipation of a successful season. The air is filled with French chatter and Cajun music in traditional households. Gumbo and *bourré* (a particularly lethal form of Cajun poker) cover the tables as final preparations are made. Honored guests, photographers, and reporters may even go along in a gala mood when the first hunt of the season gets under way just before daybreak the following morning.

The real preparations, however, actually have been going on for months in advance. During the previous fur-trapping season, the hunter has probably stashed away a freezerful of nutria carcasses that will serve as alligator bait when thawed and butchered (less frugal hunters may buy chicken for this purpose). The hunter has made sure that his boats and motors are in good repair, and, if his camp is remote, laid in a good supply of gas, oil, and spare parts. He has also stocked up on coarse salt, unless he sells his 'gators whole for meat as well as hides. He has cut and trimmed enough forked branches to serve as props for the lines of his 'gator traps.

Besides all these activities, the serious hunter has made sure his skinning table, knives, and scrapers are in good order if he plans to dress out his own catch. And the containers for storing the salted hides have been cleaned and readied. He has prepared the right number of lines and heavy hooks, often tying his tackle in such a way that the hooks can be released easily once the 'gator is taken. He may even emulate the type of lead used on big-game fishing expeditions. Most important, however, he has spent many hours ranging his assigned trapping area, reading the marsh for the telltale signs of alligator activity, and pinpointing the locations where his traps will have the best chance of hooking the biggest 'gators.

Guests at that carefree house party aren't always aware that they actually have arrived to celebrate the middle, not the beginning, of the alligator-hunting process. The next day's hunt may be the first of the season, but is only a success if all the plans have been well laid over the preceding months. Even the afternoon before the house party begins, the hunter has been busy setting his traps. After all, the harvest can't begin until the traps are in place, and the law is very strict about when they can be set. He suspends the bait

about a foot above the water to encourage the 'gators to lunge and become more firmly hooked, and to keep the baited hooks clear of rising water in areas of tidal fluctuation.

It is by the dawn's early light that the hunter and his party set out for the first, and subsequent, days of the alligator season. The law is very careful in stating that all traps must be checked daily. In near subtropic heat and humidity, that's best done in the cool of the morning. The law is equally clear that it can't be done at night; shine-a-'gator methods are now entirely prohibited. The hunter often times his departure so that he will arrive at his first trap just as the sun clears the horizon. Expertly, he wends his boat through the intricate web of *trainasses*, those narrow, shallow watery passages through the luxuriant growth of the marsh that also serve the alligator as both hunting ground and highway.

Checking the traps is easy. If the line supported by the forked stick is down, something, hopefully a 'gator, has taken it. The boat approaches the marsh bank, the line is grasped by a knowing hand, and a quick tug tells the hunter whether anyone's home. A seasoned trapper knows by the resistance he feels whether the 'gator is large or small, and he begins to play the line and tire his quarry before pulling it up for the coup de grace.

Sometimes the line is still up, but the bait is gone. This happens when a bird of prey has raided the trap.

ALLIGATOR-HUNTING HOUSE PARTY AT POINTE-AUX-CHÊNES.

BY THE DAWN'S EARLY LIGHT 161

Sometimes the line is down and the bait is gone. This indicates that a bird or leaping 'gator has knocked it into the water without becoming hooked. Once submerged, turtles, fish, crawfish, or other scavengers may have cleaned it off. These traps are reset from the bait bucket, and the disappointed hunter continues his daily run. Since alligators are perfectly happy to have their meals a little *faisandé*, it is not necessary to rebait untripped hooks that still hold their slowly ripening offerings. They may be moved to other, more promising locations if the bait isn't taken in another day or two.

When tension on the downed line tells the hunter that his alligatorship is tethered to the submerged end, a duel ensues. The 'gator usually remains underwater as the hunter plays the line to tire it. The trapper must leave enough line for the 'gator to struggle and fatigue itself, but not enough for a wily 'gator to entangle it in underwater snags or retreat into his den.

Occasionally the hunter may detach the line from its anchoring tree or stake in order to have more freedom in manipulating it. If the 'gator is big, the result may be the southern version of a Nantucket sleigh ride as the 'gator, heading for the security of deeper waters, tows boat, hunter(s), and all down the *trainasse* or across the clearing. It's surprising how fast and far a good-sized 'gator can go under such circumstances.

The marsh-time minuet of hunter and 'gator draws to its formal close, a sort of waterborne pas de deux, as the 'gator reaches exhaustion and the hunter inexorably pulls it boatward. The 'gator breaks water. The hunter eyes its head, judging size by the visible space between eye and nostril. The rule of thumb is one inch of snout for every foot of 'gator. The 'gator may spy the hunter and dive again with renewed vigor. Relentlessly, however, it is brought closer and closer to the boat. The hunter, line in one hand, .22 in the other, waits until the 'gator is within inches of the gun barrel. He squeezes off a round that sends a sudden watery geyser skyward as the 'gator is killed with a clean shot to the brain. It is an elegant ritual, as quick, painless, and humane as can be devised in the taking of such wild aquatic prey.

Some hunters load their 'gators into the boat at this point. Others trail them from the stern. Regardless of the choice, the dead or comatose 'gator is pulled to the side of the boat and its jaws are firmly secured with a trusslike set of knots and half-hitches executed while its mouth is held tightly closed. If the hook is attached to a releasable lead, it is detached. If not, the trap cord is cut. In either case, the trap is reassembled and reset in hopes of another day's catch. In the event that the 'gator has been stunned rather than killed outright, the twine muzzle that the hunter has created may well save life or limb of those who handle it later. Some hunters may take the extra precaution of severing vertebrae at head and hip with a large knife to forestall a boated 'gator's wild thrashings that may precede death. Now is the time, according to law, that the official tag, making the catch legal, must be affixed to the 'gator's tail. In practice, some hunters wait until the 'gator is docked at camp to do so.

When the rounds have been made of all the traps, the hunter and his 'gators head back to camp, threading their way through the endless maze of *trainasses*, usually arriving about midday. The docked 'gators are tagged at the end of the tail, if this hasn't been done in the marsh, and the hunter records all pertinent information necessary to provide their legal documentation. If the hunter is selling his 'gators whole to a processor who will deal with both meat and hide, the 'gators are iced in a shaded area and covered with a tarp. The dealer is called to arrange a rapid pickup, as time is of the essence in conveying the 'gators to the processing facility to ensure freshness.

If the hunter dresses his own take, the 'gators are brought to the skinning table. There each is hoisted into place and the hide is carefully removed. The skinning technique has not appreciably changed since Victorian times. The designated season's flap of back skin is cut in its proper shape and place as the hide is stripped. Skillful hands are needed to peel away the skin, usually beginning at "wrists" and "ankles." Nicks and cuts are avoided at all costs because they will significantly lower the value of the hide when it is sold. Once free of legs, tail, and sides, the skin can literally be ripped from the belly—where there are very few attachments—with one continuous, violent yank. After removal from the carcass, the hide is carefully scraped to remove any fat or flesh that may have adhered. The cleaned, elastic hides at one time were stretched and tacked to a board in an attempt to pull them out as long as possible

Left to right:
Top:
Cutting an Alligator's Tail for Tagging; Making the Record: Determining Sex of an Alligator.

Center:
A Delicate Touch, Essential to Proper Hide Skinning; Saving for Later: Salting the Hide.

Bottom:
Preparing for Storage: Rolling the Salted Hide; Hung Out to Drip Dry: Alligator Hides in Bag Storage.

in the hope of getting a better price for greater length. Richard Yancey explained in 1959 that "While the trapper may get a little more by carrying out this measure, the stretching separates the scales or plates and greatly reduces the quality of the skin . . . it is harmful to the industry as a whole." Such stretched hides today are downgraded by dealers because the leather they yield is of lessened quality. Lower prices are offered for such hides and the practice has virtually ceased.

Cleaned hides with tags still attached to their tails are wiped free of any debris, blood, or body fluids and then lavishly salted on the raw side. A few inches of the long side of each hide are then folded over toward the center of the salted surface. The hide is tightly rolled from the head end, most often on a small stick that allows the hunter to use it like a rolling pin to drive off as much of the remaining liquid as possible. Last to be wound on is the tail tip with its identifying tag. Rolled, salted hides are stored—frequently in sacks that allow fluids to drip—in a clean, dry place until purchased by dealers or offered at auction. Some hunters still use the old method of brine-pickle storage, and in Louisiana, the Wildlife and Fisheries Commission even offers helpful hints to avoid or cure bacterial problems that may occur in barrels or vats.

At each step, trapping, sale to dealer, and ensuing sales to brokers or tanneries, careful records are kept every time the hide changes hands. These are recorded by tag number. All transactions are reported to the Louisiana Wildlife and Fisheries Commission, the issuing agency, which enters them into a computer system. From the time an alligator leaves the marsh until it becomes a belt or handbag, the movement of each hide can be computer-traced to its point of origin in the ongoing effort to prevent poached or otherwise illegal hides from entering the market.

Each hunter is responsible for all the tags issued to him. When the thirty-day season is over, the hunter must present his records and surrender all unused tags. The number of hides he has taken, plus the number of unused tags he returns, must tally with the exact number of tags he received when the season began.

After each arduous day of the season, the hunter is usually glad to eat and rest. At season's opening, he may happily "pass a good time" with his house party, but he's generally early to bed in order to set off again the next morning, by the dawn's early light.

THE GREAT AGE OF DISCOVERY, PART II

HOW YA GONNA KEEP 'EM DOWN ON THE FARM?

Beginning in 1958, the Louisiana Wildlife and Fisheries Commission initiated a serious program of alligator-management studies, augmented in 1964 by a program of alligator-farming investigations. These, coupled with the work of university-based scientists, have made Louisiana a world leader in both theoretical and practical alligator knowledge. This experimentation, supplemented by work conducted in other states (notably Texas and Florida), has resulted in everything from medical advances to the modern alligator farm.

Inquiries started as early as 1953, when Drs. R. A. Coulson, Thomas Hernandez, and Fred Brazda of the LSU biochemistry faculty began looking into the value of the alligator in medical research. According to LSU's *Daily Reveille*, they were "making a complete study of the alligator's biochemistry, thus increasing science's knowledge of processes and changes similar to those in the human body. They explained that the cold-blooded alligators function just like mammals, including man, but about eight times slower. That's an advantage as far as medicine is concerned, because fleeting changes in man become prolonged activities in alligators. Scientists, therefore, get a slow-motion picture of body mechanisms."

Pioneering studies of this kind pointed out that the basics of alligator research, conducted and reported by researchers and scientists of the sixteenth, seventeenth, eighteenth, nineteenth, and early twentieth centuries had

"ALLIGATOR ET ALYSINE PLANTAIN D'EAU." COPPER-PLATE ENGRAVING BY DE SAINSON FROM *DICTIONNAIRE PITTORESQUE D'HISTOIRE NATURELLE ET DES PHÉNOMÈNES DE LA NATURE*, VOL. 1, COMPILED BY M. F.-E. GUÉRIN, 1834.

FACING PAGE: MARSH ISLAND EXPERIMENTAL SPRING ALLIGATOR HARVEST, APRIL 1986.

provided a framework and broad outlines that now could be filled in with many specifics due to mid-twentieth-century contributions. As the crisis in declining alligator populations seemed to worsen, it became evident that great parts of the alligator's biochemistry and behavior were still gray areas. Many answers were needed if the nation was successfully to protect and manage the alligator as a renewable natural resource. Even research methodologies had to be devised to investigate this unknown territory.

Robert Chabreck of the Louisiana Wildlife and Fisheries Commission was among the first to start supplying the missing data. Between 1958 and 1963, his research team captured and tagged more than 1,600 alligators on the Rockefeller Wildlife Refuge. Tagging an alligator for future identification wasn't easy, and a method had to be invented. Mike Cook reported Chabreck's solution: "By clipping a toe, removing dorsal tail scutes and inserting a self-piercing monel tag to the tail scutes (scales or ridges lying dorsally and posteriorly to the tail) there is a possibility of more than 3,000 separate marks."

Trapping and tagging were used to discover such basic information as sex ratios, growth rates, mortality rates, and the size of an individual alligator's range. Tracking alligators even more closely became possible with the perfection and application of telemetry techniques—the ways in which alligators are fitted with radio collar devices and their movements traced by using various types of tracking antennae and radio receivers. Leading men to emerge in this field were Ted Joanen and Larry McNease, also with the Louisiana Wildlife and Fisheries Commission, who published several major studies in this and related areas from the early 1970s onward. Joanen has served as research leader at the Rockefeller Refuge for over twenty years. He and his colleagues are regarded as world authorities and are often called to other states and countries to advise on crocodilian problems and research.

As early as 1969, they outfitted eight female alligators with telemetric devices, and as Cook said in 1970, "This spring and summer the bull 'gators have gone electronic. . . . The 'beep' comes from a tiny radio transmitter—no larger than a pack of cigarettes—which has been waterproofed and is firmly attached to a sturdy plastic collar placed around the neck of an animal. The transmitters, operating in the 150 megacycle range, cost about $90 each and send a signal which can be picked up a mile to a mile and a half away. The battery in the unit lasts anywhere from 120 to 180 days, depending on the size." The alligators sported their new wardrobes about the marsh quite happily. Joanen and McNease were able to document carefully courtship, mating, and nesting behaviors as never before.

J. D. Nichols and a team composed of Lynn Viehman, Robert Chabreck, and Bruce Fenderson, associated with the Agricultural Experiment Station of Louisiana State University, employed the painstaking procedures of constructing a model "to simulate the dynamics of a commercially harvested alligator population" in 1976. Such constructs, with application of carefully crafted formulae to factor in the elements of "nesting effort, nest flooding, desiccation mortality, and predation on alligator eggs and young," and others such as climatic disasters, are enormously difficult and tedious to prepare.

After completion, the results were summarized as follows:

Simulations were utilized to examine population response to various differential harvest rates in which age and sex-specific proportions of animals taken were similar to those observed in 1972 and 1973 Louisiana harvest seasons. These simulations demonstrated that under existing habitat conditions a base population of 100,000 animals should be maintained for at least 20 years when subjected to an annual differential harvest rate slightly greater than 5 percent. Simulations were conducted using proportional harvest rates in which animals of various sizes were taken in proportion to their relative abundance in the population. Comparison of proportional and differential harvest strategies indicated that proportional hunting can result in increased yields of alligator hide and resultant income. Simulations with egg collection management programs produced greater population increases than similar simulations with no management.

This rather terse, dry language is appropriate to a scientific report, but it does not convey the excitement of the findings. Scientists and wildlife managers now were provided with a mechanism that would allow them to predict, with greater accuracy than ever before, how the wild alligator population would react when placed under harvest pressures and environmental stresses.

New technologies in electronic records management were applied in 1980 by scientists at LSU, allowing quicker and more accurate information reporting, sorting, and analysis. Joan Duffy explained that "Scaly green Louisiana alligators, long the anonymous residents of secluded bayous and lakes have entered the modern world of data processing. . . . With the help of computer hardware and expertise supplied by LSU, state wildlife experts have developed a data processing program to efficiently keep track of the number of hunters wading into Louisiana marshes each September to hunt the giant lizards [*sic*] and the number of gators taken. . . . [Allen] Ensminger said information about the alligator—where it was caught and its size—is fed into the LSU computer. More information is added when the skin is sold, shipped to a tanner and fabricated into leather goods." This advance, drawing on the tagging system required of alligator hunters, allowed an ever-more vigilant policing of the hide business, as LSU staff worked cooperatively with the Louisiana Wildlife and Fisheries Commission.

An unusual hunt for a large number of alligators was staged on the Russell Sage Wildlife Refuge at Marsh Island in the spring of 1986. J. B. Angelle, secretary of the Department of Wildlife and Fisheries, said that one of the reasons for the out-of-season activity was "evaluating an alternate harvest technique for specific-sized alligators." The Sierra Club charged that such hunting was not permitted by deed of gift, and might threaten the state's title to the refuge property. Lawyers for the Russell Sage Foundation worked diligently with Wildlife and Fisheries, overruling the Sierra Club objection.

Johnie Tarver, of Wildlife and Fisheries, told the

Baton Rouge *Morning Advocate* that "The main purpose of the harvest is research. . . . One of the things the department is trying to establish with the harvest is that it is profitable for alligator hunters to sell their catch whole to companies that use both the hide and the meat. In the past, meat often has been wasted by hunters who were just interested in the hides . . . the department also hopes to show landowners that by protecting their wetlands they can make a profit. Biological information obtained from the project will help the department make decisions on alligator management, including whether a spring harvest is wise."

This and related research did indicate that the hunter made more money, and was spared the extra work of dressing out his catch, by selling his tagged alligators whole. Many began to do so, changing traditional marketing procedures. It also demonstrated the value of marsh preservation and maintenance for economic reasons, discouraging landowners from draining or developing privately owned wetlands, and thereby protecting extensive areas of alligator habitat. Consideration of a spring harvest, however, was rejected in favor of the by-then-traditional fall season, which had been timed to take place well after the natural breeding season.

Controlled spring and summer hunts at Marsh Island were conducted by Wildlife and Fisheries research coordinator Dave Taylor through subsequent years. Taylor said, "Our primary goal is to have the maximum harvest with no impact on the population." Ted Joanen, research leader, amplified the issue: "This is what wildlife management is all about. As we learn more, we understand better how to harvest a population. If we are harvesting at a lower rate, then the rest of the animals out there are dying from natural causes. We should be using that segment of the population. . . . " "The alligators harvested on Marsh Island are the largest sample size in the world," Taylor told reporter Victoria Dawson in 1989. "The results obtained from these sample sizes are more meaningful than those from anywhere else on the subject of alligator ages and reproduction."

During this same period, biologists in Texas and Florida, with the support of the National Geographic Society, were looking into such seemingly esoteric topics as those mysterious musk glands found under the alligator's jaw and near the tail. Paul Weldon, at Texas A&M University, learned that alligators rely on a sense of smell to communicate. "We think the scents emitted by the glands near the tail are used to attract mates. Those in the throat probably mark territories," Weldon indicated to Donald Frederick. An entertaining possible outgrowth of this research might be development of an alligator repellent. Frederick thinks "this could be good news to wary fishermen, swimmers, divers—even golfers—in alligator territory such as Florida and Louisiana."

These, of course, are only a sampling of the many and varied alligator studies that have been conducted since the 1950s. The work of these and other scientists has greatly expanded available knowledge concerning the alligator, often revealing highly detailed information of great use. The data that scientists have obtained has become the basis for the determination that alligators can be managed as a renewable natural resource. Much of the research was conducted in Louisiana by game-management professionals of the Louisiana Department of Wildlife and Fisheries, the Louisiana State University's Department of Forestry and Wildlife Management, and the Louisiana Cooperative Extension Service. They deserve a great deal of recognition and credit for their important contributions to a fuller

SA-6—One of the Breeding Pens at Casper's Alligator Jungle, St. Augustine, Fla.

ABOVE: ICING EXPERIMENTALLY HARVESTED 'GATORS ABOARD A SHRIMP BOAT AT MARSH ISLAND, 1989.

LEFT: AN EARLY FLORIDA BREEDING PEN. POSTCARD BY THE CURT TEICH CO., CHICAGO, CA. 1947.

THE GREAT AGE OF DISCOVERY, PART II 171

understanding of the alligator and the development of management strategies utilizing the findings of their research.

The modern annual alligator hunt is a direct result of their hard work. Their success is recorded by the Louisiana Fur and Alligator Advisory Council: "Louisiana's first program to manage the alligator on a sustained yield basis was initiated in 1972. This alligator harvest program was initiated in one parish, expanded to three parishes in 1973, nine parishes in 1979 and was further expanded to a statewide harvest in 1981." Their work was also controversial, playing a major technical role in the legal and legislative battles of the "alligator wars" of the 1970s. Their solid, provable, pioneering results won the ultimate victory that would see the eventual opening of alligator seasons in other states, as well.

The lack of success in breeding alligators in captivity was evident to the United States Department of Agriculture as early as 1929: "That those engaged in alligator farming are not propagating these reptiles on an extensive scale is apparent from interviews with the owners. On one of these farms it has been observed that the captive females do build nests and lay their eggs therein, but with no degree of regularity," read a technical report issued that year.

Anthony Mullet managed a six-year-old alligator farm in New Orleans in 1937, and he regarded it as "more an experiment than a business venture." It had been started as a hobby by F. C. Luthi in 1931, with an original stock of about twenty-five adult alligators "and several hundred young, which were taken in the main, from surrounding swamps and marshes." By 1937 it had reached an "awkward stage, too big for a hobby and not big enough for financial profits." At that point, Mullet had six hundred alligators in stock, and was shooting for one thousand. Sales were few and far between. Katharine Daly wrote in 1937, "[Mullet] does sell the babies sometimes, to curious tourists who want them for pets, and once in a while he sells the hide of a medium-sized alligator, keeping the larger ones for breeding purposes." His goals in the late Depression years? "What I want to do is catch them, keep them and breed them. Later on, I'll think about profits."

Some of the information and answers needed to achieve greater success were provided through trial-and-error experiments by the alligator farmers. The Louisiana leader in this field was the Kliebert Turtle and Alligator Farm, near Ponchatoula, which was established in the 1940s. More of the necessary information came from studies in the 1950s and 1960s at the Rockefeller Refuge. A great deal was learned about wild alligator behavior that could be applied to alligator farming. Kliebert's worked closely with Wildlife and Fisheries staff in developing such applications. It was in 1964 that the Louisiana Wildlife and Fisheries Commission tackled the specific problems of saurian farming on a systematic basis. Their findings were convincing.

Shortly after the program began, isolated commercial alligator farms began to appear (as opposed to the old roadside tourist attractions). Some of the earlier "snake farm" variety, catering largely to tourists, began to take heed and change or expand their operations to include large and well-managed breeding populations. By 1970, the American

Alligator Council was encouraging scientific alligator farming "to eliminate part of the pressures on wild populations," as A. W. Cooper, Jr., told New Orleans's Wyvern Club.

Ted Joanen was among the earliest to approach farming studies. The Baton Rouge *State-Times* credited him as the first: "Ted Joanen, state wildlife biologist, started the state's research into the feasibility of raising gators commercially. . . . Joanen said he learned in his research that the alligator is an efficient animal. At the younger stages in its life, a gator will grow a pound for every two pounds of feed."

There were, of course, critics as well as supporters. In 1972, the National Audubon Society reported, "Louisiana's Dr. Leslie L. Glasgow . . . and some other conscientious wildlife biologists have long argued that the only way in the long run to save the species is to harness the profit motive through legitimized 'alligator farming.'" The Audubon Society, however, supported the divergent view of Dr. Archie Carr, "whose preeminent knowledge and understanding of the ecology of the world's exploited great reptiles is undisputed." Dr. Carr wrote in *Audubon*, "I have yet to see or hear of a work plan for any reptile ranches that shows in realistic detail how it expects to achieve a volume of production so great that it will do anything other than *increase* both demand and prices. If the enterprise is a commercial one, it will obviously do everything possible to create new markets. Just as obviously, it will not be able to satisfy these, and so will exacerbate, rather than relieve, the predicament of the natural populations."

The editors of *Audubon* were apparently not aware that the Louisiana scientists were a jump ahead. Efforts were being made not just to determine growth rates but also to discover optimum temperatures for both accelerated growth and breeding. An experiment maintaining pens at eighty-two degrees Fahrenheit was begun at the Rockefeller Refuge. Scientists had to wait a full alligator generation (about nine years in the wild) to see whether it worked. The Baton Rouge *State-Times* reported its success in only six years: "One of the biggest problems when the program started in 1972 was whether they would reproduce. But now [1979] about 30 offspring of the first batch of super gators, born [*sic*] earlier this year, live in the same heated pens where their parents grew up."

The idea was not a new one. It had been among the trial-and-error investigations attempted, without success, by commercial farmers in the early part of the twentieth century. "The proprietor of one of the largest alligator farms in the country" had communicated to Albert Reese by 1915: "We have experimented with our stock to see if we could get them to eat in the winter, and found that by keeping the water in the tanks at a certain temperature they would eat, but we found out that the warm water would make their bowels move, and that they would not eat enough to keep themselves up . . . and as a result they would become very poor and thin, so we do not force them to eat [in the winter]." The job of later wildlife managers of the 1970s was to adjust the formula so that it did work.

While the first batch of scientific hot-tub 'gators of the 1970s was growing up, there was simultaneous

examination of a second option, beginning in 1975 when the initial generation of "super 'gators" were only three years old. Leonard Gray reported, "It has since been converted from a brood stock closed operation to an open system in which smaller gators are harvested instead of being allowed to breed and new eggs are brought in from the wild." Farmers, however, were required to release some of the babies they hatched in order to maintain the wild population.

Joanen told the press something about the "super 'gators" in 1979: "You refer to them as super gators. . . . The only difference is that they are grown 12 months of the year and they don't go into hibernation [*sic*] for six months. . . . An alligator living in the wild grows about 1 foot per year, but the super gators kept in water tanks heated to 82 degrees and fed a steady diet of fish gain about 3 feet per year. Regular alligators reach sexual maturity [breeding age] in nine years and 10 months; super gators in five years and 10 months." In other words, "They look just as ugly and ornery as their naturally grown counterparts, but about 2,000 super gators raised by the state Wildlife and Fisheries Department got that way in half the time." At this time, the country's most successful commercial alligator hide ranches were located at Ponchatoula, Louisiana, and West Palm Beach, Florida. Many more were soon to crop up—particularly in Louisiana, but in other southern states, as well.

The advantages of the new method to farmers were obvious. Heated ponds, or even suspended tiers of heated trays, are now widely accepted by alligator farmers as a means of stimulating growth, allowing harvest in about two and a half years as opposed to four or five in unheated environments. Harvest size is approximately five feet; the finer scale patterns of smaller animals are essential for smaller alligator goods. Large scales may be dramatic on luggage but are not effective for watchbands and wallets. Steele McAndrew, an alligator farmer at Ville Platte, explained another benefit of the system: "gators kept inside have better quality hides because the animals aren't as susceptible to scarring injuries to their hides."

The alternate approach, harvesting smaller, nonbreeding animals and bringing in wild eggs to be incubated, hatched, and "super grown," might at first appear to be decimating the wild alligator population. Regulation of alligator farms not only prevents this but significantly enhances the wild population. The techniques of alligator-egg incubation had been well-established, particularly in Florida, since the turn of the century, as a result of the large market for the sale of souvenir baby alligators to Edwardian tourists. Albert Reese wrote in 1915 of "the collection of eggs for sale and hatching purposes . . . such eggs may readily be hatched by simply keeping these moist and at a fairly constant temperature. . . . " In 1922, Karl Schmidt recommended "maintaining them at a temperature of 80 degrees F., and moistening them daily to prevent drying." The practice was not helping the wild alligator population; as Schmidt found, "the robbing of their nests for eggs [and sale of wild babies] . . . have decimated the species to such an extent that few places are now [1922] left where it [the alligator] can still be said to be

abundant." Reese had an even bleaker view, saying that such profiteering would "tend towards the annihilation of the species in the course of time." This, of course, was just the opposite of the intent of the wildlife managers championing the gathering of eggs a half century later.

In the early years of its egg-gathering program, the Louisiana Wildlife and Fisheries Department actually collected and distributed alligator eggs, and has continued to do so. Later this effort was supplemented by delegating authority to licensed farmers to gather wild eggs, as well. In the carefully regulated program, farmers are required to release 17 percent (1989 figure) of their successful hatchlings when they reach four feet. This is a larger percentage than normally survive the rigors of baby alligatorhood (they are eaten by birds, raccoons, large fish, and even other alligators). Alligators that reach four feet, however, have few natural enemies; releasing more than would normally survive to this size augments rather than decreases the total wild population.

Alligator farming got another boost at the end of the 1970s when processing and sale of alligator meat for human consumption was legalized. Food scientists at LSU, working through the Louisiana Cooperative Extension Service, determined its wholesomeness and even developed recipes for preparing it. Carcasses of harvested 'gators were allowed to enter the state's seafood market, adding substantially to both hunters' and farmers' incomes.

Experiments also were made concerning alligator-egg incubation, yielding some odd results. It had been known that the incubation temperature determined sex of hatchlings in some reptiles. Ted Joanen teamed with Mark Ferguson of Queen's University in Belfast, Ireland, in 1982 to see whether this might be the case with alligators. They found that it was. Their findings were that nests kept at thirty degrees centigrade (86°F.) produced females, while nests maintained at thirty-four centigrade (93.2°F.) hatched males. Eggs kept at less than twenty-six centigrade (78.8°F.) died and did not hatch. This useful information would allow breeders to produce male or female alligators at will and as needed. Faster-growing males would be more profitable to most farmers. More females could be induced if needed to augment the wild breeding stock.

The study also led to the speculation, according to the Baton Rouge *State-Times*, "that if the sex of dinosaurs was also determined by incubation temperatures, then this may explain the selective extinction of these groups in response to a relatively sudden, continuous change in climate to one that is [*sic*] hotter or colder." Dinosaurs finding themselves with a single-sex population would have been hard put to guarantee survival of their species.

Louisiana-researched farming methods were so successful that by 1984, Jack Scott wrote, "state-regulated farms are thriving in Florida and Louisiana, based on the belief that the reptiles are a renewable resource that can be raised in captivity both for profit and for the benefit of the species." He added, "Some wildlife specialists agree, and are convinced that the farms will not only relieve pressure from hunters, but that wildlife management can control, and even direct, future alligator populations for the reptiles' benefit."

By March of 1986, thirteen Louisiana alligator farms had been stocked with state-supplied eggs. Another three dozen would-be alligator farmers were waiting in the wings to receive eggs, but Joanen warned that it might take several years to supply them all. Nine more had been served by November, bringing the in-state total to twenty-two operating farms that year. And there was still much to learn. "Alligator farming is still in the infancy stage," Joanen was quoted as saying. By that time, Louisiana's farms were contributing 4,000 hides to the state market annually (or about 20 percent), while about 17,000 were being taken from the wild population. Joanen estimated that the gap could be bridged in ten to fifteen years, when "The farm harvest could equal the wild harvest."

Things moved faster than anticipated. By the end of the 1980s, the number of farms had more than doubled, numbering about fifty-five. Louisiana was well on the way to producing a majority of farm-raised hides. The Louisiana Fur and Alligator Advisory Council announced, "During the 1988 season approximately 12,500 farm-raised alligators were harvested." By 1989, the waiting list for state licensing stood at over two hundred, and alligators had gotten to the classroom. Mark Robichaux wrote that "Alligator sections have been added to aquaculture classes in state universities." At LSU, the Louisiana Cooperative Extension Service even issued an alligator aquaculture videocassette. The state's newfangled ranchers were estimated to be raising 75,000 head of stock for future markets. In September of 1990, marine advisory agent Paul Thibodeaux of the Louisiana Cooperative Extension Service put the number of licensed farmers at one hundred and anticipated they would export fifty thousand hides that year alone.

Research continued in Louisiana and other places, notably on Florida's alligator farms, several of which were cooperating with that state's biologists. Kent Vliet, one of the major Florida researchers, has been investigating hormonal cycles and their effects on breeding. Vliet's work has been based on the earlier investigations of Ruth Elsey and Valentine Lance, who had looked into the same topics, using both wild and captive alligators at the Rockefeller Refuge as their research subjects.

In 1988, Vliet told Diane Ackerman, "We've developed a threefold project. The first part is just to look at the effect our taking blood [samples] and handling the alligators has on their hormones. The second part is to look at alligators in different population densities and compare hormone concentrations. The third part is a sort of background check to make sure that alligators in captivity cycle hormonally the way wild alligators do."

Vliet hopes his findings will help to promote knowledge about breeding and to improve it: "The basic problem we're concerned with is that alligators, like many other animals, reproduce much less successfully in captivity than in the wild. It might be a result of how densely the animals are crowded together. When animals are under stress, reproduction drops. . . . When you capture an alligator, its stress hormones sometimes go screeching up, and its reproductive hormones can plunge for days."

Alligators continue to suffer from an image problem. As recently as 1989, over 350 citizens gathered at a public meeting in the small town of Paradis, Louisiana, to "declare their opposition to a proposed alligator ranch." The residents objected to approximately one thousand new reptilian neighbors for a number of reasons: (1) "the wind would be noxious and would travel for miles"; (2) "the fear of alligators could cause psychiatric problems among local children"; (3) "hurricanes and floods . . . could send 500 alligators running around the neighborhood"; (4) wild alligators might be attracted to the facility; and (5) waste water from the proposed farm might contaminate the local drainage system. Leonard Gray reported in the *River Parishes Guide* that parish president Albert Laque "announced that planning and zoning 'will issue no such [building] permit under my administration.'"

Alligator farming is fraught with its own special situations. Robichaux described one attempt to move a herd. The rancher was "Skeet" Rogers of Natchitoches: "He first thought to move them through a 'chute' made from sheets of tin. 'We were going to herd 'em like cattle with sticks,' he says. 'It was a mess. They tried to climb over each other and they started fighting.' With the help of 14 leery volunteers, each wearing two pairs of thick gloves to protect his hands, Mr. Rogers hand-carried the [1,000] alligators from barn to barn." Ranchers had to learn by doing that special methods are needed to deal with unique alligator situations.

Selling them can be equally troublesome. Robichaux says, "At market time, Mr. Rogers loads some 200 live four-foot gators into an old, gutted school bus. . . . Only a sheet of plywood separates the driver from his passengers. The

 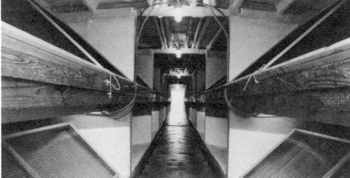

driver is 'usually the guy who draws the shortest straw . . .' says Mr. Rogers, adding: 'Usually a car follows—just in case.' "

Feeding time on the commercial alligator farm can be an ordeal to the uninitiated. In Robichaux's words, "The smell takes some getting used to . . . the 17-year-old Stelly twins, Velma and Thelma, daily plop gobs of feed mix to the gators as part of their farm chores [at Kaplan, Louisiana]. The feed is one part nutria . . . one part croaker [a kind of fish] . . . and one part vitamin-fortified dry food that a producer packs in sacks labeled Alligator Feed. 'The first time we did this, I couldn't believe it,' says Thelma, her arms sunk in a bucket of bloody nutria carcasses."

Alligators thrive on nutria, and the farmers are now friends of the trappers. They buy fresh nutria carcasses during the fur-trapping season and freeze them to use for feed throughout the year. This is very different from the early days of the century when trappers claimed alligators were destroying their livelihood by eating too many muskrats. However, that was also at a time before the prolific nutria was inadvertently introduced to the state.

Joanen maintains that "the farmers who skin alligators also are returning healthy four-footers to the wild. If you want to help the marsh, and the alligators, buy an alligator handbag." Dr. Glasgow had been Joanen's principal professor in the graduate program of wildlife management studies at LSU during Joanen's student days. Had he lived, the professor (nicknamed "Bwana" by his students because he could walk them into exhaustion on field trips) would have been proud that his former student proved the wisdom of his own contention that scientific farming would be the alligator's salvation.

Robichaux reports, "There are alligator farms in Florida and Texas, too. But alligator-farm technical knowledge and state support is [sic] centered here; for nearly 20 years, Messrs. Joanen and McNease did their research on alligators in captivity in the marsh at Rockefeller Refuge. . . . Foreign countries, mainly in Africa, have engineered their alligator and crocodile farming enterprises on the Louisiana's [sic] model."

Phil Massey also credits the academic institutions: "The Louisiana State University Agriculture Center, through its experiment station and extension divisions, has been a key factor in this expansion [of alligator farming]." The university's chancellor, Dr. H. R. Caffey, added, "aquaculture has top priority for research and extension, because it offers the best opportunity for economic development of our renewable natural resources, and because we feel that aquaculture will create new jobs and improve the economy."

The Louisiana Fur and Alligator Advisory Council takes justifiable pride in the fact that: "The Louisiana Department of Wildlife and Fisheries is known as the world leader in both wild and captive alligator research and management. The Department recognizes the value of this renewable, natural resource and will continue to harvest and manage alligator populations on a sustained yield basis."

The 1990 state of affairs was summarized by Massey: "Alligator farming is a small but growing industry. The early entrants into the business now have brood stock and are hatching their own eggs, and with the attractive prices, lack of serious diseases and ready availability of nutria as food, the future of the industry looks bright." It appeared so bright, in fact, that the Louisiana Fur and Alligator Advisory Council predicted, "Farm alligator production is expected to double again [from 1988] by 1990."

The development of alligator management, including both wild and farm populations, has been a remarkable success story. Facing opposition from such groups as the Sierra Club and the National Audubon Society, Louisiana researchers conducted their scientific investigations and utilized their data to devise programs that have worked to the benefit of both man and alligator.

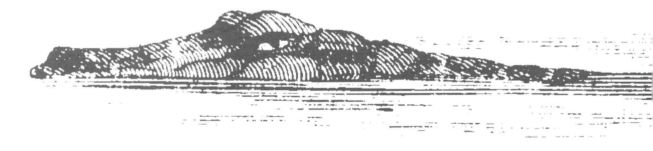

ALLIGATOR, INC.

SAURIANS IN BUSINESS

The alligator holds an honorable position in business and advertising, dating back to its emergence in the commercial world in the early nineteenth century. Promoters found it had special appeal to tourists seeking the unusual in the South, and the additional benefit of selling well at home. The earliest manifestation of the alligator in business names may have been the Alligator Line, an interconnecting system of rail, steamboat, and coach transportation linking New Orleans with Georgia destinations in 1839. Alligator Pure Louisiana Molasses was being tinned and marketed by 1912, with a label copyright protected by the New Orleans Coffee Company.

Nationally, the best known is doubtless the "alligator shirt." The Lacoste line of tennis apparel was originated by René Lacoste, a championship player, in France in 1933. Serious exportation to the United States began following World War II. The original crestlike "alligator" was actually a crocodile, but Americans promptly misidentified it. Izod/Lacoste, now manufacturing and distributing the line, had to give in to a self-righteous public that knew an alligator when it saw one; as a result, the crocodile suffered a sea change. There have been alligators on those trendy tennis togs ever since. One Asian manufacturer even clandestinely produces fake Lacoste crests that the less affluent can sew onto less costly clothing; while others have fraudulently manufactured fake Lacoste shirts including the emblem.

THE "ALLIGATOR" SHIRT: CROCODILE THAT SUFFERED A SEA CHANGE.

FACING PAGE: GATORADE—DEVELOPED AT THE UNIVERSITY OF FLORIDA TO SUSTAIN EX-HAUSTED ATH-LETES.

 ALLIGATOR, INC. 181

In addition to logos, alligators have served as shop signs. A "cigar store alligator" was carved of oak by the "wood butcher" of Minnesota at the time of the 1984 New Orleans World's Fair, and the seven-foot saurian, dubbed "W.C." because of its resemblance to Mr. Fields, now resides at a Decatur Street bar. Many businesses use alligator images on signs and cards to identify the regional character of their merchandise. A sporty alligator in spats graces those of the Wehmeier Belt Shop in the French Quarter, a leading retailer of alligator leather goods.

Gatorfoam is produced by the International Paper Company of Statesville, North Carolina. It came onto the market in 1976 as a stiff but lightweight sheet that has many applications. It is often used as a backing material in

fine picture framing and for panel construction in traveling exhibitions. The logo for the product is an alligator silhouette, and according to company officials, the name was chosen to remind the customer of "toughness like the skin of an alligator."

The Lowdown Alligator Jass Band (using the original spelling of *jazz*) markets its music from Cornell University in Ithaca, New York. The band's albums are nationally distributed and can be found everywhere at record shops featuring a strong jazz section.

Not surprisingly, Florida seems to contribute the most "alligator" products (ones neither made from nor in the shape of alligators) to the national market. A small sample illustrates their wide range. Gator Roach Hives is a household pesticide product, manufactured and distributed by the trademark holder, the DeSoto Chemical Company of Arcadia. Gator Eggs are masquerading bubble gum, packaged in miniature milk cartons, distributed by Lenny's Sales, Inc., of Lake Wales, Florida (they also add place names to the label, depending on which city or locality the "eggs" will be sold in).

Best-known of these products is Gatorade. Developed by a team of researchers headed by Dr. Robert Cade in the early 1960s at the University of Florida, the formula was ready for testing in 1965. What they had concocted was a quickly absorbed vitamin and mineral supplement meant to be a healthy and legal pick-me-up to refurbish exhausted collegiate athletes by replacing salts and alleviating dehydration. It worked. The University of Florida 'Gators enjoyed winning football seasons. The secret got out.

 ALLIGATOR, INC. 183

Gatorfoam ®
Laminated Foam Panels

Vanquished Georgia Tech head coach Bobby Dodd told reporters at the 1967 Orange Bowl, "We didn't have Gatorade. That made the difference." It was marketed. It became a huge national success, even though the original formula didn't please everyone's palate. America had entered the jogging age; the new era of physical-fitness awareness encouraged such products.

Stokely–Van Camp of Indianapolis, Gatorade's first commercial producer, promoted it to the National Football League, beginning in May 1967. That manufacturer was acquired by The Quaker Oats Company of Chicago in 1983, at the price of $230 million, including the Gatorade brand. Product effectiveness and superb marketing have made it the "official sports beverage" of the NFL, the NBA, Major League Baseball, the NHL and the PGA, among professional organizations. It has become a corporate sponsor of the NCAA, the NAIA, and national high school athletic groups. Gatorade, gulped down by millions of weekend athletes as well, has

brought the alligator name into countless American homes.

Among the most entertaining products is Growlin' Gator Lager, advertised as "the beer with a bite—favorite of lounge lizards everywhere." It is "brewed and bottled in Alligator Alley," by the Gator Lager Company at the Florida Brewery in Auburndale, although the company is headquartered in Orlando. The story behind Gator Lager is the tale of marketing genius recognizing and filling a need, drafting into service the recognition value and widely salable image of the American alligator.

Actually, Gator Lager wasn't the first version of saurian suds to be marketed. That honor seems to go to a pair of students at the University of Florida in Gainesville, who originated Alligator Beer, named in 1985 for the university mascot. The collegiate brew seems to have lasted but a single season. It, too, was produced at the Florida Brewery, but their spokesman says they haven't heard from the college kids since they placed their original order.

Gator Lager was actually a sort of sideways creation of Bill Burrer, a Michigan-born and -educated businessman, who moved to Florida in 1972. Among other enterprises, he owned and operated companies producing garments for the tourist trade. In September 1987, Burrer developed a logo for T-shirts and caps. It consisted of a jazzy alligator drinking an entirely fictitious brew. Reporter Tom Henry says, "he put some sunglasses on the cartoon reptile and gave it the grin of a cat that swallowed the canary—or perhaps, in this case, an alligator sipping suds after taking a bite out of a tourist." It worked. A landslide sale of shirts, caps, and mugs featuring the "growler" got a great response.

By early 1988, Burrer's mailbox was swamped with demands for the nonextant beer itself. Recognizing an opportunity when it came knocking, Burrer (who has been called a marketing whiz, and in fact holds a degree in marketing) called on informal knowledge of the brewing business that was part of his Michigan heritage, and he made plans about supplying the demand.

Nine months were spent in development. During that time Burrer successfully interested five major backers. Burrer recalled that in reality the hardest part of getting started was coming up with funds for the initial advertising budget.

The brew that was selected was among the samples proposed by a third-generation brew master. It has been described as reminiscent of Japanese beers (Kirin, in particular), but it is also said to be "a brew of Czechoslovakian hops with a distinct European flavor." With the blessing of his investors, Burrer ordered the first batch to be made up and bottled in long-necks at the Florida Brewery, and he put it on the market in November 1988. "We did it for the state of Florida," he claimed, "and for Floridians to have something to call their own."

The first full year of production for Burrer was 1989. During those twelve months, he introduced cans in addition to the original long-necks, received inquiries from as far away as Japan, Oman, the United Kingdom, and the Canary Islands, distributed Gator Lager to twenty-three states, and grossed over $1 million. That amount was expected to triple in the following year. Burrer saw the handwriting on the wall (or on the label) and by midyear

added phrasing admonishing consumers to partake in moderation—several months in advance of the federal requirement to do so, which took effect in November 1989. In a company press release, Burrer said, "To our knowledge, we are the only brewery to voluntarily take on this responsibility, and we are certainly proud to do so."

Order forms for the original T-shirt are distributed with each six-pack of Gator Lager sold. When an intrigued customer sends one in, along with the shirt he (or she) is sent a copy of the *Gator Gazette*. This regularly updated catalog masquerading as a periodical advertises Burrer's

"GROWLIN' GATOR LAGER" ADVERTISING MEMORABILIA: MARKETING GENIUS AT WORK.

THE QUEEN AT THE FLORIDA ALLIGATOR FARM, JACKSONVILLE, FLA.

FLORIDA ALLIGATOR FARM

PABLO QUEEN.
AGE ABOUT 350
WEIGHS 784 LBS.

 Alligator, Inc. 187

related logo products, which include everything from sweatshirts ($18.00 in 1990) to can coolers, glasses, mugs, key chains, clocks, caps, coasters, tank tops, matchbooks, aprons, beach towels, visors, luggage tags, and neon signs ($350.00) to the "finishing touch at your next party," which is, believe it or not, toilet paper at $5.00 a roll. We hope it hasn't got the "bite" of the brew that unleashed all this upon the sunny South. And, one must remember, it was the popular image of our native saurian, built over centuries, coupled with Burrer's perception and imagination that transformed a nonextant product into a multimillion-dollar industry.

Florida also leads the nation in alligator farms, most of which use some form of *alligator* in their business names. This rich legacy of roadside attractions dates back to the late nineteenth century. The oldest is the St. Augustine Alligator Farm, founded in the 1890s. Datable postcards

recall some of the stellar examples of the early twentieth century, such as Alligator Joe's (Miami) and the Jacksonville Alligator Farm (Jacksonville), the Tampa Alligator Farm (Sulphur Springs), Ross Allen's Reptile Institute (Silver Springs), and even the Musa Isle Indian Village (where Seminole 'gator wrestlers entertained the tourists). The current Gatorland Zoo (between Orlando and Kissimmee) originated as the Snake Village and Alligator Farm in 1948, and Casper's Ostrich and Alligator Farm did a roaring business in the 1950s. Everglades Gatorland at South Bay opened about 1960, according to Jack Barth. The Alligatorland Safari Zoo is in Kissimmee, and Gator Jungle is located in Christmas.

Competition between Florida farms led to squabbles in 1982 and 1989 as to who could have what kind of self-advertising entrance, according to *Orlando Sentinel* reporter Mike Oliver. The 1989 dispute was between Gator Jungle and Gatorland Zoo, both in Orange County. Both also had monster alligators out front, with doors in their mouths, enticing tourists to pass through the monumental maws (or have their pictures taken there) as they entered these roadside attractions. Gatorland Zoo, though, did it first, erecting its saurian version of "Jaws" in 1963, registered the entrance as its trademark in 1982, and promptly sued to force Alligatorland Safari Zoo to terminate its construction of giant jaws in Kissimmee. Barth recommends staying in Room 220 at the Gator Motel in Kissimmee, overlooking Gatorland Zoo for a remarkable "unimpeded view of the statue's blinking red eyes."

188   *A Social History of the American Alligator*

In 1989, Gator Jungle, on the other hand, installed its gaping doorway on "Big Swampy"—a 210-foot-long architectural alligator that houses an entire building—in Christmas, Florida, in 1989. Gatorland Zoo maintained that the similar entrance violated its trademark and would lure tourists to the wrong alligator farm. Judge Frederick Pfeiffer was not entirely convinced they were so similar, and he regaled the court by observing that the situation "might be misleading to someone in Poland or Podunk." "Big Swampy's" architect, Donald Morgan, was called to the stand. Being a nature artist, he attested that his creation was the more anatomically correct of the two competing monsters.

After hearing the attorney's arguments, Judge Pfeiffer finally decreed that indeed "Big Swampy's" jaws could be confused with those at Gatorland Zoo, thus misleading tourists, and that the doorway must be moved. Gatorland Zoo actually seemed to have wanted the judge to rule that "Big Swampy" had to be demolished. Heaving a sign of relief, Gator Jungle agreed to transfer the entrance to their gigantic alligator's neck. Gatorland Zoo's lawyer did admit, "Quite frankly, the logical place to enter an alligator would be through the mouth." To this, the judge riposted, "You don't think you should enter through the other end?"

Such farms existed in other states, as well. The Alligator Farm at Hot Springs, Arkansas, was a going concern by 1905, and the Los Angeles Alligator Farm in California was operating by 1910. The breeding farm at Michaud, on the outskirts of New Orleans, was well established by the mid-1930s. C. C. McClung operated one at Laplace, Louisiana in the 1950s, and Kliebert's Turtle and Alligator Farm, near Ponchatoula, Louisiana, has combined tourism with hide ranching and has been in business since the 1940s.

Purveyors of lodging, souvenirs, food, and potables have found the alligator a fitting device to advertise their goods and services. The earliest such insignia found to date is the 'gator brandishing a ribbon bearing the name of the Prairie Cottage, a resort hotel near New Orleans in the 1840s. Louis Ruhe's New Orleans Bird Store illustrated a baby 'gator in 1893 to push its line of souvenirs and curios. And those cans of Alligator Pure Louisiana Molasses were labeled with a 'gator in a cane field in 1912.

A rash of advertising 'gators appeared in the 1980s after the establishment of the modern alligator hunt and the legislation that legalized the sale of alligator meat. Tipitina's, a popular New Orleans music club, began issuing fans in 1980 to the overheated clientele. These depicted a sunbathing 'gator (taken from an earlier published illustration) and carried the slogan "hottest bar in town." Marciante Brothers manufactures alligator sausage—with appropriate labels—which it has marketed since 1986. The Alligator Hurricane, a potent potable at Drusilla's Seafood Restaurant (later renamed the Crystal Seafood Cajun Cafe) in the old Jax Brewery, is advertised by a second-lining alligator, complete with umbrella.

The upscale, uptown Upperline Restaurant in New Orleans has a menu printed on a fan, much like Tipitina's, with a mod 'gator's portrait on the back (management reports that the waiters color them with Marksalots between

"UNCLE ALLIGATOR'S" KIDDIE MEALS. ADVERTISEMENT FOR RAX RESTAURANTS IN *GAMBIT*, NEW ORLEANS, FEBRUARY 20, 1990 (MARDI GRAS SEASON).

ALLIGATOR BUSINESS LOGOS.

INCLUDING OVERLEAF: ALLIGATOR LOGOS FROM BUSINESSES IN NEW ORLEANS AND HARVEY, LOUISIANA.

course servings). For Carnival of 1990, Rax fast-food restaurants publicized its "Uncle Alligator Kid's Meal" with an illustration of said uncle reclining in regal splendor atop a Mardi Gras parade king's float, visually punning *Rax* and *Rex*.

A cursory examination of sixty-four Louisiana telephone directories in 1989 turned up twenty-three business entries under *'gator* or *alligator*. This is certainly an incomplete compilation, since if a business was called Harry's Alligator Bar, it was excluded because no search was made under *H*. What this informal survey does indicate is that 'gators sell in the late twentieth century and that they share their names and likenesses with many who would like to profit from them.

Many of the businesses using a 'gator name have a logical geographic or water-related reason for doing so. These include the Gator Pool Service (Jefferson Parish, which also has an alligator nuisance officer to remove

'gators from pools when necessary); Gator Boats, Inc. (Minden); and, playing on the old New York legend, the Alligator Drain and Sewer Cleaning Service (New Orleans). A number are related to Louisiana's petrochemical industry, a great deal of which is located in the coastal zone. Representatives in this category are Gator Hawk, Inc. (offices in both Jefferson Parish and Monroe); Gator Energy Corporation and Gator Supply Co. (both in Harvey); and Gator Service (Galliano).

Other businesses use the alligator to express regional identity, such as Gatorgraphics Screen Printing and Gatorland Distributors (both Jefferson Parish); Gator Moving and Storage and Gator's Used Cars (both on Bayou Tèche); Gator Plastics Co. (Baton Rouge); Gatorland Bike Shop (Donaldsonville, where the Mississippi meets Bayou Lafourche); various Gator Stops (Napoleonville, Houma, and other places); Gator Ready Mix (supplying concrete to Lockport and Leeville); and Gator Park, Inc. (Livingston).

A certain number of local watering holes bear names such as Gator Corner (Napoleonville) and the Alligator Bar (Dutchtown). A neighborhood newspaper even appeared in New Orleans called *The Uptown Alligator*. Most of these businesses feature an alligator on their signage or corporate logos, and many often illustrate their advertisements with them.

Like Louisiana, Florida has many 'gator-named businesses, often in the same categories. The Miami directory divulges no less than sixteen in the community, including three watery references: Alligator Pool Service, Inc., Gator Pools of Miami, and (shades of the farm-raised "supergators") Gator Hot Tubs, Inc.

Miami businessmen also have found the 'gator name useful in establishing the regional identities of their enterprises. In that city are found Alligator Graphics, Inc., Gator Doors & Millwork, Inc., Gator Glass Laminating, Gator Office Supply and Furniture, and Gator Plastics, Inc. For some unknown reason, alligators have become associated with automotive and transportation concerns in particular. These include Miami's Gator Express, Inc., Gator Freightways, Inc., Gator Leasing, Inc. (as well as the Gator Leasing Used Truck Center), and Gator Towing. Most prestigious-sounding among these concerns are Gator Industries, Inc., and Gator Investments.

The Gator Club of Miami, one suspects, supports the 'Gators of the University of Florida. By name alone, only the Gator Shoe Corporation seems to have a relationship to the fashion industry dealing in alligator-skin products. Neither organization, however, answered telephone calls made to inquire.

Jacksonville beats out Miami, with thirty *gator* listings, the most apt of which is perhaps Gator Carwash Equipment, Inc., remembering that an awful lot of four-legged "nuisance" 'gators have, in fact, required eviction from damp domains they have established in the car washes of the Gulf Coast. Gainesville, home of the 'Gators of the University of Florida, is the undisputed leader according to this very informal inquiry. It has sixty-four *gator* entries in its directory. Like Miami, many of them are associated with the automobile business. Others are water-related, and include Gator Culverts, Gator Plumbing and Improvements, and Gator Pools. Particularly intriguing are the Gator Telephone Company and Gatoropoly.

Directory surveys of the remaining southern states would doubtless prove just as enlightening. Even New York has a few such listings. A cursory glance at the 1990–1991 Manhattan directory revealed two businesses in the garment district (the Alligator Clothing Store and 'Gator Girl of Miami, Inc.), both on West Thirty-fourth Street. In addition, 'Gatorbelts, Inc., was located on Pitkin Avenue in Brooklyn. Obviously, in the Big Apple, it is specifically the high fashion value of the alligator that has given rise to such names.

There is no apparent end to the ever-increasing use of the alligator in business names, products, trademarks, and logos, particularly in the southern states. The alligator has become so entrenched as a regional symbol—popular at home and exuding exotic appeal on the national and tourist markets—that its place in the world of commercial exploitation seems assured.

 ALLIGATOR, INC. 191

THE SHAPE OF **GUCCI**

GIMME SOME SKIN*

MODERN ALLIGATOR TANNING

The appeal of alligator, as determined by Frank and Ada Graham, lay in that "Fine leather has always been a status symbol . . . alligator skins proved to yield a superior leather. When these skins are properly tanned, they are strong and long-lasting, yet the scales and other markings on the skins form attractive patterns. It is pleasant just to run one's fingers over this elegant leather."

By 1902, the demand for alligator was so great and prices so high in the wake of the late-Victorian vogue for the saurian that it became profitable to fake it. According to the report of

the United States Commissioner of Fish and Fisheries in that year, "Imitation alligator leather is now prepared in large quantities, principally from sheepskin or the buffings from cowhides. These are tanned according to the usual process, and before the skins are finished they are embossed with the characteristic alligator markings by passing them between two rollers." This is the classic method, still in use after nearly a century. Later "fakers" would invent other alligator substitutes as well, made from resin-impregnated fabrics, plastics, and other materials.

Production of the real thing was also impressive. The American South was said to have produced 126 tons of alligator hide in 1908. This was at a time when Florida dominated U.S. production; chief trading centers were at Cocoa, Melbourne, Fort Pierce, Miami, and Kissimmee.

FACING PAGE: HANDBAG FROM THE GUCCI FALL 1990 COLLECTION.

*TITLE PHRASE *GIMME SOME SKIN* COURTESY OF REBECCA VENABLE.

Skins were classed as Floridian, Louisianian, or Mexican. Long-bodied Florida skins were especially suited for handbags but were often marred by "buttons" or "corn marks," calcium deposits, and "imbedded hornlike tissue," which made tanning difficult, produced scarred leather, and reduced the Florida hides to the least valuable on the market. Louisiana skins were the most pliable, and the scale patterns were "more artistically curved and shaped," so they were considered excellent for card cases, pocketbooks, and the like; marked with fewer "buttons" than Florida hides, they commanded the market's highest prices. This superiority has been noted ever since.

The caiman hides from Mexico had a natural set of "four small dots or markings like pinholes" on each scale, and were generally dressed out by splitting the abdomen down the center to retain the full dorsal surface intact, producing what was called "horn" or "hornback" alligator. American hides were split down the back to preserve the smoother ventral, or belly, surface for use.

As alligators became less plentiful, many early conservationists voiced alarm that the demand for alligator leather was a major factor leading to the alligator's ultimate extinction. Manufacturers, habituated to larger hides (five feet and longer), were reduced to finding ways to utilize very small ones (in the two-foot range) by the mid-1920s. This continued until well into the 1940s, when Thomas Barbour found they were being used for "cigarette cases, and similar novelties."

Most tanning operations seem to have been located in Europe or in the northern states. France and prerevolutionary Russia had been major consumers. Alligator farms, of course, were natural sales outlets for American goods. The U.S. Department of Agriculture observed the following in 1929: "In the past none of those engaged in alligator farming manufactured the goods on display in their showrooms, but acted merely in the capacity of retailer for some leather-goods firm. Recent developments have led one or two of these alligator farms to attempt the manufacture of some of their own goods."

Increasing tanning and manufacturing took place throughout the South. By the 1940s, it was regarded as big business. Among the most vocal entrepreneurs was Maximilian Rinow, who worked in conjunction with the Zimmerman Tannery in New Orleans, where it was said alligators had been tanned since the end of the Civil War, "laying the initial foundation for the alligator leather business in Louisiana." Zimmerman came from a family of tanners, each generation adding to that of its forebears. One acquaintance insisted, however, that Zimmerman had no quality control on color—what you got was what you got in a batch of Zimmerman-tanned hides. Fabrication took place in the upper story of the tannery.

Martel McNealy lauded Rinow's efforts: "He has brought to the industry some of the country's ablest designers and he is now promoting the training of wounded servicemen whose injuries prevent them from returning to their former occupations, into the designing and making of beautiful things from the finest grained and most beautiful leathers to be found anywhere in the world. Being widely experienced in worldwide merchandise distribution, Mr.

Rinow has developed the already healthy demand for Louisiana alligator leather and is bringing to the area the work of making the finished products."

In 1946, Maud Ronstrom touted Rinow's product: "Today some experts consider the hide of the Louisiana alligator to be the most luxurious leather in the world." At that time, she found that Zimmerman was tanning 1,200 to 1,500 hides each month for the products that Rinow marketed. She described the process: "After an alligator is skinned, its hide is measured, put into a lime pit to remove scales, then pickled, tanned, dyed, glazed, finished, and finally made into a luxury product. Each of these procedures is an exacting process which has been perfected through the years. . . . Once a hide has been pickled it will keep indefinitely, awaiting the subsequent processes whenever convenient." Tanners have traditionally been jealous of their methods; fearing industrial espionage, they have seldom revealed more than this list of steps in the tanning procedure.

The factory above the tannery, by then managed by George Hirdes (a former employee of the Crescent Belt Company who had just returned from military duty), was taking those 1,200 to 1,500 hides each month and turning out "high-quality alligator belts, wallets, keypieces, watchbands, compacts and cigarette cases, all expertly handcrafted." Ms. Ronstrom enumerated the steps in manufacturing: "Mr. Hirdes designs the different products, makes the dies, and is foreman in charge of production."

Hirdes soon left to open an independent plant, located at his home in the later 1940s, moving to Chartres Street in

FIG. 15. ALLIGATOR SKINS; UNDER-SURFACE AND HORN-BACK.
(From Report of Commissioner of Fish and Fisheries, 1902.)

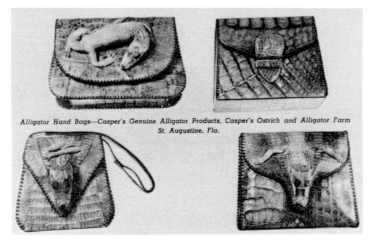

Alligator Hand Bags—Casper's Genuine Alligator Products, Casper's Ostrich and Alligator Farm St. Augustine, Fla.

"ALLIGATOR
PRODUCTS AT
CASPER'S OSTRICH
AND ALLIGATOR
FARM, FLORIDA."
POSTCARD ILLUS-
TRATION BY THE
CURT TEICH CO.,
CHICAGO, CA.
1951.

the French Quarter in the early 1950s. With a staff of six to eight employees, he produced belts and wallets to satisfy orders from retailers, and accepted commissions for special one-of-a-kind pieces. Among his regular clients were Brooks Brothers, Bullock and Jones, and Neiman-Marcus, according to his widow. His primary production was in alligator, but Hirdes also worked in cordovan leather, cowhide, ostrich, and occasionally snake. His creations can be identified by the Hirdes stamp, which also may be accompanied by that of the retailer.

Rinow himself claimed international distribution and top U.S. retailers: "Our beautiful products so far have carried the fame of the Louisiana alligator to Paris and London. New Orleans–made alligator goods are sold in fine shops on New York's Fifth Avenue and in leading stores all over America. One notable retail outlet is Brooks Brothers of New York, 127 years in business. . . ."

Rinow felt that business was promising enough for him to plan complete modernization of the factory over

Zimmerman's and to predict expanding production into overnight bags and other men's and women's leather furnishings in both calfskin and alligator. The need for workers was so great that McNealy reported in 1947 that "the Delgado Trades School of New Orleans is instructing and training many wounded veterans in the creation of this kind of industry, which will provide employment for many as new craftsmen in the field."

In the fall of 1947, Rinow had some competition. The New Orleans *Times-Picayune* reported that one Charles Vagabond had "recently opened the small glove factory on the second floor of his photography studio and import shop at 322 Royal. He launched the business after studying manufacture of gloves at Gloversville, N.Y., and after research in tanning alligator hides. Mr. Vagabond received the aid of the Association of Commerce after he explained that a tanning plant at Tarpon Springs, Florida, had perfected a process for rendering flexible the stiff hides. . . ." Mrs. Hirdes recalled that her husband had purchased many tanned hides from a firm operated by two brothers from the Greek community of Tarpon Springs and made "plenty trips" to secure them.

Vagabond thought big, and "said his new product is aimed mainly at the 'carriage trade' and that he plans to have only one retail distributor in each of the 50 largest cities in the country. He expects at the outset to turn out about 30 dozen pairs of gloves a week." To assure the quality of his product, he was dependent on local hides: "He pointed out that only the Louisiana alligator [pliant and largely free of "buttons"] could produce the type of hide needed for making gloves since it is extremely 'smooth-bellied.' "

By the 1950s, Rinow, too, had turned to out-of-state tanners. Richard Yancey wrote in 1959 that "One of the most interesting features of Rinow's business is the fact that he ships the raw hides to Paris where they are processed, tanned and returned from France to his factory . . . . There they are made into the finest quality leather goods and bear the labels of such establishments as Brooks Brothers, Sulka, Abercrombie and Fitch, Marshall Fields, Sakowitz, I. Magnin, and others."

Hunting had taken its toll. In the spring of 1960, a journalist reported, "The great demand and resulting high prices for these elite articles, and the declaration of these wonderful creatures to be outlawed quadrupeds, are the basic causes of their near extermination." Louisiana closed down in-state alligator hunting in 1963, although poaching continued unabated. The Rinows and the Vagabonds, with no legal supplies of sufficiently high quality hides, had to suspend their operations. Actually, Rinow had suffered financial reverses and his entire stock was purchased by Al Wehmeier. By 1967, Archie Carr was hoping that "If the vogue for alligator bags, belts and shoes should pass, the profit would go out of poaching, and it would stop."

The dictates of fashion, however, didn't change. Although wearing alligator was frowned upon in the United States as chic armchair urban conservationists took up the causes of endangered species, the craze for crocodilians flourished in other countries. France and Italy, longtime producers of fine quality crocodilian leathers (including

alligator), already had demonstrated the superiority of their technical knowledge in alligator tanning over that of the United States, and they weren't sharing any trade secrets.

About 1965, Mr. Zimmerman renovated the old upstairs plant for George Hirdes, who transferred his operation from the French Quarter to the tannery premises. Hirdes remained there until his death in 1971. His manufactory was continued by his wife and brother-in-law for a short period before its final closing. Rinow reentered the alligator business, operating from new facilities through the 1970s. Although he attempted to buy out the Hirdes enterprise when George Hirdes died, the family resisted. The largest New Orleans manufacturer of all was, and remains, the Crescent Belt Company, located in Chalmette. Several generations of the Montegut family have operated it, and by sheer quantity it has dominated the alligator belt business in New Orleans. Opened well before World War II, it has continued to produce belts ever since. Formerly located in conjuction with Zimmerman, it moved to the French Quarter, and later to its current address.

During the years of the "alligator wars" of the 1960s and 1970s, virtually all legal U.S. processing ceased, although Carr estimated as early as 1967 that illegal hides on the Miami market (black or otherwise) garnered hundreds of thousands of dollars each year. During that period, Peter Brazaitis of New York's Central Park Zoo explained, "Any of the animals that had a beautiful classic [crocodilian] skin, which made the best leather, were right on the brink of extinction. You see, the industry would use a species until it exhausted it, and then switch to another

species, and just go on down the line." During that time, and even later, the terminology appearing on crocodilian leathers was misleading. *Alligator* was used in the United States for virtually any crocodilian species (with the general exception of true Nile crocodile). *Domestic Alligator* simply meant that it was tanned in this country, and not that it was from a true alligator at all. Stamps and labels of the period are not to be trusted, unless the jargon of the trade is known by the reader.

Louisiana's alligators were well managed, through the expertise of the state's Wildlife and Fisheries Commission, and recovered nicely. In 1972, an experimental season was reinstated to harvest the surplus of the state's natural abundance. The alligator, however, was still an endangered species in other states, and while legal domestic hides could be transported within the United States, federal and international law forbade exporting or importing hides of endangered species, no matter what the demands of a voracious international market.

The Louisiana alligator season of 1978 was canceled because of the small call for domestic hides, while negotiators worked to allow the legal Louisiana skins back into world commerce. As Congressman John Breaux explained, "There's no market because the best tanning people are in France." As far as Breaux knew, the only plant in the United States then processing alligator hides was in South Carolina. The largest U.S. manufacturer was alleged to be a fabricator of expensive cowboy boots in Texas. Americans needed only so many costly masculine high heels.

Louisiana was successful in its bid to have alligator reintroduced to the world market in 1979. This meant that legal hunters again had a viable economic situation within which to work. The advantages were explained by the Baton Rouge *State-Times*: "Hides are sold to European buyers for tanning. . . . Some tanning has been attempted in the U.S. but the efforts have fallen short of achieving the high gloss known as a Bombay finish. . . . [Ted] Joanen doubts the U.S. could establish a gator tanning industry. 'Tanning is a very guarded secret,' he said. 'It will probably never be let out.'"

Even today, tanners will not tell you exactly how the "bombay" or "bombé" finish is achieved, although a promotional brochure of the late 1980s explained it thusly: "This relief effect is accomplished by applying heat to the flat, polished skins and slightly raising the center of each scale." The result is a deep reflective surface, and rich coloristic effect. One tanner intimated that a certain common piece of hair-care equipment could be used in the process. Al Wehmeier's experience reveals that farmed Florida hides are stiffer than those from Louisiana and tend to "wrinkle" after the bombé treatment, while the softer Louisiana skins do not deform in that manner.

Letting legal Louisiana hides loose in the global marketplace resulted in a bonanza for the local hide hunters. At that time, the Baton Rouge *State-Times* reported, "The U.S. doesn't buy many finished alligator-skin products." Joanen clarified this: "We still have this endangered-species stigma that this is a poached skin." In fact, selling any alligator products in certain large markets such as New York had been prohibited by local law. This type of legislation during the "alligator wars" was supported by well-meaning but misguided conservation-oriented organizations such as the National Audubon Society.

Among those taking advantage of the new situation was the Plott family of Griffin, Georgia. There a family hide and fur business had been in existence since 1923, dealing in skins of many species, including alligators, but not involved in tanning. In 1980, the enterprise was reorganized as American Tanning and Leather and began processing alligator hides. Mr. Zimmerman, from the old New Orleans tannery, had gone there and helped to establish the new operation.

Zimmerman's last days in New Orleans had not been happy ones. He purchased a shipment of alligator skins from a Georgia dealer, allegedly *before* interstate shipment became illegal, but unfortunately they arrived in New Orleans *after* punitive measures had gone into effect. The feds nabbed him, and at the hearing, despite remarkable character witnesses in his defense, he was found guilty and was given a year and a day's suspended sentence.

After a decade, according to the manager of American Tanning and Leather in 1990, the firm was tanning about 12,000 hides each year. These skins came from all the alligator-producing states, including Louisiana, Florida, Georgia, Texas, and South Carolina. By his estimate, about half the hides were from wild alligators and half from farmed animals. The finished leather was sold to fabricators in the United States, Asia, and Europe.

European tanneries, however, were also delighted to have legal skins, and prices rose dramatically—from twenty dollars per foot to fifty dollars per foot for raw, salted hides—in the decade between 1980 and 1990. Alligator farming quickly became a burgeoning industry; the large number of farmed hides entering the market in the late 1980s fast approached 50 percent of the annual Louisiana total. This supplement from the farms allowed the market to expand without placing any increasing hunting pressure on wild alligator populations. Careful tagging, tracking, and policing of the hides also kept poaching down by making it extremely difficult, if not impossible, for illegal hides to be bought, sold, or transported within the state.

A system of hide auctions was introduced in Vermilion Parish in 1984, and expanded to other parts of the state by 1986. Lisa Martin investigated the phenomenon in 1986. She felt it steadied the market and worked to the hunter's advantage: "Hunters at the auction [in St. Bernard Parish] said that some buyers try to panic them into selling their skins cheaply. 'They'll say they can pay us $22 today, but maybe only $19 or $20 tomorrow,' one said. . . . The competition among buyers that an auction encourages generally raises the price a skin commands. . . . " These sales were staged under the jurisdiction of "the Louisiana Cooperative Extension Service and State Department of Wildlife and Fisheries to help hunters get a better price for their catch."

At such an auction, rolled, salted, tagged hides are brought in by the hunters and put on public view under the watchful eyes of Extension Service and Wildlife and Fisheries personnel. Hides are unrolled, shaken free of salt, and placed on examining tables. Along with his staff, each bidder inspects the hides, notes tag numbers, verifies lengths, and grades them for quality (using such factors as clean-liness, whether they have been artificially stretched or not, whether there are any nicks, cuts, or other flaws, and so on).

Then, as Martin says, "After the viewing, buyers submitted sealed bids for each lot of hides. The winning bidders arranged directly with the hunters to pay for their purchases. The buyers work for dealers who will send the hides to tanneries, mostly in other countries. . . ." Arrangements are also made to resalt and reroll the hides, then pack them for transport to the buyer's facility for storage until shipment. Hunters' profits increased again in the later 1980s as they began to sell their catch whole to dealers who processed the meat, as well.

The "other countries" soon came to include more of those in the Orient. Zachary Casey, of Pelts and Skins in Belle Chasse, Louisiana, negotiated the first sale of hides to Korea in 1986. The initial shipment of five hundred was purchased by H. L. Kim, of Sauvage Korea, Ltd., in Seoul. Lower Asian labor costs, according to the New Orleans *Times-Picayune*, meant that "Korean-made alligator products should be available for about half the price of similar products made in France, Italy and Japan, where Louisiana alligator has been traditionally processed. . . . Next year [1987], Casey plans to export about 2,000 alligator hides to Korea. Eventually he hopes half of Louisiana's hides go there for processing." Critics said the Korean-tanned hides came back "flat," that is, tanned but without a glaze. Casey maintained they were "stylish," but New Orleans alligator retailer Al Wehmeier didn't find the "classic, timeless" qualities he sought, and, feeling that "alligator outlasts 'style,' " refused to buy.

As a result of international enthusiasm, the Baton Rouge *Morning Advocate* could advise its readers in 1986, "Louisiana's gator hides are known worldwide as the best crocodilian hide because the coastal marsh is well suited to producing a good, lustrous hide. The majority of the harvest is shipped to tanneries in France and Spain, but [Robert] Love said he expects a tannery or two to open in South Louisiana."

The New Orleans area was rife with rumor in following months that an Italian firm did intend to

establish an alligator tannery in the region. By the late 1980s, however, such talk was no longer current. Perhaps, it was thought, the economic advantages of placing a tannery at the source were not as great as investors had hoped. Perhaps, it was speculated, the Europeans feared losing control of their closely guarded alligator-tanning technology if it was exported to the New World. The former seems more likely than the latter. Chris Dumestre remembered that the state's Commissioner of Agriculture, Bob Odom, laid a number of enticements before the Italians but failed to win the tannery because the Europeans were playing a numbers game—not in dollars but in skins. The delegation of Italian businessmen felt that they would be better off placing such a facility in Africa or South America because they processed a much larger number of crocodile and caiman hides each year than Louisiana was yielding in alligator skins from the American South.

During this time, one unscrupulous wholesaler was selling an Italian roller-imprinted product as "real" alligator at National Luggage and Leather Goods trade shows. Al Wehmeier examined it and found it labeled something like "bidenti cocodrillio," meaning "printed crocodilian." The dealer insisted that it was "reprocessed" from real hides, although close observation revealed it to be resin-finished and therefore subject to eventual cracking as the resin hardened into inflexible rigidity. Any economic advantage in destroying "real" alligator in order to manufacture a "fake" was never properly explained.

Things improved somewhat on the domestic scene when New Yorkers challenged their infamous Mason-Smith Act and it again became legal to sell alligator in Manhattan. By the late 1980s, however, alligator and its allies were not cheap. The *Times-Picayune* gave examples: "A Gucci handbag made from crocodile starts at $2,500, according to Gucci's store in Manhattan. Crocodile handbags start at $500 at Saks Fifth Avenue's New Orleans store." Prices continued to climb as alligators acquired more and more designer labels. By 1988 and 1989, fashionable American magazines routinely carried advertisements listing designer bags at up to four thousand dollars. Exceptional designers, such as Judith Leiber, could command as much as ten thousand dollars for a single creation. *Vogue* announced "An accessory that's a once-in-a-lifetime purchase: the genuine alligator bag," and proclaimed that "the sweet little alligator

DESIGNER AND CUTTER EXAMINING HIDE AT SAUVAGE KOREA, LTD., SEOUL, KOREA, 1990.

handbag expands into a once-in-a-lifetime 'investment' tote."

These new designer delights were described by *The New York Times* in late 1989: "Another difference in today's alligator bags is that they come in a variety of shapes and styles—envelope, hand-held, over-the-shoulder—they are generally larger than their forerunners. The metal frames of yore have also been discarded in favor of a flap, which can be either buckled closed or fastened with a strap. The shoulder models have chains or beltlike alligator-hide straps."

More and more alligators appeared to accessorize outfits in fashion photography of new styles from European and American haute couture houses. Articles were written about individual alligator designers. The appeal of the exotic was apparently strong and mysteriously met some human psychological need. Diane Ackerman analyzed the growing fad: "By wearing their skins on our feet or over a shoulder like talismans, we have, I suppose, domesticated them in a strange way. Some people carry alligator briefcases and luggage, in which they tame part of their lives."

As the decade ended, alligator was once again firmly ensconced as a fashionable status symbol. And Louisiana reentered the tanning business for the first time in nearly thirty years. From New Orleans, *Gambit* reported, "An alligator production plant is beginning construction in Baton Rouge and should be opening its doors toward the end of this year [1989], according to Greg Linscombe,

program director for the Louisiana Fur and Alligator [Advisory] Council. The plant will process skins year-round from alligator farms and dress them for manufacturers around the nation. The only other competing plant in the U.S. is in Georgia."

Louisiana's first processing plant in a quarter of a century was called the Cocodrie Tannery, aptly named with the special Louisiana Cajun word for *alligator*. The technology that the Europeans feared loosing had become available. The fabled "bombay" finish was being produced in Baton Rouge and some of the home-tanned hides began to bear the signature of Ralph Lauren.

At the same time, the Memphis Tannery was in its organizational stages. Created as a closely held corporation in 1989, it began a combined tanning and fabrication operation in 1990. Most of the hides for its initial season came from Louisiana, with a few from Florida—and most of them were from the rapidly increasing number of commercial alligator farms. The Memphis Tannery had not reached full production by September 1990, so statistics on volume were not yet available at that time. Inquiries had been received from both domestic and foreign fabricators, but few tanned hides could be made available, because the tannery's own fabrication program required the bulk of its leather. Manufacturing primarily purses, belts, and several other small items for retail, it was supplying various U.S. outlets, with Saks Fifth Avenue as the largest taker. The alligator business was looking up for the 1990s.

PENNIES FROM HEAVEN

ALLIGATOR ECONOMICS

The alligator has been an important factor in the personal economies of hunters since the eighteenth century. Its economic significance spread as commercial dealing, handling, processing, and tourist-industry development increased throughout the nineteenth and twentieth centuries. That this was fated to be was first queried by Job, speaking of the biblical Leviathan: "Shall they part him among the merchants?" Part him they did as over a period of two centuries markets developed for alligator oil, alligator teeth, alligator hide, baby alligators, alligator souvenirs, and more.

That the alligator had acquired commercial interest was indicated by H. M. Brackenridge in 1814, who said that Southerners "value their skins." John J. Audubon agreed: "It had become quite an article of trade, and many of the squatters and strolling Indians [on the Red River], followed, for a time, no other business." This was sporadic, however, as the vogue for alligator waxed and waned.

Betsy Swanson found that "In 1858 . . . a man had killed 400 alligators in Jefferson Parish. The skins brought 75 cents each." Wenzel Zimmerman is said to have established America's first tannery to process alligator about 1865. An Austrian tanner-by-trade, trained in Bohemia, he came to the United States in 1856. During the Civil War, he worked for the Ulmeier Tannery in New Orleans, and he opened his own business when the conflict ended. Oral tradition says that he tanned the hides later sold to Mrs. Vanderbilt by Shattuck and Binger, New York dealers in skins.

ASIAN ALLIGATOR.
PRODUCTS OF
SAUVAGE KOREA,
LTD., SEOUL,
KOREA, 1990.

FACING PAGE:
ALLIGATOR
SHOOTING IN THE
SWAMPS. WOOD
ENGRAVING IN
HARPER'S NEW
MONTHLY MAGA-
ZINE, 1855.

With the exception of such isolated incidents, little is available to document actual volume of sales or prices for the antebellum uses of the alligator. It provided marketable elements such as oil (medicinal uses, as an ingredient in indigo processing, as a lubricant, and as an ingredient in soap making), teeth (powder chargers, babies' teethers, and talismans), meat (to a small market), musk glands (mentioned as used in perfumery), and hide (in early nineteenth-century tanning efforts and subsequent antebellum fashion crazes).

View of State Street, Abbeville, La.

Alligator hide became an article of international commerce as European tanneries (first those of France and Russia and later those of Italy and Spain) began an increasing manufacture of saddles, luggage, gun cases, wallets, and other top-of-the-line furnishings. These contributed to the alligator's "snob appeal" as status-symbol leather, as did the early Vanderbilt alligator-upholstered chairs in New York. One hide dealer is said to have shipped as many as seven thousand skins in 1871. In addition, alligator teeth "had a small market value" in the 1880s, apparently as curios and souvenirs. At that time, "Green hides were worth 75 cents to one dollar according to size."

The trade in hides was such that fur dealers began to handle alligator skins in quantity in the coastal and port cities of the South in the late Victorian era. Louisiana centers of this commerce developed in Lake Charles, Abbeville, New Iberia, Morgan City, Houma, and New Orleans. By 1875, Edward King wrote of "an alligator hunter in Jacksonville," and the development of alligator hunting as an occupation was complete by 1885 when the *Historical Sketch Book* reasoned that "There are not as many alligators . . . as there were before the skins of the mighty saurians became [a] commercial commodity, and hunters went to work to kill them as a profession. . . ." E. A. McIlhenny confirmed that the peak harvests in the Avery Island area were realized in the late 1800s.

Florida became a major alligator producer, eventually surpassing Louisiana. Reports indicated large catches; twelve men at Fort Pierce were said to have taken four thousand skins in 1889 alone. Thirty dealers handled hides and souvenirs in Jacksonville in 1890, and another forty individuals were involved in stuffing alligators and polishing their teeth in the manufacture of souvenirs. Dr. Hugh Smith estimated that in the fifteen years spanning 1880 to 1894, 2.5 million alligators were killed to satisfy the late-Victorian hide and curio trade, "an important factor in the thinning of its numbers," according to Raymond Ditmars.

T. E. Dabney has written that according to *Harper's Magazine* in 1892, there were "about 500 men who in the summer months made their living by killing and skinning alligators in South Louisiana." The alligator business was, and is, seasonal, as that account indicates. In considering alligator economics, it is well to remember that most persons engaged in the various aspects of the alligator trade, with the exception of farmers, followed other economic interests for six to eight months of the year. The alligator season was further shortened when later twentieth century hunting regulations were developed.

LOUISIANA TAXPAYER WITH ITS CAPTORS. PHOTOGRAPH FROM THE *LOUISIANA CONSERVATION REVIEW*, DECEMBER 31, 1931.

A better idea of the value of the hide crop is known after 1890. Albert Reese reported that "According to the United States Bureau of Fisheries the hunter in 1891 averaged about 60 cents for the skin, while in 1902 the price averaged about 90 cents, varying between 15 cents and [$]2.00, depending on size and condition. . . ." According to Reese, "In 1890, three firms at Kissimmee [Florida] handled 33,600 hides," although the annual total is said to have diminished thereafter. Reese also reported that, "Ten men at [Cocoa, Florida] took, in 1899–1900, 2,500 skins; one man took 800 skins in one year; another man collected 42 skins in one night."

Louisiana and Florida supplied a combined 42 percent of the 280,000 hides processed yearly in the United States in 1902, with the remainder coming from Mexico and other places. That two-state total of 117,600 hides (said to have been worth $176,400, tanned) did not include the large number of hides supplied to European tanners. The *Brooklyn Eagle* told New Yorkers in 1902, "Dade County, on the east coast of Florida, sends to market about 50,000 skins annually, while the number from the counties on the west coast reaches fully 125,000 each year. There is one firm in New Orleans that handles over 500,000 skins annually." It seems likely that Brooklyn's faith in Louisiana's turn-of-the-century productivity may have been overestimated. However, if these figures were accurate—which would be extremely difficult to verify—simple subtraction suggests the immense quantity that must have been shipped to foreign tanneries at that time.

Reese indicated that "In 1908, there were marketed

from the South Atlantic and Gulf States 372,000 pounds of alligator hides, valued at $61,000." Methods of selling and pricing hides varied in the early twentieth century, making figures difficult to compare. A report prepared by the U.S. Bureau of Fisheries explained that "Although the raw skins are sold according to length, the tanned hides are sold by the width of the leather at the widest part." To contribute to the confusion, the 1908 figures were given not in numbers but in pounds, and little information is available concerning the validity or accuracy of such statistics. Regardless, it is apparent that well before 1910, the alligator was exerting a very strong economic influence.

Stanley C. Arthur collected figures for 1917 for a single New Orleans hide dealer. The dealer bought a total of 2,436 hides. The majority (1,425 skins) were three and four feet long, indicating that the larger hides (only 157 were seven feet) were becoming scarcer. Arthur also noted prices, confirming that Louisiana hides were the most valuable. In 1926, a six-foot Louisiana skin was valued at $3.00, while a comparable hide from Alabama was worth $2.50, one from Georgia, $2.00, and a six-footer from Florida, only $1.85.

The maximum size for hide-buying purposes in 1928 was seven feet. The hunter was paid no premium for extreme length, presumably because such large hides were good only for luggage, the scale pattern being too big for use in small articles. As Arthur said, "A hunter does not get any more for a 10, 12 or 14 foot hide than he does for a seven-footer."

The alligator farm, supplying alligators for zoos, scientific specimens, and the like was still largely a tourist attraction. In 1922, Karl Schmidt assessed the situation: "It would not be practical to raise alligators for their skins alone, on account of their relatively slow rate of growth, but when the sale of baby alligators to tourists, the sale of larger specimens to zoological parks, and possibly an additional fee for visitors to the establishment are combined, the raising of alligators becomes a practical business." On these grounds a limited number of farms flourished, particularly in Florida. It was not until the 1960s that scientific advances in alligator farming began to make this enterprise extremely lucrative to the hide rancher.

Purchasing from alligator hunters and farms were the biological supply houses that in turn distributed live or preserved specimens to a market composed primarily of schools and universities. In 1926, the Southern Biological Supply Co., Inc., was providing live alligators in five sizes (from number one, "babies, less than 12 inches" at $1.25 each up to number five, "33 inches average," which cost $4.50 apiece). This was a small but important segment of the alligator market, and one that, because of the nature of science classes, was predictably steady from year to year.

The public sector found its first economic advantage in alligators through taxation. Severance taxes were in place by the mid-1920s, possibly established as early as 1915. Dealers were required to pay a few cents on hides entering into legal commerce. The amount depended on hide length. Exactly 21,885 such hides were handled in 1925 in Louisiana, and 36,041 were taxed there in 1926. That year, state law regarding wild animals hunted or trapped for skins was recodified. The alligator levy was set at one cent for

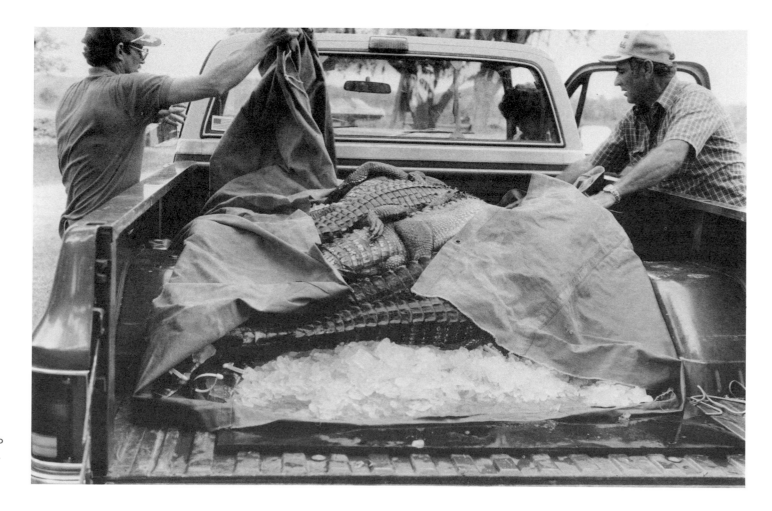

ICED 'GATORS
LOADED IN
PROCESSOR'S
TRUCK FOR
TRANSPORT TO
BUTCHERING AND
SKINNING FACIL-
ITY.

each hide not over five feet, two cents for each between five and ten feet, and three cents on all hides over that length. In comparison (and contrast) to these numbers, we have Remington Kellog's report that "information received from a Georgia hide and fur company indicates that the average catch in that State for the 5-year period, 1922–1926, has been in the neighborhood of 10,000 skins."

Prices for hides continued to fluctuate, but in general they rose slowly—with notable amounts being paid in 1926 and 1927, following a severe dry period—but declined the next year. A five-foot skin brought the hunter $2.00 in 1926, $2.25 in 1927, but fell to $1.25 in 1928. Part of that price depended upon the degree of care exercised in dressing the hide. The U.S. Department of Agriculture admonished in 1929, "Any injury or defect that detracts from the appearance of the finished article, or adds an additional burden to the work of the tanner [cuts, nicks, and so on], will lower the market price for raw alligator hide."

The Louisiana wild alligator crop of 1929-1930 was reported as 20,646 but dropped in 1930-1931 to only 1,828. The remarkable discrepancy was credited to the Great Depression. The Department of Conservation (forerunner of the current Louisiana Department of Wildlife and Fisheries) observed, "Due to conditions of depression and the low price of furs, there were not as many fur buyers in the 1930-31 season as usual." The fur buyers, who were suffering, were also the hide buyers. Percy Viosca explained, "Since the alligator is captured almost solely for its hide, it is treated by some authors along with fur-bearing animals." It was also legislated by the state in the same category.

Regardless of its "legal" designation, the number of alligator hunters appeared to have increased during the Depression as more and more Americans were forced to live off the land. The technological advance of the marsh buggy rendered remoter 'gator habitat increasingly accessible to the hunter. As a result, the market declined along with the alligator population, reaching a low ebb in the later years of the Depression. In 1937, *The Progress* inferred, "The 'gators have since become so few that there is no profit in hunting them for their meat or their skins and most of the hunts now staged in the marsh are for sport. . . ."

On the eve of World War II, the situation had not improved. "During the 1940-41 season, for example," pointed out the *Roosevelt Review*, "when alligator skins brought low prices, total production in Louisiana was only 2,928 gators." As the war ended, however, the demand went up. The United States boomed with postwar prosperity and European trade was reopened. Thomas Barbour could say in 1944, "I am informed . . . that at the Gainesville [Florida] hide brokerage about 80,000 skins are received each year. . . . Gators from four to seven feet long furnish the highest-priced hides, but much smaller ones are also killed. . . ." Martel McNealy asserted in 1945 that alligator leather "brings many millions of dollars annually."

Tanneries and factories were established in the South to keep some of the profits at home. Alligator farms began to manufacture more of the goods they sold to visitors on their own premises. Among the chief promoters was Maximilian Rinow, and McNealy found the business particularly suited to a certain group: "The local tanning and manufacturing of alligator skins into finished products is especially fitting to the specific artistic talent of South Louisiana people." Why they were gifted in this special endeavor was not explained. Prices increased as these good postwar times rolled. The Louisiana alligator catch for 1945 was "now estimated by men of the industry to reach between 25,000 and 30,000 and to bring the trappers alone more than a half million dollars."

By then, those hunters were being paid by the foot rather than by the piece, and they became more enthusiastic. During the 1946 season, according to the *Roosevelt Review*, "alligator skins brought an average of

$1.40 per foot, largest price in recent years." Because of this boost to the profit motive, "production reached 33,409, largest take in recent years."

The alligator's payroll began to number far more than trappers. "In addition," wrote McNealy, "there is remuneration to the tanner and his employees, and last, but not least, the alligator goods manufacturing industry provides employment for craftsmen and other workers." Louisiana artisans were supplying so many national and international retailers that Maud Ronstrom could wryly muse, "If you see an alligator belt on President Truman, or observe him using an alligator wallet, cigarette case, keyholder or watchband, you can presume it came from New Orleans."

Although more alligators were being hunted and processed, the total national consumption in the United States, including imported crocodiles, was estimated at 250,000, slightly down from 1902! The local alligators were still on the tax rolls, providing dedicated funds to the Louisiana Conservation Department's game-management and biological-studies efforts. The *Roosevelt Review* gave impressive statistics in 1947: "Included in the revenues of tax collected from fur dealers is a tax on 33,409 alligator hides taken . . . last season. These alligators, if placed head to tail would cover a distance of 213,415 feet or 46 [*sic,* 40.2] miles which is more than one half the distance by the Airline Highway [from New Orleans] to Baton Rouge." At 1946 prices, they brought hunters just under $300,000. The rate of state income had slightly increased. Severance taxes now amounted to two cents on each hide up to five

feet, five cents on those between five and ten feet, and twenty-five cents on all those exceeding the ten-foot mark.

Prices continued to rise. Edgar Poe noted in 1949, "The hide brings $2.50 per running foot. . . ." Olen LeBlanc commented in 1950, "the unique alligator trapping industry maintains a steady pace and provides added dollars for those who annually seek the reptile in the marshlands . . ." By 1951, the New Orleans *Times-Picayune* reported, "The bigger ones, up to eight feet, bring as much as $2.80 a foot. . . ."

During the 1950s prices steadied ($2.75 per foot in 1954). Total income to Louisiana hunters for the first four years of the decade amounted to $395,326. This four-year total was less than a single good year's figure in the late 1940s, indicating the continuous decline in the alligator population. Prices began to fall in the later 1950s. Ed Waldo discovered in 1957 that "Alligator hides do not attract high prices on the market. . . . Pricing today is based upon a per-foot-of-alligator basis, with prices ranging from $1.25 to $2.50 per foot."

The remarkable expansion of the 1957–1958 catch (climbing to a total of 28,600 skins) was the result of alligators stranded and made vulnerable by the tides and winds of Hurricane Audrey rather than a population explosion. Richard Yancey was concerned that 23,115 of the storm victims "were under 5 ft. in length and this is much the same as if a farmer were to harvest a crop before it had reached the income producing stage."

As the decade ended, Yancey pointed out that prices were $2.25 or more per foot for medium hides, and $3 for those of six feet. The storm-augmented catch had sold for nearly $300,000. An ever more worrisome situation, however, was the small size of many of the hides. That the public was not aware of either the benefits or the problems concerned Yancey: "The value of the Louisiana alligator is one that is not widely recognized. . . . Only the hunters, dealers, and manufacturers, who profit from the skins are fully aware of the amount of money that is annually derived from the alligator hide business."

By 1963, the price had risen to about four dollars per foot of raw, salted hide, and, according to Yancey, "Because of this high value many other people in addition to the regular trappers have sought alligators on a commercial basis. Large numbers had been taken [in the late 1950s] from the marshes by [petroleum] exploration crews working from marsh buggies."

In order to get the highest prices possible, hunters had taken to "stretching" hides by pulling them to extreme lengths and nailing them down until the deformation was permanent. These "lengthened" hides brought more money because a five-foot-eleven-inch skin, for example, might be extended to get a six-foot price. Yancy explained that the practice, while profitable to the hunter, "separates the scales or plates and greatly reduces the quality of the skin." Because this was generally a detriment to the whole industry, dealers later began paying lower prices for stretched hides, which discouraged the practice.

In conservation-oriented efforts, alligators were protected by shortening seasons and hunting was forbidden in Florida starting in 1961 and in Louisiana beginning in 1963. Black-market hides, poached or stolen, could be sold for about $3.25 per foot to unscrupulous dealers, and stock was even snatched from alligator farms by thieves hoping to reap such profits. By 1965, poachers were receiving five to six dollars per foot, which proved to be irresistible to the unethical. Archie Carr estimated in 1967 that "the profits from bootleg hides marketed in Miami alone run close to a million dollars annually."

The "alligator wars" of the late 1960s through the 1970s attempted legislatively to determine the alligator's fate and to control the poachers' black market. With the expert leadership of biologists from the Louisiana Department of Wildlife and Fisheries, the crisis in Louisiana was resolved by 1972, when a limited alligator season was reinstituted. The three-parish hunt that year produced 1,300 hides, sold for just under $75,000. The state also stepped up its efforts to develop knowledge, techniques, and strategies about alligator farming that would lead to a very profitable renaissance in hide ranching.

The experimental alligator hunting season of 1973 saw a larger catch of 2,900 hides, bringing in $268,500. Things were looking up for the alligator hunter, but the 1974 season was canceled when the alligator was given nationwide federal protection, despite the overpopulation in Louisiana. Federal approval was given for a 1975 season that yielded 4,300 hides, valued at $252,000.

This decrease from $92 per skin in 1973 to $58.50 two years later also was largely due to federal legislation. "Legal" alligators could be transported within the United States to processors, but international convention governing

endangered species, upheld by the United States, prevented them from crossing international boundaries. The important international market had been lost. By this time, most reputable United States manufacturers of alligator goods, dependent on forbidden foreign tanneries to make the best leather from homegrown 'gators, had simply gone out of business, or substituted other leathers for alligator at their plants.

At home, public opinion opposed alligator goods all throughout the United States, considering the animals endangered over the whole country, although that was not the case in Louisiana. As a result, the domestic market declined while the international market evaporated. The U.S. market fluctuated for the remainder of the 1970s. In 1976, Louisiana produced 4,300 legal hides valued at $511,000. The per-foot price to the trapper reached the unheard-of figure of $16.50, which persisted through 1977. The following year, the legislative "blockade" of the world market resulted in a total cancellation of the annual alligator season. The Baton Rouge *State-Times* reported that "trappers felt a hunt would be unprofitable."

Successful negotiations allowed reentry of "legal" Pelican State hides into the world market in 1979. Representative John Breaux said, "International trade will greatly increase the value of alligator products and will allow trappers and landowners who have worked hard in the recovery program to benefit from their conservation efforts." He was correct. Over 16,000 alligators were trapped that year. And public opinion began to change. Frank and Ada Graham found that "Many Americans

believe the alligator is a product to be managed wisely for business profits." Louisiana's sound philosophy of a controlled harvest to maintain a sustained yield was beginning to take hold. With the international market restored, local prices rose to over eighteen dollars per foot for raw, salted hides, and have continued the dramatic ascent, soaring to twenty dollars in 1986 and forty-eight dollars in 1988.

State-sponsored research on alligator farming kept abreast, as well. New methods were developed that accelerated growth rates and revolutionized hide ranching. Competition was keen to obtain licensing and an initial hatching stock of eggs in order to enter what was fast becoming a very lucrative form of aquaculture. Fifty-four farms had eighty thousand head of stock growing in Louisiana by 1988.

Both hunters and farmers benefited economically from regulations effected in 1979 that allowed alligator meat to be sold for human consumption within the state. By 1980, the way was paved for legalized interstate commerce and alligator for the table could travel freely to new markets as far away as Hawaii or even to foreign countries. This brought new profits to food processors, sausage manufacturers, seafood distributors, and restaurants as products and recipes to tickle the gourmet palate were developed. In 1982, alligator meat retailed for about three dollars per pound at seafood markets and grocery stores in Louisiana.

The 1984 price in Florida for prime cuts of alligator was five dollars per pound, and meat sales ($40,000) exceeded hide sales ($26,000) in that state. Between 150,000 and 175,000 pounds of alligator meat were sold throughout the United States in 1985, and international markets were developing in France, Italy, Japan, and Singapore. Farmers and hunters wholesaled it at four dollars per pound. Three years later, it was retailing in Hawaii at as much as $10.95 per pound for tenderloin, while the poorest cuts were not less than $5.95. Cyrus Tamashiro, the Hawaiian retailer, proclaimed, "It's a gourmet item like escargot or caviar." In 1989, *Cooks* reported, "production of alligator meat in Florida topped 220,000 pounds last year; in Louisiana almost 750,000 pounds of 'gator meat was [*sic*] harvested."

Worldwide numbers of other crocodilians continued to dwindle as farmed and wild alligators begat a mushrooming population in the 1980s. This meant that as hide prices grew, so did the available U.S. domestic supply. The burgeoning trade contributed $2.5 million to the Louisiana economy in 1986. Hides brought twenty-five dollars per foot in a new state-instituted system of silent public auctions that began in 1984.

Twenty-four thousand Louisiana hides were harvested in 1988, valued at $8 million ($333 each) and 600,000 pounds of meat at $3.50 per pound produced an additional $2.1 million, making that year's crop worth $10.1 million. *Cooks* had slightly overestimated the meat total. As early as the 1960s, Dr. L. L. Glasgow foresaw that the alligator would become the basis of a $25 million industry. With the dramatic rise in hide prices in the late 1980s, that prediction may be more realistic than many once believed.

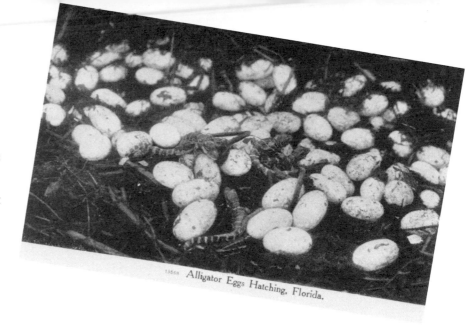

13568 Alligator Eggs Hatching, Florida.

By 1989, the world market in all crocodilian hides was alleged to have regenerated to only half its 1975 volume. This was the excellent and effective result of legislation designed to protect endangered crocodilian species within the United States and internationally. It did leave legal United States hides in the 1980s in something of a bind, though. Mercifully, tanners, designers, fabricators, distributors, and retailers were delighted to have the legal hides that came from areas where the alligator had been removed from the endangered-species lists, even though these hides and their resultant products still brought frowns from those who remained unaware of the dramatic alligator comeback in well-managed southern marshlands. In spite of the misplaced stigma, the price paid to legal hunters of wild Louisiana hides had increased from $16.50 in 1976 to $50.00 per foot at the end of the 1989 season, up by a whopping 300 percent in fewer than fifteen years.

"GOLDEN EGGS" OF THE ALLIGATOR INDUSTRY. POSTCARD ILLUSTRATION BY THE CURT TEICH CO., CHICAGO, CA. 1902.

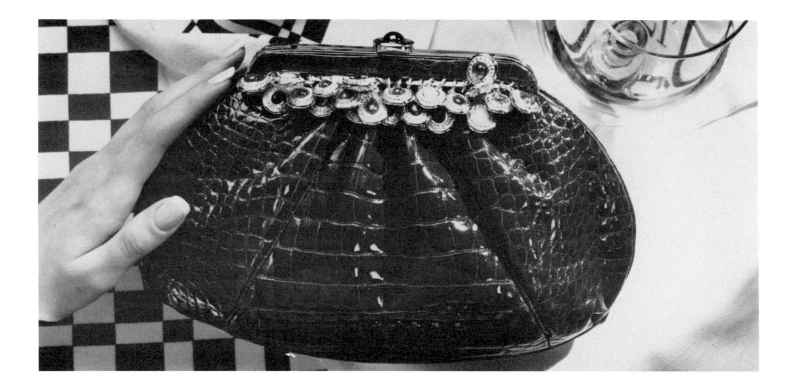

The explosive economic success of the Louisiana alligator bonanza of the 1980s naturally attracted attention and envy from other places. Entrepreneurs began to want some of the alligators and some of the action for themselves. The Louisiana Wildlife and Fisheries Commission clamped down in order to protect the state's investments and its profits. John Tarver, director of the commission's fur and refuge division, explained, "It seems [that] if they'll be breeding them in other countries, this will hurt our alligator industry—it's foolish to give up the goose that lays the golden egg." The commission's firm recommendation was that neither "geese" nor eggs should be given passports.

An unfortunate aspect of alligator economics in most alligator-producing areas is that only the prices paid for raw products remain within the region (with the exception of "parts" such as teeth and skulls, sold as souvenirs). Efforts begun as early as 1979 to attract European tanners, with their closely-guarded secret processes, remained unsuccessful.

Regrettably, the immense profits of brokerage, most tanning, manufacture, distribution, and retailing are dispersed worldwide. These convert the millions paid to hide producers to the multimillions, since with each step in its international trek, the hide nearly doubles in value. The result is investment-quality goods such as designer handbags, which cost the fashion-conscious from four thousand to ten thousand dollars each in 1989. The processing plant constructed in Baton Rouge is an attempt to retain the untapped profit from alligators for the greater benefit of one state. Another has begun operation in Tennessee and new life has been breathed into existing businesses in Georgia and Florida. If they are successful, others surely will follow.

There is another aspect to alligator economics that should not be overlooked and this is tourism and its associated souvenir sales. Florida leads in the number of alligator farms that profit from admissions. In Gulf Coast states, there are many "swamp tours" that whisk the uninitiated in life preserver–clad safety into the swamps and marshes, where the main attraction is often a quasidomesticated alligator population that is only too glad to swim right up to the boat to be fed when they're called. A significant number of tickets is sold each year.

In addition, tour operators, alligator farms, and gift shops at zoos, as well as establishments purveying regional souvenirs and curios, do a landslide business in alligator souvenirs. The goods in question include a wide range of merchandise, and the manufacturers and retailers literally make millions. Among the most outrageous recent offerings are Gator Shoes. Available in just one size that "fits just about all," these saurian toe-ticklers are made of molded vinyl with alligator faces and appended tails, making them a whopping seventeen and a half inches long. So desirable are these oddities that the 1989 Archie McPhee catalog, from Seattle, Washington, claimed, "You cannot have a satisfying life without wearing or giving a pair of these at least once before you die." McPhee was willing to part with them at $12.95 a pair—"Made proudly in the U.S.A."

As a footnote to alligator economics, the scientists, game-management professionals, and enforcement personnel of the various Gulf Coast wildlife and fisheries commissions and universities, as well as the local game wardens, should not be forgotten. Some of those folks owe their salaries and their livings, at least in part, to solving the alligator's problems in dealing with twentieth-century American society.

CHAPTER SEVENTEEN

THE EYES OF THE BEHOLDER ARTISTS AND ALLIGATORS

Artists have been intrigued and inspired by alligators for many centuries. Native Americans, particularly in the Deep South, made stylized icons of them in a variety of forms. The Chitimacha, west of New Orleans, created "the alligator's entrails," one of the most complex and beautiful of their intricate basketry patterns. From the sixteenth through the eighteenth centuries, Europeans were interested primarily in capturing the likeness of the alligator for scientific and educational purposes. Draughtsmen and engravers worked from written descriptions or sketches made in the New World to create plates for books on the geography and natural history of exotic American colonies. Results were not always terribly accurate. The Baton Rouge *Morning Advocate* justly noted that the alligator "was depicted in earlier steel [copper] engravings as a fire-breathing dragon, lying in wait to attack every man, woman or child who came within his reach."

The earliest surviving European depiction of an American alligator seems to be John White's watercolor drawing *Allagatto,* painted in 1585 on the American East Coast. The most entertaining (and inaccurate) may well be the *Crocodil* [*sic*] engraved from a written description—by an artisan who had obviously never seen an alligator—to accompany LePage du Pratz's *Histoire de la Louisiane* in 1758. The unknown engraver gave the animal doglike legs and fish scales.

During the nineteenth century, more exacting anatomical illustrations were made, sometimes in the spirit

"LE FAUTEUIL CROCODILE." BRASS AND COPPER ARMCHAIR BY FRENCH SCULPTRESS CLAUDE LALANNE, 1987.

FACING PAGE: "ALLIGATOR SHOES (THOM MCAN, EAT YOUR HEART OUT)." OBJETS D'ART BY GEORGE FEBRES, 1975.

THE EYES OF THE BEHOLDER 219

RIGHT:

"AN ALLIGATOR
SEIZING A CRANE."
WOOD ENGRAVING
FROM *HARPER'S
NEW MONTHLY
MAGAZINE*, 1855.

BELOW:

LIDDED, DOUBLE-
WOVEN, FOUR-
COLOR CHITIMACHA
STORAGE BASKET
IN THE
"ALLIGATOR'S
ENTRAILS"
PATTERN. HAND-
WOVEN NATURALLY
DYED RIVER CANE,
NINETEENTH
CENTURY.

of true medical studies. M. F.-E. Guérin's engraver combined flora and fauna in such a plate, entitled *Alligator et Alysine Plantain d'eau,* which appeared in his multivolume compilation, *Picturesque Dictionary of Natural History and the Phenomena of Nature* of 1834. This was the same year that John J. Audubon prepared the oversized plate *Whooping Crane,* for his monumental *Birds of America.* In the hand-colored aquatint engraving, the bird is shown, scientifically accurately, eating baby alligators, which are taxonomically exacting in their delineation. The crane even has placed its alligator dinner obligingly so as to provide both dorsal and ventral views. Drs. John Holbrook (1842) and Bennet Dowler (1846) included nitty-gritty illustrations of alligator taxonomy and dissected anatomy in their detailed studies.

Alligators made early appearances in the works of illustrators of various forms of popular literature that included tall tales, folk stories, novels, and popularized science, as well as receiving a wide variety of newspaper and magazine coverage. Among the writings making science safe for the masses was *The Book of Reptiles,* published in 1835. It included *An Alligator Destroying a Snake.* The artist of this remarkable image was almost as ill informed as LePage du Pratz's engraver had been in the preceding century.

Pictures in the popular illustrated press were often taken from a field observer's sketch or description and then executed as woodblocks for the publisher. Such illustrations range from the dragonlike *Alligator Seizing a Crane* in *Harper's New Monthly Magazine* in 1855 to the astonishing battle scene of the intrepid Savannah Walston saving her mother from the huge invading monsters, which accompanied a sensationalized account of the same incident in the *Chicago Tribune* of 1900.

LEFT:

SWAMP IVORY:
ALLIGATOR-TOOTH
NECKLACE
DESIGNED BY
VIRGINIA MOSELEY,
CA. 1988.

RIGHT:

ALLIGATOR JUJU.
MIXED-MEDIA
FETISH BY LOIS
SIMBACH, 1988.

Famed illustrator Gustave Doré gilded a few lilies for an 1863 luxury edition of Chateaubriand's romantic novel *Atala.* Doré obligingly graced Louisiana with mountains sporting palm jungles, while alligators bask on a sandbar in the river flowing through this lush but unrealistic scene. Twenty years later, an artist named Church supplied an entire spiky, anthropomorphized saurian family (with all the babies in a bed, no less) to illustrate "How the Bear Nursed the Little Alligator" in Joel Chandler Harris's *Nights with Uncle Remus.* These and countless more nineteenth-century depictions, with all their inaccuracies and anthropomorphisms, had a strong influence in shaping the general public's image and misconceptions of the alligator.

It was also during the nineteenth century that the alligator first appeared in advertising, breaking into commercial art. The cartoon was developing at the beginning of the century as an amusement and alligators occasionally graced them from as early as the 1840s and 1850s. The ubiquitous animal even inspired costume and float designs for New Orleans Carnival and Mardi Gras before the century ended.

By the twentieth century, the camera had largely replaced the draughtsman in the production of scientific and technical illustrations. Photography itself had become an art form and nature photography an accepted genre. Alligators posed for countless nineteenth- and twentieth-century photographers, some of whom published their work as souvenir postcards or other memorabilia for tourists to collect and take home.

The alligator has become so embedded in the lore,

mythology, and customs that define the South, artists have utilized it as a means of expressing a regional identity in their works. Elements of humor or whimsy often reign in such creations. George Febre's *Alligator Shoes (Thom McAn, Eat Your Heart Out)* of 1975 parodies serious footwear and fashion by replacing the toes of traditional alligator pumps with snapping jaws, appropriately "open." The work is reminiscent of Salvador Dali's highly entertaining surrealistic jewelry.

Elizabeth Shannon's *Camille* and her later *Petite Camille II* of 1989 put the alligator in the preposterous but amusing stance of climbing a ladder. These large-scale works evolved from her use of native materials, harvested directly from the landscape, in her earlier sculptures of the 1970s. In addition to palm fronds, cane, and other materials, she now occasionally harvests an alligator, as well.

Mickey Mclean's whimsical polychrome furniture, stabile sculptures and other creations such as toys present stylized alligators in imaginative narrative contexts. The *BonneIdée Cow Bandit* presents a saurian version of the wolf in sheep's clothing. Mclean explained, "For twenty years up and down Bayou BonneIdée, cows disappeared at the hands of an unknown perpetrator. The culprit avoided capture these twenty years by use of an extremely clever disguise. During a routine check of cows, the owner became suspicious by the way this particular cow chewed its cud."

James Maurice Schexnaydre has taken chain saw to log, converting ancient "sinker cypress" into sculpted 'gators by the yard. His largest—over forty feet in length—has been nominated for the *Guinness Book of Records*. Jack Barth

THE BONNEIDÉE
COW BANDIT.
POLYCHROME
WOODEN SCULP-
TURE BY MICKEY
MCLEAN, 1989.

FACING PAGE:
SCULPTOR JAMES
SCHEXNAYDRE
ASTRIDE MONU-
MENTAL CHAIN-SAW
CARVED CYPRESS
ALLIGATOR.

224   *A Social History of the American Alligator*

and his traveling companions, however, have found one they think is larger: "Right next to [the Gator Motel in Kissimmee, Florida] in the parking lot, is probably the world's largest gator statue." Schexnaydre's saurian may also lose to the fifty-foot fossil ancestors of the modern alligator, but the concept is novel. In 1989, the artist appeared, chain saw in hand, work in progress, at the New Orleans Jazz and Heritage Festival. Schexnaydre considers cypress as a material to be part of his regional heritage. "Sinker cypress," his favorite, consists of felled logs preserved underwater on swamp bottoms, sometimes for centuries. The artist has said, "I chose the alligator because it's such an exotic, ancient creature and because it represents Louisiana so well." His giant saurians have been created for a restaurant in Burnside, a store in Laplace, and for Lafayette's Festival International de Louisiane.

Artists from outside the region, and even outside the country, have become fascinated and occasionally incorporate the alligator into their work. Sculptress Claude Lalanne, for example, has visited Louisiana and also has furnished her garden in France with a most unusual bronze and copper alligator armchair.

Alligator humor has become a twentieth-century standard. Alligators appeared in occasional comic drawings before the Depression. Since that time, and with the further development of the cartoon strip and comic book, "Albert" became a national favorite. The creation of Walt Kelly, "Albert" dominated the opening frame of *Animal Comics No. 1* in 1942. "Pogo" played only a supporting role and both looked quite different than they did in the 1950s and

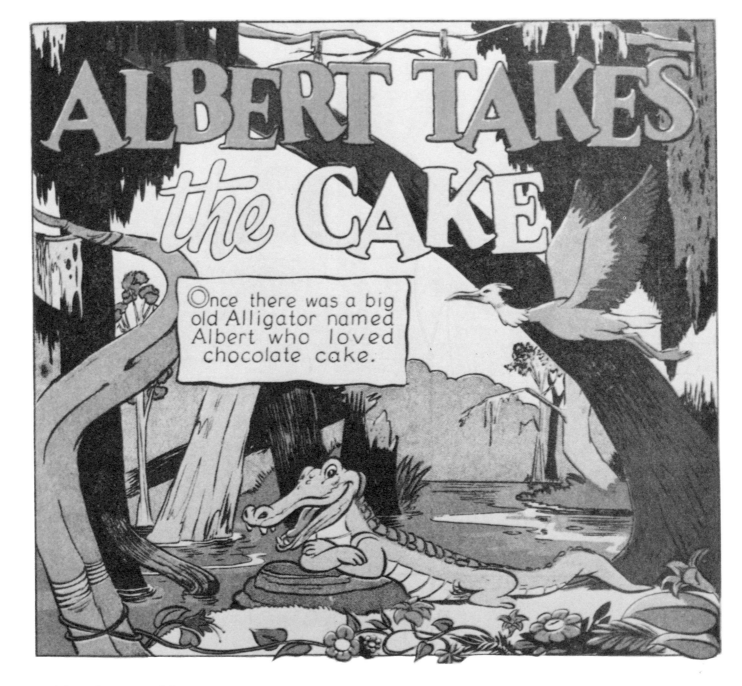

1960s. Over the next decade, Kelly refined the characters and visual appearances of these candid purveyors of swamp wisdom, folk philosophy, and occasional universal truths. The "Pogo" comic strip, with "Albert" garumphing around the swamp, became a regular newspaper feature in 1949 and has entertained millions of Americans since that time, earning Kelly a warm spot in the collective national heart.

Alligators have appeared in other nationally syndicated comic strips, usually for single installments or short-run episodes. In "Brenda Starr," the short-lived saurian character objected to alligator shoes and bags during the time that the nation was preoccupied with environmental and endangered-species issues. Ray Billingsley has used children, with their concrete, literal thought patterns, in his "Curtis" to add a deft twist to traditional alligator humor. Alligators, or alligator subjects, have made cameo appearances in other single comic strip sequences, too.

In "The Far Side," a syndicated individual daily "spot" cartoon feature (also collectively issued in yearly calendar format), Gary Larson has utilized alligators in witty and wacky situations. Larson generally portrays them as either man-eating monsters or as anthropomorphized off-the-walls commentators. His 1989 calendar included a cartoon for Ash Wednesday showing two armchair-bound saurians in front of a television, with one reading a newspaper horoscope to his buddy: "Leo: You will eat well this summer, but hard times are ahead. . . . Poachers figure big in your future."

Political and/or editorial cartoonists have discovered the joys of the symbolic, allegorical alligator. It is frequently used in such a context to represent a powerful force or adversary. In the 1970s, Byron Humphries often allegorized as alligators the personal and political woes besetting Louisiana's Cajun governor in cartoons for a New Orleans newspaper. In these usages, the alligator usually represents the exaggerated or mythologized aspects of strength, voraciousness, aggression, or greed (better and more realistically attributed to crocodiles) that have come to dominate much of alligator imagery.

In the realm of commercial art, a surprising number of

designers have been involved in the creation of souvenirs of all kinds, camera-ready advertising materials, and the conception of insignia, logos, and the like. Seemingly limitless souvenirs range from statuettes to posters to printed T-shirts and beyond. Advertising artists, for the most part, have resided in the communities in which product labels, printed ads, or other promotional materials have been commissioned or produced and manufactured for clients. These locations span the globe from the Gulf Coast to Hong Kong.

Especially creative artists have been known to concoct special alligators for special occasions. Multimedia artist Lois Simbach, touched by the hospitality of Dovie Naquin, a traditional alligator hunter, at his camp in 1989, made an alligator shaped juju instead of the traditional human-shaped fetish as her handcrafted personal expression of thanks. Shortly before his untimely death that same year, neon artist Josh Caffey created the initial design for a multicolored flashing alligator as a gift to the author. It was among his last conceptual works.

Each viewing of an "artistic" alligator subtly influences the viewer's concept of that animal. Viewing many images over time results in a composite mental idea of an alligator that is different from that conveyed by the written word. Artists speak in a strong visual language that does not depend on verbal skills to communicate and thus they exercise a power over us of which we are often unaware. While we are warned not to believe everything we see in print, no one in our usual process of education tells us to beware of the work of the visual communicator as well.

228   *A Social History of the American Alligator*

Unquestioningly, we gaze at alligator art, and guilelessly store away impressions that such work communicates to us. Probably without realizing it, the artists who have depicted alligators have had a deep influence on the conceptual archetype that we all carry around in our heads.

The reality of the alligator—its size, shape, form, and color—was made widely known by the works of the earliest of these artists, those whom we would think of today primarily as scientific illustrators but who brought great talent to their work, which was often of high quality. They educated a broad public in a time before Monsieur Daguerre had perfected his "magic box" and made photography available to the Western world in 1839. The legend of the alligator—the fearsome man-eating beast—was also brought to reality by another school of illustrators, those for the popular press, especially in the nineteenth century. They let us visualize the alleged attack on Savannah Walston and their renderings reinforced the impact of such events described in other richly colored journalistic verbiage. The anthropomorphism of the alligator reached its apex in the work of artists of the mid to late twentieth century who transformed the words of authors into palpable images of highly humanized saurians.

Regional artists of the American South utilized the alligator much as a moviemaker might use an establishing shot to firmly identify locale. They also entertain us through cleverness of original thought and occasionally preposterous concept. Their abilities allow them to bring purely imaginary and mental ideas to concrete two- or three-dimensional form that in reality may not exist at all. Often their work is disseminated in printed form: The books, magazines, and periodicals in which it appears are frequently national or international in distribution and are produced in immense quantities, reaching and influencing a vast number of people in all geographic areas.

OFFUTT INNS

Our Specialty is People

THANKS FOR THE MEMORIES (AND THOSE SENSATIONAL SOUVENIRS)

FACING PAGE: SOUTHERN SHENANIGANS, CA. 1910, AND DETAIL (BELOW) FROM "OUT FOR A RIDE, FLORIDA," CA. 1905. NOVELTY POSTCARDS BY THE CURT TEICH CO., CHICAGO.

The already-ancient American alligator began the "social" aspects of its history with the rise of Amerindian civilizations in the lower Mississippi Valley and the American Southeast—a process well advanced 12,000 years ago, if not a few millennia earlier. Those first families of America respected the alligator, even to the point of worship, utilized its meat and hide, enjoined it in song and dance, made it the tribal or clan totem among select groups, produced tools from its skeletal remains, looked to it for artistic inspiration, depended upon it for protection and medication, built it an occasional monument, and even bathed in its company. This harmonious balance of the centuries continued unabated until the intrusion of European explorers. It is, in fact, the longest and perhaps richest era of man-and-alligator interaction, but the one for which we have the shortest record.

When Europeans arrived in the fifteenth century, they came saddled down with mental preconceptions and legends that immediately clouded their vision of the alligator and got them off to a false start in their budding

THANKS FOR THE MEMORIES 231

relationship with America's ruling reptile. Since then, all degrees of Southerners, from Native Americans to explorers, ethnic groups, and the general population have created additional beliefs and legends that mythologized and anthropomorphized the alligator, making it the subject of folktale, symbol, and allegory.

Best known of the alligator folktales is that of the alleged saurian inhabitants of the sewers of New York. Apparently based on a crumb of fact found in a mid-1930s newspaper, the legend grew. It was spurred on by popular literature and popular entertainment, and its vestiges remain today. "Leave It To Beaver," among the television sitcoms that had graduated to infinite rerun status by 1991, reaired a segment in which one of Beaver's jealous friends told his mother that he hoped Beaver would "fall down a manhole and get eaten by a great big old alligator in the sewer."

Confounded by the currency of misinformation, legends, and folk practices, European and American investigators floundered for over three hundred years until, with the aid of newly developed scientific method, they finally sorted things out and good common sense prevailed. During that time, scientists observed, examined, studied, documented, dissected, analyzed, experimented with, learned from, and published about the alligator, often competing, arguing with, and refuting each other in the race to acquire alligator knowledge.

As the new Americans began to better understand the alligator in the South, they, too, began to utilize it as the Amerindians had done for thousands of years. The alligator provided them medicine, lubrication, food, tools, useful and decorative objects, and even totems for their clubs and institutions of learning. This nouveau population of colonists and settlers had made America the world's melting pot. Various dominant groups of Western European origin—notably the Spanish, French, and British—participated in the arduous and sometimes audacious importation and implantation of their own thought patterns and technologies, supplemented by African knowledge and traditions; these created new visions and new utilizations of the alligator.

Both visions and utilizations changed, relatively rapidly, as newer technologies developed. Such advances made tanning and production of alligator leather both practical and profitable, contributing to the decline of the saurian population. New modes of transportation let the living alligator travel ever more widely. Novel approaches to animal husbandry allowed the alligator to be farmed and later ranched. Further scientific inquiry developed the management methods and procedures that "saved" the alligator from the onslaught of man himself—at least temporarily.

Over this most recent five hundred years, while all these activities were occurring, the alligator earned an important place in "modern" American life. Headlines for the month of January 1991 alone might read, "Alligator Farmers Victims of Own Success," "Saurians on National Television," "New York Designer to Release Radical New Bags," "The Nightmare Continues," and "Skin Treatment Scorns 'Gators." In fact, all these things happened and this

LOVE AT FIRST SIGHT.

plethora of news certainly demonstrated the alligator's continuing success at grabbing the national spotlight, and its concomitant significance to various aspects of contemporary American society.

Economically, the alligator has given employment and income to all those who have hunted, poached, farmed, skinned, butchered, sold, tanned, fabricated, cooked, wholesaled, and retailed it, as well as to the agents who have protected, managed, and policed it and its captors in its native southern environment, not to mention hosts of others. It has occupied the thoughts, strategies, and practices (some forthright, others devious) of legislators, lawyers, politicians, conservationists, and customs agents on every continent, particularly during the "alligator wars" of the 1970s.

An economic crisis among alligator farmers was brought on by their own immense productivity, which

"LOVE AT FIRST SIGHT." LITHO-GRAPHIC CARTOON POSTCARD BY H. HORINA, POST-MARKED 1914.

FACING PAGE: EDSEL AND CLARA FORD ON A FLORIDA VACATION. SOUVENIR POST-CARD, CA. 1905

jumped into sudden focus in late 1990 and early 1991 when the market for farmed hides suffered its own recession, parallel to that of the national economy. Contrary to the earlier opinions of Dr. Carr and the Audubon Society, alligator farming did succeed in producing so many hides that it not only met the demand for four-footers but surpassed it, creating a glut on the market. American and foreign producers unwittingly exceeded the industry's need for skins with small scale patterns to make small-scale leather objects.

As a result, prices for farmed hides dramatically declined, according to Fred Kalmbach in the Baton Rouge *State-Times*. Longer, wider hides from wild alligators, suited for the manufacture of large objects, continued to bring increasing prices—up to seventy dollars per foot—while the shorter farmed hides fell from the 1990 high of thirty-six dollars to as little as twenty-eight dollars in the new year. Farmers were hesitant to "grow" larger alligators because of another kind of diminishing return. Food and heating costs to produce "super 'gators" accelerated on a per-foot basis after the fast-growing youngsters passed the four-foot mark and their growth rate slowed. Relative costs of producing slow-growing footage of over four feet increased exponentially, eating into profits.

Farmers and biologists alike tackled the problem and sought new ways to guarantee the financial future of ranched alligator. The more progressive and the more optimistic looked upon the situation as only a temporary setback. New management procedures, they hoped, would allow farmers to raise longer 'gators more economically and to jockey their way into the ongoing market for larger hides.

Throughout this long process, the patient alligator became ever more familiar. Public fancy was caught first by the size and exotic appearance of the alligator and its relatives, and attempts were made to connect this mysterious, frightening, and occasionally dangerous link with the great age of dinosaurs to the European mythology of dragon and Leviathan. News and media coverage, beginning with nineteenth-century periodicals and ending with national television networks, brought the alligator into virtually every American home. Popular opinion, however, influenced by all these human activities, remained riddled with exaggerations and inaccuracies, intermingling alligator fact with saurian fantasy.

Such alligator fascination naturally gave the alligator star power in the constellation of southern tourist attractions from the early nineteenth century to the present. Early tourists sought out the saurians as sights to be seen or quarry to be hunted. Victorian tourists admired alligators by the hundreds at the earliest alligator farms. Modern tourists fill excursion craft to the gunwales in search of the elusive alligator on contemporary swamp and marsh tours. Alligator souvenirs of all types are sold by the thousands to these visitors as the alligator continues its selfless labors, workin' for the Yankee dollar.

Showmen have exhibited, promoted, filmed, exaggerated, and sensationalized the alligator in their attempts at commercial exploitation, with results that are sometimes fine, sometimes pure chicanery. This is ably illustrated by two diametrically opposed television appearances that *Alligator mississippiensis* made during the first weeks of 1991. *Newton's Apple*, a popular public-television science series, presented a snapping baby saurian over national airwaves in a segment that explained several facets of alligator science and lore. Just nights before, network television had regaled American insomniacs with *Curse of the Swamp Creature,* starring John Agar, on an all-night movie broadcast. Originally released by Azalea Films in 1966, this less than B movie fare featured an overcrowded alligator pond as the mad scientist's solution of how to deal with the evidence. Bodies were merrily pitched to the cry of "Feed him to the alligators," with ineptly directed saurians shown shredding sheets presumably shrouding the corpses of hapless victims of scientific experiment gone awry. Special effects were not terribly sophisticated, but the intent to support the alligator's popular image as primordial monster was clear.

Alligator luggage turned up again, too. About a week later, a rerun segment of *M*A*S*H* dealt with a famous practical joker who had served as best man at B.J.'s (Mike Farrell) wedding, where he turned up in white towel and black tie. B.J. further shared by saying, "On my honeymoon, he put a lizard in my alligator bag." To this, Hawkeye (Alan Alda) laconically inquired, "So it wouldn't be lonely?" *Nova,* another popular public television series, had an alligator on a treadmill, studying "arm" motion that might help establish the ancient relationship between fossil saurians and the ancestors of modern birds. The segment aired on Mardi Gras (February 12) of 1991.

Artists, writers, composers, and designers have been inspired by our native saurian in the creation of sculpture, painting, cartoons, drawings, engravings, photographs, novels, songs, sound tracks, and stories that have entertained and edified the nation. In the world of American fashion, New York designer Barry Kieselstein-Cord was busy planning another type of alligator assault in early 1991. This remarkable artist previously had made an international hit with his alligator-motif jewelry, ranging from bracelets to earrings, and he confided to the author that he was planning to introduce his own line of high-fashion alligator bags, as well. Barry's wife is from Shreveport, Louisiana, home of the beloved Charlie Bob. Barry visits the state on recreational and social occasions, hunting in "Sportsman's Paradise," and visiting friends and relatives.

"BRINGING HOME SOME REAL MEMORIES." CARTOON POST-CARD BY THE CURT TEICH CO., CHICAGO, CA. 1946.

Bringing Home Some Real Memories

The alligator's nightmare status was admirably upheld, as well. A New Orleans friend confided in late January 1991 (several days *before* the 1982 film *Cat People* was televised) that he had just experienced a remarkable dream in which four people metamorphosed into extraordinarily terrifying panthers and tigers, except for one who changed—you guessed it—into an alligator. According to his wide-awake memory, the alligator was the ugliest in animal form but the most alluring of the lot as a person—one to whom our dreamer was terribly attracted. As Rebecca Currence, director of the Louisiana Museum Foundation, observed, "Freud and friends would have had a field day with that one."

The alligator also continued its starring role in American advertising in both real and fanciful ways. Among motorists' hazards were "alligator crossings" in ads for an allegedly superdependable automobile that would not break down and leave driver and passengers at the mercy of such ferocious wildlife. A brand of skin lotion (Lubriderm) stylishly touted its abilities to prevent dry, cracking skin by showing an alligator (shades of our New Orleans dreamer) sensuously crawling out of a curvaceous model's bed, down a staircase, and into the distance, while a narrator intoned, "See ya later, alligator."

None of this was the intent of the innocent and much maligned alligator. Much older than mankind and content to survive as it has done for 70 million years, the alligator has seldom initiated human contact. It is man who began the process that so firmly has ingrained the alligator into the collective national identity. It has even been adopted as the official state reptile in Louisiana. During that time, *Alligator mississippiensis* in all its manifestations—handbag, legend, nightmare, pet, experimental subject, main course, souvenir, and many more—has acquired an unsought but impressive social history. Today, more than at any other time, "the earth trembles with his thunder."

This compendium of alligator lore and history is an outgrowth of exhibition planning in the Office of Special Projects at the Louisiana State Museum in New Orleans. It began when the author was generously included in alligator-hunting house parties at the home of Mr. Dovie Naquin at Pointe-aux-Chênes, Louisiana, during the 1988, 1989, and 1990 alligator seasons. There, Dovie, his son, Mark, daughter, Grace Daigle, and son-in-law, Harry Daigle, treated everyone to South Louisiana's famed hospitality, extraordinary Cajun food, and shared a lifetime's experience of traditional fur trapping and alligator hunting, recounted in spirited, melodious conversation drifting back and forth between Louisiana French and southern English. Environmental sculptress Elizabeth Shannon and textile conservator Rebecca Venable first introduced me to Dovie and his family, and thereby greatly enriched my life.

It soon became apparent that this unique lifestyle and rich cultural heritage were worthy subjects of documentation and exhibition at the Louisiana State Museum, which showcases the state's history and culture. Preliminary research promptly revealed a surprising and largely unknown trove of historic materials that yielded a fascinating picture of man's relationship with the alligator over a period of several centuries, as well as some remarkable antique illustrations. It also became apparent that alligators were not yet aware that they had a social history, one in which they had interacted with people since before recorded time began on the North American continent. As a result of this reticent collaboration, the alligator unwittingly had become an integral part of the U. S. national personality. By the fall of 1988, I was as hooked on the subject as one of Dovie's alligators at the end of his line.

Over a year's time, additional information was collected from Dovie, his family, friends, and neighbors. Their generous sharing and lively personal warmth were the inspirations for this project. It was made possible by the strong support of Jim Sefcik, director of the Louisiana State Museum; Tamra Carboni, the museum's director for public programs; and Rebecca Currence, director of the Louisiana Museum Foundation. Jim and Becky undertook the fund-raising required to mount the exhibition and facilitated the extraordinary measures necessary to pull together an enormous number of illustrations in an incredibly short time. Their contributions in this regard are sincerely appreciated.

It is difficult to describe the sense of excitement and discovery that permeated the research and writing phases of *A Social History of the American Alligator.* Ms. Rebecca Venable shared many of these experiences as our communal research into American alligators progressed. Traveling by jeep across south Louisiana, navigating by water towers, we ventured back and forth between New Orleans and Pointe-aux-Chênes, constantly discussing the latest subject of investigation. New sources, curious information, confirmations of dubious material, negations of incorrect findings, recording Cajun alligator vocabulary, and the dawning of the broader implications of the social history of the alligator all contributed to the feeling that attention to this neglected area of U. S. culture that we were focusing on was overdue. Ms. Venable's contributions to this project have been significant and her own work on the creation, manufacture, and conservation of alligator products will be a unique contribution to both artifact conservators and toward the education of the consumer public.

Research that located the approximately four hundred published and manuscript sources utilized in reconstructing the alligator's social history was performed by many people. Kathryn Page, curator of the museum's Louisiana Historical Center, found many rare publications in the Center's library. Her volunteer staff, and in particular Mary White, kept their eyes open for uncataloged alligator references in the manuscript and historic newspaper holdings of the Center's archive. Through their enthusiastic participation, sources that have never appeared in existing alligator bibliographies were made available.

The rich resources of the McIlhenny Collection and the extraordinary vertical files formerly maintained by Evangeline Lynch, now housed in the Louisiana and Lower Mississippi Valley Collection at the Hill Memorial Library of Louisiana State University in Baton Rouge, Louisiana, provided additional materials and illustrations that otherwise would have remained untapped. I am extremely grateful for the highly professional and occasionally high-spirited cooperation of Kathy Morgan, formerly at the McIlhenny Collection, Barbara Aldrich, library associate for the rare books collection, and Faye Phillips, head of the Louisiana and Lower Mississippi Valley Collection, and their staffs for preliminary work that maximized the research time in Baton Rouge and for providing photocopies and photographs that facilitated work in New Orleans.

Frank de Caro, professor of English at LSU, put me on the right track to unravel the mystery of the alligators in the sewers of New York, as well as providing valuable references to other aspects of alligator folklore. Scientific and popular publications from the university were provided by Ashley Laborde in the Editorial and Publications Department of the Louisiana Agricultural Experiment Station. Harriet Callahan and Virginia Smith, successive librarians of the Louisiana section of the Louisiana State Library in Baton Rouge, assisted with photographic reproductions from their holdings. One of the oddest documents, an affidavit for a singing alligator, was obtained through the good offices of Milton R. Skyring, clerk/judicial administrator of city court of Baton Rouge.

In the Office of Special Projects, dedicated volunteers Gertrude Burguières, Rosemarie Fowler, and Barbara Reed were invaluable in preparation of the manuscript, establishing and maintaining research files and assembling the bibliography. I hope that their many hours of demanding labor are rewarded, in part, by this result.

Students participated, as well. Interns from Tulane University, notably Brian Rich and Brad Lebow, each spent a semester immersed in alligators, locating sources at Tulane's Howard-Tilton Memorial Library and Special Collections and cataloging an enormous number of alligator images and objects. Two students from the Amoco Summer Employment Program, administratively facilitated by the Friends of the Cabildo, underwent a similar ordeal. Richard Bates and Ann Schnieders were enthusiastic French translators, photographer's assistants, and more during their summer at the museum. I would like to think that they have profited as much from their internships and work experience in the Office of Special Projects as this project has from their participation.

Highly specialized work in law libraries was undertaken by Janet Williams, a volunteer lawyer through the Friends of the Cabildo. The alligator's legal history could not have been traced without the solid access to alligator legislation that she provided. Ms. Sandra Hotard-Peairs, archivist at the State Division of Archives, Records Management, and History in Baton Rouge very kindly retrieved the text of the legislation authorizing the alligator as Louisiana's official state reptile. Dr. George Shannon, director of the museum's branch in Shreveport, Louisiana, contributed his knowledge of Native American archaeology and bibliography to provide the prehistoric information and prototypes that set the stage for European intervention into alligator affairs. Mr. and Mrs. Al Wehmeier in New Orleans shared their considerable experience with and knowledge of crocodilian leathers. Mrs. George Hirdes of Chalmette recalled her late husband's career in alligator manufacturing for my benefit. Dr. Ted Joanen, of the Louisiana Department of Wildlife and Fisheries, stationed at the Rockefeller Wildlife Refuge at Grand

Chênier, Louisiana, very kindly gave the manuscript a reading for scientific and contextual accuracy. This review, by a leading expert in alligator biology and management, has greatly strengthened the entire project. These specialists are due my considerable thanks.

Christine Pyle, assistant curator for special collections at the Lake County Museum in Wauconda, Illinois, probed the enormous holdings of the Teich Collection for delightful and often hilarious alligator imagery. The Collection's *Image File* published the first article documenting this rewarding collaboration. Dr. Bruce Erickson, curator of paleontology at The Science Museum of Minnesota, made his expertise and collections available so that the fossil history of the alligator could be presented, as well as reviewing portions of the project narrative. Dr. John Bolt, at the Field Museum of Natural History in Chicago, was of special assistance in the search for fossil alligators, as were Professor Wann Langston in Texas, Dr. C. R. Schaff of the Museum of Comparative Zoology at Harvard University, and Dr. Judith Schiebout of the Louisiana State University Museum of Geoscience.

Sarah Granato, reference librarian at the American Museum of Natural History, accessed the important historic work of the Count de Lacépède, to the project's benefit. Mary Lynn Stevens Heininger, curator of the collections division of the Henry Ford Museum, gave enthusiastic assistance and arranged special photography of objects from their extensive collections. Bill McCarthy, research historian of Circus World Museum in Baraboo, Wisconsin, delved into collections and research files to aid in developing the story of the alligator under the big top. Brenda Nelson-Strauss of the archives of Traditional Music at Indiana University made many harmonious references available. Barbara A. Shattuck, from the National Geographic Society in Washington, D. C., provided prints of photographs made for *National Geographic* in the 1930s.

In France, Thierry Lefrançois, director of the Museums of Art and History of La Rochelle, very kindly located the du Ru account of Iberville's voyage of 1700 and provided photographs of the Indian and alligator *pendule au nègre* at the Musée du Nouveau Monde. Additional references and photographs came from Dr. Duguy, director of the Natural History Museums of La Rochelle. Jean Favier, Director General of the Archives of France, served as much-needed traffic director, forwarding my specific requests to the appropriate departments of the National Archives. The earliest known view of New Orleans, drawn in 1726 and including an alligator, was made available through the assistance of Mr. Camara in the overseas section of the National Archives at Aix-en-Provence.

Catherine Hustache, curator of manuscripts at the Central Library of the National Museum of Natural History in Paris, was generous in her correspondence concerning rare French publications. Véronique Wiesinger, curator of the National Museum of Franco-American Cooperation, and Ludovic de Beaugendre, at the photographic service of the French National Museum System, were instrumental in obtaining photographs of Sebron's 1861 *View of Lake Cocodrie*. From Marly-le-Roi, Claude and Annie Luter sent alligator negatives taken while the famous musician was making a rare U. S. appearance.

In London, with the coordination of Julie Oldfield, the staff of the British Museum rephotographed John White's "allagatto" of 1585, earliest-known European depiction of an alligator. In Copenhagen, Marianne Poulsen at the National Museum of Denmark made arrangements for reproduction of the frontispiece of the *Museum Wormianum* of 1655, showing crocodilians in a European cabinet of curiosities. *A Social History of the American Alligator* is all the richer for this close international collaboration.

Librarians throughout the United States were unfailingly helpful in the search for hard-to-find publications. Thomas A. Horrocks, associate librarian for historical collections of the Library of the College of Physicians and Surgeons of Philadelphia; Dr. Samuel T.

Huang, head of rare books and special collections at Northern Illinois University; Janice Riggs at the Sims Memorial Library, Southeastern Louisiana University in Hammond; and Margaret Cook, curator of manuscripts and rare books at the Earl Gregg Swem Library of the College of William and Mary, are among them.

In New Orleans, Curt Burnette, senior curator of the Audubon Zoo, provided images of and access to the rare leucistic and albino alligators in his keeping. It was the only known place in the world where living alligators in three color phases could be photographed in a single negative. Ms. Ann Mason at the Gallier House discovered and made available a remarkable mid-nineteenth-century illustrated article from *Harper's New Monthly Magazine*. Francis Roger Kelley prowled the city's flea markets, bargain basements, and secondhand bookshops in a relentless quest for alligator goods, memorabilia, and publications. His more unusual finds have become part of the Louisiana State Museum's permanent holdings, and his extraordinary goodwill in the undertaking is very greatly appreciated. Mrs. Dode Platou, director, and John T. Magill, assistant curator, at The Historic New Orleans Collection, facilitated imagery research and photography of rare nineteenth-century views. Paul Tarver, curator of traveling exhibitions at the New Orleans Museum of Art, assisted with

reproductions of George Febres's outrageous *Alligator Shoes (Thom McAn, Eat Your Heart Out).*

Bruce Raeburn, curator of the William Ransom Hogan Jazz Archive at Tulane University, added grace notes to the remarks about musical saurians, as did Don Marquis, curator of jazz at the Louisiana State Museum and jazz historian Al Rose. Artist Wade Welch opened his reference files of historic humor. Ms. Rosemary Loomis opened her library of Orientalia to assist with the alligator-versus-dragon question. Producer Al Volker at WVUE-TV, the ABC affiliate in New Orleans, provided videotapes of " 'Gator Goldmine," a news series on Louisiana's contemporary alligator industry. Helen Perry undertook a one-woman patrol of uptown garage sales, producing a wide array of odd and wonderful alligator toys and souvenirs. Her good food and sense of humor bolstered the project at critical junctures.

At the Louisiana State Museum, thanks are due to J. Burton Harter, director for collections, for lending his vast knowledge of the museum's holdings, and for locating various intriguing alligator memorabilia, as did Oscar Lee Bates and Tamra Carboni, of the public programs staff, and Mrs. Isidore Cohn, Jr., president of the Louisiana Museum Foundation.

The delightful illustrations created by

Chuck Siler and the alligator ephemera located by Maureen Krail and Pat Hand, all of the public programs staff, have added materially to the success of the project. Very special mention must be made of Deena Bedigian, museum registrar, whose accessions vault was constantly invaded by alligators as the project progressed, and who diligently sorted out records and receipts as gifts and loans of alligator materials entered and left the museum.

Others who have aided with information, illustrations, and their goodwill have been Lolita Cortes of the Marisa del Re Gallery in New York City; James Pate, executive director of the Mount Dora Center for the Arts in Florida; Michael Kim at Sauvage Korea, Ltd., in Seoul; Zachary Casey of the Pelts and Skins Export Company, Ltd., in Belle Chasse; Steele McAndrew, alligator farmer in Ville Platte; and Julia McLaughlin of New York City. Artists Lois Simbach and Mickey Mclean provided illustrations of their alligator-inspired creations. Virginia Moseley lent her handsomely designed alligator-tooth jewelry. Professor Ron Todd, at Central Connecticut State University in New Britain, and Mary Connors, courageously undertook the demanding task of printing both exhibition and publication photographs from field negatives that were not always of professional caliber. In New Orleans, photographer Neil Hurd generously made pictures of unusual three-dimensional items from the collections of the Louisiana State Museum and from private collectors to grace these pages and the exhibition. Elizabeth Shannon thoughtfully included the project in her conceptual piece "Caught," performed for the 1989 annual meeting of the American Association of Museums, and encouraged continuing alligator research in numerous ways. Alligator tanners Chris Dumestre at the Cocodrie Tannery in Baton Rouge and Doug McPherson at the Memphis Tannery in Tennessee were generous with information. Many publishers, literary agents, illustrators, and authors freely gave permissions to quote from, reproduce, and exhibit their works.

Photographers Don Allen of Baton Rouge, Greg Guirard of St. Martinville, and Jim Segreto of New Orleans entrusted me with their valuable negatives of the Louisiana alligator and the annual hunt. Many businesses lent the use of their alligator products, logos, and trademarks, for which I am grateful. Bernard "Randy" Guste of Antoine's, New Orleans's oldest restaurant, wrote down for the first time the recipe for praise-winning alligator soup. Famed Louisiana chefs Paul Prudhomme, Tommy Wong, John Folse, Paul Gambel, and Andrea Apuzzo made the secrets of their alligator creations available. Others were arriving as we went to press. Ernest A. Liner, in Houma, provided the astonishing contribution of over two hundred alligator recipes that it had taken him decades to collect.

And then there were those remarkable authors – the encyclopedists, the explorers, the travelers, the scientists, and more who began to write and publish about the American alligator in the sixteenth century. They have left us, since that time, a steady stream of impressions, observations, misinformation, adventures, anecdotes, scientific discoveries, and other accounts that make fascinating reading. It was the historic record they created, their contributions to alligator science, lore, and history, which provided a foundation for this book. Peter Miller of the Peter Miller Agency in New York believed in their work and mine, and his efforts to bring *A Social History of the American Alligator* to publication are very greatly appreciated. The enthusiasm of my editor, Robert Weil, and the general helpfulness of everyone at St. Martin's Press, from secretaries to legal counsel, made the business of getting out a somewhat complicated book as painless as possible. Editorial assistant Richard Romano, copy editor Carol Edwards, and production editor Tom Noonan were exceptionally helpful. Remarkably talented Carol Haralson put my words and pictures together to create a wonderfully orchestrated whole.

A Social History of the American Alligator would not have taken form without the participation of all those named above, as well as many more who aided in other ways. I am particularly appreciative of those who provided much-needed information as the manuscript neared completion, whose contributions came too late to be recognized here. Respect, thanks, and appreciation are tendered to all who have helped bring the project to reality.

VAUGHN L. GLASGOW
New Orleans
May 1991

Prologue

pg. x. Feeding Her Pet: Courtesy Lake County Museum, Curt Teich Postcard Archives, Wauconda, IL.
Alligator Lamp: Collection of the Louisiana State Museum, New Orleans, gift of Mrs. Arthur Q. Davis and Mrs. Beauregard L. Bassich. Photo by Neil Hurd. Courtesy Louisiana Museum Foundation.

Chapter One

pg. 1 The Natchez: Courtesy The Historic New Orleans Collection, Museum/Research Center Acc. No. 1974.25.10.72. (Detail page 2.)
Native American Awl and Vial: Collection of Benward L. Treadaway, Jr. Photo by Neil Hurd, courtesy Louisiana Museum Foundation.
pg. 2 Diagram of the Alligator Effigy Mound: Illustration from *Louisiana, Its Land and People* by Fred B. Kniffen, 1968. Courtesy Louisiana State University Press, Baton Rouge, and Dr. George Shannon.
Pre-Columbian Crocodilian Figurine: Collection of the Middle American Research Institute, Tulane University, New Orleans, 70118. Photo courtesy M.A.R.I.
"Medicinal" Alligator Tooth: Private collection, New Orleans. Courtesy Dovie Naquin and the author. Photo by Neil Hurd. Courtesy Louisiana Museum Foundation.
pg. 3 Courtesy the E.A. McIlhenny Natural History Collection, LSU Libraries, Baton Rouge.
pg. 4 Courtesy the E.A. McIlhenny Natural History Collection, LSU Libraries, Baton Rouge.

pg. 5 Courtesy Lake County Museum, Curt Teich Postcard Archives, Wauconda, IL.
pg. 6 Photo by Neal Foy. Courtesy Morton M. Goldberg Auction Galleries, Inc., New Orleans.
pg. 7 Courtesy Louisiana State Museum, New Orleans.
pg. 8 Courtesy Lake County Museum, Curt Teich Postcard Archives, Wauconda, IL.
pg. 9 Collection of the Louisiana State Museum.
pg. 10 Collection of the Gallier House, a museum property of Tulane University, New Orleans.
pg. 17 Leucistic Alligator: Courtesy Audubon Park and Zoological Garden and Louisiana Land and Exploration, Inc., New Orleans. Photo 1988 © Curt Burnette. Courtesy the photographer.
pg. 20 Courtesy Research Files, Lake County Museum, Wauconda, IL.
pg. 21 Collection of the Louisiana State Museum. Photo by Neil Hurd. Courtesy Louisiana Museum Foundation.

Chapter Two

pg. 22 Courtesy the E.A. McIlhenny Natural History Collection, LSU Libraries, Baton Rouge.
pg. 24 Collection of the Department of Prints and Drawings, British Museum. Courtesy Trustees of the British Museum, London.
pg. 26 Collection of the Louisiana Historical Center, Louisiana State Museum.
pg. 27 Courtesy the E.A. McIlhenny Natural History Collection, LSU Libraries, Baton Rouge.
pg. 28 Collection of the Louisiana

Historical Center, Louisiana State Museum.
pg. 29 Collection of the Louisiana Historical Center, Louisiana State Museum, gift of Mrs. Leon Wolf and the Friends of the Cabildo.
pg. 31 Neg. #2A 17483–Plate "Le Crocodile. . . ." Courtesy Photographic Collections, Department of Library Services, American Museum of Natural History, New York.
pg. 33 Courtesy the E.A. McIlhenny Natural History Collection, LSU Libraries, Baton Rouge.
pg. 34 Collection of the Louisiana State Museum, purchased from the artist by legislative act.
pg. 35 Courtesy Special Collections, Howard-Tilton Memorial Library, Tulane University, New Orleans.
pg. 36 Heads of Alligator and American Crocodile: Courtesy Special Collections, Howard-Tilton Memorial Library, Tulane University, New Orleans.
Cross Section of Crocodilian Tooth: Courtesy Special Collections, Howard-Tilton Memorial Library, Tulane University, New Orleans.

Chapter Three

pg. 38 Based on an illustration by William Hutchinson in *Who Needs Alligators?* by Patricia Lauber, 1974. Courtesy U.S. Educational Publishers, Dallas.
pg. 40 Illustration ©1978 Jean Zollinger, reproduced by permission of Morrow Junior Books, William Morrow & Co., Inc., New York.
pg. 41 Collection of the Gallier House, a museum property of Tulane University,

New Orleans.
pg. 42 Skulls of *Albertochampsa langstoni* and *Wannaganosuchus brachymanus.* Collections of the Science Museum of Minnesota, St. Paul. Courtesy Dr. Bruce R. Erickson.
pg. 44 Courtesy the E.A. McIlhenny Natural History Collection, LSU Libraries, Baton Rouge.

Chapter Four

pg. 46 Collection of the Louisiana Historical Center, Louisiana State Museum.
pg. 48 Sculpture: Collection of the Henry Ford Museum and Greenfield Village, Dearborn, Michigan. Woodcut: Collection of the Louisiana Historical Center, Louisiana State Museum.
pg. 49 Collections of the Musée du Nouveau Monde, La Rochelle, France.
pg. 50 Collection of the Louisiana State Museum, gift of the City of New Orleans.
pg. 51 Collection of the Louisiana Historical Center, Louisiana State Museum, gift of the Hon. John M. Wisdom.
pg. 52 Courtesy Lake County Museum, Curt Teich Postcard Archives, Wauconda, IL.
pg. 53 Albert the Alligator: Photo courtesy University of Florida, Gainesville.
Charlie-Bob: Courtesy *The Times,* Shreveport, and the artist.

Chapter Five

pg. 56 Collection of the Louisiana State Museum, gift of the Louisiana Museum Foundation.
pg. 58 Collection of the Louisiana State Museum, gifts of Miss Marguerite

Chiapella. Photo by Neil Hurd, courtesy Louisiana Museum Foundation.

pg. 59 Collection of the Louisiana Historical Center, Louisiana State Museum, gift of Mrs. Leon Wolf and the Friends of the Cabildo.

pg. 60 Courtesy Louisiana State Museum.

Chapter Six

pg. 62 Collection of Dr. and Mrs. Robert Judice, New Orleans; 19th-century paisley shawls courtesy Louisiana State Museum, gifts of Mrs. Emile N. Kuntz, Mrs. Carlo Capomazza Di Campolattaro, Mrs. Paul T. Westervelt, and the Darien Historic Society. Photo by Neil Hurd, courtesy Louisiana Museum Foundation.

pg. 64 Collection of the Louisiana Historical Center, Louisiana State Museum, gift of Mrs. Leon Wolf and Friends of the Cabildo.

pg. 65 Collection of the Louisiana State Museum, gift of the Fashion Group of New Orleans.

pg. 66 Japanese Print: Collection of Dr. Edwin L. Wade. Photo courtesy The Philbrook Museum of Art, Tulsa, OK. Alligator-shod Soldier: Collection of the Louisiana State Museum, gift of Ron Levert.

pg. 67 Courtesy Francis Roger Kelley, New Orleans. Photo by Neil Hurd, courtesy Louisiana Museum Foundation.

Chapter Seven

pg. 68 Courtesy Lake County Museum, Curt Teich Postcard Archives, Wauconda, IL.

pg. 70 Collection of the Louisiana Historical Center, Louisiana State Museum.

pg. 71 Collection of the Louisiana State Museum.

pg. 72 Collection of the Louisiana Historical Center, Louisiana State Museum, gift of Max Keella.

pg. 73 Courtesy The Historic New Orleans Collection, Museum /Research Center Acc. No. 1974.25.31.203.

pg. 74 Courtesy The Historic New Orleans Collection, Museum /Research Center Acc. No. 1979.338(v).

pg. 75 Photo by an unidentified photographer, September 1980. Courtesy Roy Rogers, Sr.

pg. 78 Courtesy Lake County Museum, Curt Teich Postcard Archives, Wauconda, IL.

pg. 79 Affadavit: Courtesy Milton "Mickey" Skyring, clerk/judicial administrator, city court, Baton Rouge. "Charl" Bazil: Courtesy *Morning Advocate* and Louisiana and Lower Mississippi Valley Collections, LSU Libraries, Baton Rouge.

pg. 80 Collection of the Louisiana Historical Center, Louisiana State Museum.

Chapter Eight

pg. 82 Collection of the National Museum of Denmark, Copenhagen. Photo by Niels Elswing.

pg. 84 Courtesy the E.A. McIlhenny Natural History Collection, LSU Libraries, Baton Rouge.

pg. 85 Photo courtesy Dr. R. Duguy, director, Muséum d'Histoire naturelle, La Rochelle, France.

pg. 86 Photo courtesy Ringling Bros. and Barnum & Bailey Circus.

pg. 87 Courtesy Louisiana Museum Foundation and the artist.

pg. 89 Courtesy Mrs. Michael Carboni.

pg. 90-91 Collection of the Louisiana State Museum.

Chapter Nine

pg. 92 Published by Théodore de Bry. Courtesy Rare Book Collections, Earl Gregg Swem Memorial Library, College of William and Mary, Williamsburg, VA.

pg. 93 Collection of the Louisiana State Museum, New Orleans, gift of the West St. Charles Rotary Club.

pg. 94 © Estate of Walt Kelly, courtesy O.G.P.I. and Vaughn L. Glasgow.

pg. 97 Photo ca. 1989, courtesy Gator Lager Beer, Inc., Orlando, FL.

pg. 102 Courtesy Antoine's, New Orleans. Photo by Neil Hurd, courtesy Louisiana State Museum Foundation and Mrs. Michael Carboni.

pg. 103 Photo © 1989 Vaughn L. Glasgow.

pg. 105 Courtesy Lake County Museum, Curt Teich Postcard Archives, Wauconda, IL.

Chapter Ten

pg. 106 New Orleans Jazz Club Collection of the Louisiana State Museum.

pg. 107 Courtesy Hot Jazz and Alligator Gumbo Society, Fort Lauderdale, FL.

pg. 108 Courtesy Lake County Museum, Curt Teich Postcard Archives, Wauconda, IL.

pg. 111 Courtesy Prof. Frank de Caro, Louisiana State University, Baton Rouge.

pg. 113 © 1987 James Stevenson, by permission of Greenwillow Books, William Morrow & Co., Inc., New York.

pg. 114 © 1984 Thacher Hurd, courtesy the artist.

pg. 115 Reproduced by permission of the Dell Publishing Co., New York, courtesy Vaughn L. Glasgow.

pg. 116 Reproduced by permission of Warner Books, New York, courtesy Vaughn L. Glasgow.

pg. 118 Mechanical Alligator: Collection of David Ross McCarty, New Orleans. Photo by Mike Palumbo, courtesy Louisiana State Museum, Marketing and Public Relations. Promotional Still: Collection of the Louisiana State Museum, New Orleans, gift of the Louisiana Museum Foundation.

pg. 119 Collection of the Louisiana State Museum. 007: gift of the Louisiana Museum Foundation. Gator Bait: gift of Dr. and Mrs. Chet Coles.

pg. 120 Collection of the Louisiana State Museum, gift of Alvin Guggenheim & Associates.

Chapter Eleven

pg. 122 Photo © Don Allen, courtesy the photographer.

pg. 123 Collection of the Louisiana State Museum, gift of Raymond H. Weill.

pg. 124 © National Geographic Society, Washington, D.C.

pg. 127 © National Geographic Society, Washington, D.C.

pg. 129 Courtesy *Louisiana Conservationist,* Louisiana Department of Wildlife and Fisheries. Night Hunters: Collection of the Louisiana Historical Center, Louisiana State Museum. Rinow: Courtesy also Louisiana and Lower Mississippi Valley Collections, LSU Libraries, Baton Rouge.

pg. 133 Collection of the Louisiana State Museum, gift of Francis Roger Kelley.

pg. 135 Collection of the late Dr. L.L. Glasgow, courtesy the Glasgow family.

pg. 136 Photo © Don Allen, courtesy the photographer.

pg. 141 Courtesy Louisiana State Museum.

pg. 142 Courtesy Louisiana State Museum.

Chapter Twelve

pg. 144 © Vaughn L. Glasgow.

pg. 146 Photo © Vaughn L. Glasgow.

pg. 147 Photo by John McCusker, courtesy *Times-Picayune*.

pg. 148 Courtesy Rare Book Collections, Earl Gregg Swem Memorial Library, College of William and Mary, Williamsburg, VA.

pg. 149 Collection of the Centre des Archives d'Outre-Mer, Archives Nationales, Aix-en-Provence, France.

pg. 151 Photo © Vaughn L. Glasgow.

pg. 152 Collections of the Louisiana State Museum.

pg. 153 "Poncho" Duhé: Photo by John McCusker, courtesy *Times-Picayune*. Hunter Poling: Courtesy the Fairmont Hotel, New Orleans, and the Louisiana and Lower Mississippi Valley Collections, LSU Libraries, Baton Rouge.

pg. 156 © National Geographic Society, Washington, D.C.

pg. 159 Louisiana Collection, State Library of Louisiana, Baton Rouge.

pg. 161 Photo © Vaughn L. Glasgow.

pg. 162 Photo Sept. 1986 © Michael J. Egermayer.

pg. 163 Courtesy *Louisiana Conservationist*, Louisiana Department of Wildlife and Fisheries and Louisiana and Lower Mississippi Valley Collections, LSU Libraries, Baton Rouge.

pgs. 164 All are photos © Vaughn L. Glasgow, except bottom right photo © Elizabeth Shannon, courtesy the photographer.

Chapter Thirteen

pg. 166 Photo 1986 © Greg Guirard, courtesy the photographer.

pg. 167 Collection of the Muséum d'Histoire naturelle, La Rochelle, France, courtesy Dr. R. Duguy, director.

pg. 171 Icing 'Gators: Photo by Ted Jackson. Courtesy *Times-Picayune*. Breeding Pen: Courtesy Lake County Museum, Curt Teich Postcard Archives, Wauconda, IL.

pg. 174 Photo by Irwin Thompson, courtesy *Times-Picayune*.

pg. 178 Photos 1990 © Greg Guirard, courtesy Steele McAndrew and the photographer.

Chapter Fourteen

pg. 180 Courtesy the Quaker Oats Company, Chicago, IL.

pg. 181 Courtesy Izod-Lacoste, a division of Crystal Brands, Inc., New York, and J. Patrick Hand, New Orleans.

pg. 182 Collection of the Louisiana State Museum, gift of the Friends of the Cabildo.

pg. 183 Courtesy Lord VJ's Drinking Establishment, New Orleans. Photo by Neil Hurd, courtesy Louisiana Museum Foundation.

pg. 184 Courtesy International Paper Company, a New York corporation, Two Manhattanville Road, Purchase, NY 10577.

pg. 185 Courtesy Gator Lager Beer, Inc., Orlando, FL, and Ms. Maureen Krail, New Orleans. Photo by Neil Hurd, courtesy Louisiana Museum Foundation.

pgs. 186-187 Courtesy Lake County Museum, Curt Teich Postcard Archives, Wauconda IL.

pg. 188 Courtesy Tipitina's Music Club (ca. 1980) and the Upperline Restaurant (ca. 1989), New Orleans, James W. Green, Ms. JoAnn Clevenger, Mrs. Margaret Harter, and the Louisiana State Museum.

pg. 189 Rax: Courtesy Rax Restaurants, Columbus, and *Gambit*. Gator Supply Co. logo: Courtesy Gator Supply Co., Inc.

pg. 190 Logos courtesy Gator Hawk and Alligator Drain and Sewer Cleaning Service.

Chapter Fifteen

pg. 192 Courtesy Gucci, New York.

pg. 195 Courtesy Special Collections, Howard-Tilton Memorial Library, Tulane University, New Orleans.

pg. 196 Courtesy Lake County Museum, Curt Teich Postcard Archives, Wauconda IL.

pg. 199 Collections of the Louisiana State Museum, gifts of Dr. A.E. Merchant, Mrs. Rosemarie Fowler, and Francis Roger Kelley. Photo by Neil Hurd, courtesy Louisiana Museum Foundation.

pg. 201 Photo 1988 © Rebecca Venable.

pg. 202 Photo by Michael H. K. Kim. Courtesy Sauvage Korea.

Chapter Sixteen

pg. 204 Collection of the Gallier House, a museum property of Tulane University, New Orleans.

pg. 205 Courtesy Sauvage Korea and Michael H.K. Kim.

pg. 206 Collection of the Louisiana State Museum, gift of Mrs. George Berry.

pg. 207 Courtesy *Louisiana Conservationist*, Louisiana Department of Wildlife and Fisheries, collection of the Louisiana Historical Center, Louisiana State Museum.

pg. 208 Photo 1988 © Vaughn L. Glasgow.

pg. 210 Photo 1989 © Vaughn L. Glasgow.

pg. 215 Courtesy Lake County Museum, Curt Teich Postcard Archives, Wauconda, IL.

pg. 216 Detail of a photo by Rocky Piliero, Peter Rogers Associates, for Judith Leiber, Inc., New York, courtesy Mrs. Judith Leiber.

Chapter Seventeen

pg. 218 Collection of the New Orleans Museum of Art, gift of Prof. Stephen E. Ambrose, courtesy New Orleans Museum of Art.

pg. 219 Photo reproduced by courtesy of the Marisa del Re Gallery, New York.

pg. 220 Basket: Collection of the Louisiana State Museum, gift of George Sillan.

Alligator Seizing Crane: Collection of the Gallier House, a museum property of **Tulane University, New Orleans.**

pg. 221 Alligator-Tooth Necklace: Photo by Neil Hurd, courtesy, Louisiana Museum Foundation. Alligator Juju: Courtesy the artist. Photo by Judy Cooper.

pg. 222 Collection of the Louisiana Historical Center, Louisiana State Museum.

pg. 223 Photo © 1990 Vaughn L. Glasgow.

pg. 224 Photo © Mickey Mclean. Courtesy the artist.

pg. 225 Courtesy *Morning Advocate*, Baton Rouge. Photo by Vicki Ferstel.

pg. 226 1942 © Estate of Walt Kelly, courtesy O.G.P.I. and Vaughn L. Glasgow.

pg. 227 1989 © King Features Syndicate, Inc., reprinted with special permission of King Features Syndicate, Inc., New York.

pg. 228 Collection of the Louisiana Historical Center, Louisiana State Museum.

pg. 229 Private collection, New Orleans, courtesy the estate of the artist and Vaughn L. Glasgow.

Chapter Eighteen

pg. 230–231 Courtesy Lake County Museum, Curt Teich Postcard Archives, Wauconda, IL.

pg. 232 Collection of the Henry Ford Museum and Greenfield Villiage, Dearborn, MI.

pg. 233 Collection of the Louisiana State Museum; gift of Joseph F. H. Voltz.

pg. 235 Courtesy Lake County Museum, Curt Teich Postcard Archives, Wauconda, IL.

SELECTED BIBLIOGRAPHY

EXTRA! EXTRA! READ ALL ABOUT IT!
PARTIAL BIBLIOGRAPHY
OF SOURCES CONSULTED

Limited space does not allow listing of all resources utilized in preparation of this volume. Complete bibliography and research data are found in alligator research files created 1988–1991 by the Office of Special Projects of the Louisiana State Museum. These may be consulted at the Louisiana Historical Center of the Louisiana State Museum, located in the Old U. S. Branch Mint, 400 Esplanade Avenue, New Orleans, Louisiana 70116. Prior appointment is required and may be scheduled by writing the Louisiana Historical Center, Louisiana State Museum, P.O. Box 2448, New Orleans, LA 70176.

Ackerman, Diane, "A Reporter at Large: Crocodilians." *The New Yorker*, Oct. 10, 1988.

Acts Passed by the General Assembly of the State of Louisiana at the Regular Session. Baton Rouge: Daily State Pub., 1908.

Adams, Ezra. "It Takes a Lot of Nerve to Catch an Alligator." *Morning Advocate*, Baton Rouge, Dec. 6, 1959.

Adams, Louis A. *Revised Register of Points and Landings* (aka *Adams' Directory of Points and Landings in the South and Southwest*). N.p.: Louis A. Adams, 1877.

Aiges, Scott, "Gators Can't Hide from the Hunters on Their Tails." *Times-Picayune*, New Orleans, Sept. 10, 1989.

"Alligator, (The)." *Harper's New Monthly Magazine*, Vol. X, Dec. 1854–May 1855.

"Alligators for Research." *LSU Alumni News*, Sept.–Oct. 1953.

"Alligators in International Commerce May Soon Be Permitted, Breaux Says." *State-Times*, Baton Rouge (undated clipping), late March or early April, 1979. Vertical file "A," Louisiana and Lower Mississippi Valley Collections, Louisiana State University, Baton Rouge.

"Alligators Not Protected in 14 Parishes." *Louisiana Game, Fur & Fish*, Feb. 1948.

"Archie McPhee" mail order catalogue. Seattle: Archie McPhee, 1989.

Arthur, Stanley C. *Audubon, An Intimate Life of the American Woodsman*. New Orleans: Harmanson, 1937.

——. *The Fur Animals of Louisiana*. New Orleans: [Louisiana] Department of Conservation, 1928.

"Asian Grazin'." *Southpoint*, Oct. 1989.

Ashe, Thomas. *Travels in America Performed in 1806*. Newburyport: William Sawyer, 1808.

Ashley, Pam, comp. and ed. *The Alligator Cookbook*. Orlando: National Alligator Association, n.d.

Audubon, John James. *Delineations of American Scenery and Character*. London: Simpkin, Marshall, Hamilton, Kent & Co., Ltd., 1926.

——. *Journal of John James Audubon Made During His Trip to New Orleans in 1820-1821*. Howard Corning, ed. Boston: The Club of Odd Volumes, 1929.

——. *Letters of John James Audubon*, Vol. II. Howard Corning, ed. Boston: The Club of Odd Volumes, 1930.

——. "Observations on the Natural History of the Alligator." *Louisiana Conservation Review*, Dec. 1931.

"Audubon View, (The)." *Audubon*, Aug. or Sept., 1972 (unidentified photocopy). Louisiana and Lower Mississippi Valley Collections, Louisiana State University, Baton Rouge.

Baird, Robert. *Impressions and Experiences of the West Indies and North America in 1849*. Philadelphia: Lea & Blanchard, 1850.

Ball, Zachary and Saliee O'Brien. " 'Gator Boy [1947]." Reprint in *TAB Animal Tales*, Hardy R. Finch and Mary Dirlam, eds. New York: Scholastic Corporation, 1953.

Barbour, Thomas. "Alligators and Crocodiles." *Atlantic Monthly*, July, 1944.

Barrier, Michael and Martin Williams, eds. *A Smithsonian Book of Comic-Book Comics*. Washington, D.C.: Smithsonian Institution Press, 1981.

Barth, Jack, Doug Kirby, Ken Smith and Mike Wilkins. *Roadside America*. New York: Simon & Schuster, 1986.

Bartram, William. *Travels Through North and South Carolina, Georgia, East and West Florida*, 2nd ed. London, 1794.

"Beauty and the Beast." *Newsweek*, May 1, 1989.

Bennet, Ed. Turner. *The Tower Menagerie*. London: printed for Robert Jennings, Poultry, 1829.

Bernard, Duke of Saxe-Weimar Eisenach (HRH). *Travels Through North America During the Years 1825 and 1826*. Philadelphia: Carey, Lea & Carey, 1828.

Bienvenu, Marcelle. "Cook Hooks Her Own Gator." *Times-Picayune*, New Orleans, Sept. 20, 1990.

Blanchard, John. "Gruntin' and Grabbin' for 'Gators, by Capt. Harry Reno as told to John Blanchard." *Louisiana Conservationist*, May–June 1954.

Book of Reptiles (The). London: John Parker, 1835.

Bossu, Jean-Bernard. "*New Travels in North America, 1751–62.*" Samuel D. Dickinson, trans. Natchitoches: Northwestern State University Press, 1982.

——. *New Voyages in North America, 1751–62*. Louisiana Historical Center, Louisiana State Museum, New Orleans. W.P.A. translation in typescript.

Bostwick, O., "ALLIGATOR LINE, Mobile to Augusta, Via Florida," advertisement. *True American*, New Orleans, Dec. 11, 1839.

Boulenger, G. A. "Remarks on the Chinese Alligator." In *Proceedings of the Scientific Meetings of the Zoological Society of London for the Year 1890*. London: Zoological Society of London, 1890.

Bowman, Val. "400 Feet of 'Gators." *Times-Picayune*, New Orleans, Dec. 30, 1945.

Brackenridge, H. M. *Views of Louisiana*. Pittsburgh: Cramer, Spear and Eichbaum, 1814.

Branan, Will, "Why I Am Not Allergic to 'Gators— Ugh!—or Am I Not?" *Louisiana Conservation Review*, Summer 1940.

Brasher, Mabel, *et al. Louisiana, A Study of the State*. New York: Johnson Publishing, 1929.

"Bringing in the 'Gators." *Terrebonne Magazine*. Sept. 1985.

Brunvand, Jan H. *The Vanishing Hitchhiker*. New York: Norton, 1981.

(de) Bry, Théodore, pub. *Historia Americae sive Novi Orbis*, Part II. Frankfurt: Théodore de Bry, 1591.

Buckley, William F. Jr. *See You Later, Alligator*. New York: Dell Publishing, 1986.

Buffon and de Lacépède. *Histoire Naturelle extraite de Buffon et de Lacépède*. Tours: Alfred Mame et fils, 1883.

"Business Class." *Vogue*, Aug. 1989.

Carr, Archie. "Alligators, Dragons in Distress." *National Geographic Magazine*, Jan. 1967.

Carrier, Cornelia. " 'Gator Paw Removal Ok'd, Purchaser Reports Some Beginning to Rot." *Times-Picayune*, New Orleans, Sept. 28, 1972.

Carter, Hodding. *Lower Mississippi*. New York and Toronto: Farrar & Rinehart, 1942.

Catesby, Mark. *The Natural History of Carolina, Florida and the Bahama Islands*. London, 1771.

Cathcart, James Leander. "Southern Louisiana and Southern Alabama in 1819: The Journal of James Leander Cathcart," Walter Pritchard, Fred B. Kniffen and Clair A. Brown, eds. *Louisiana Historical Quarterly*, July 1945.

"Chain Saw Masterpiece." *La Louisiane*, Fall 1989.

[Chapman, Isaac D. ?]. "The Editor Learns . . . About Alligator Hunting." *Roosevelt Review*, Oct. 1947 (text first published in *Louisiana Game, Fur and Fish*, Sept. 1947, by Isaac D. Chapman).

(de) Charlevoix, Pierre F. X. *Charlevoix's Louisiana*. Baton Rouge and London: Louisiana State University Press, 1977.

(de) Chateaubriand, François Auguste René (Vicomte). *Atala*. Paris: Hachette, 1863 (first published 1801).

Cohen, Kate. "Daytripping: Alligators Are the Lure at Hammond Farm." *Times-Picayune*, New Orleans, Aug. 10, 1990.

Coleman, Loren. "Alligators-in-the-Sewers: A Journalistic Origin." *Journal of American Folklore*, No. 92, 1979.

——. "Erratic Crocodilians and Other Things." *The Info Journal*, Feb. 1974.

[Connelly, Will]. "A Connoisseur's Guide to HAGS (and Other Trivia) (for use by Reporters, Interviewers and other Oppressed Classes) [1989]." Special Projects alligator research files, Louisiana State Museum, New Orleans. Press kit, Hot Jazz and Alligator Gumbo Society, Fort Lauderdale, 1989.

Cook, Mike. "Allen Apparently Did No Damage to Louisiana Alligators." *State-Times*, Baton Rouge, Aug. 14, 1980.

——. "Alligators Now Near Extinction But Federal, Texas Legislation Should Help." *State-Times*, Baton Rouge, Mar. 16, 1967.

——. "Drop Charges in Gator Hides Case in Orleans." *State-Times*, Baton Rouge, Dec. 23, 1966.

——. "1,080 'Gator Hides Confiscated At Abbeville by WLFC Agents." *State-Times*, Baton Rouge, June 9, 1966.

——. "Scientists Use Bellow, 'Beep Beep' of Gator." *State-Times*, Baton Rouge, May 14, 1970.

OFFUTT INNS

Our Specialty is People

*U.S.GPO:1996-755-009/22007

Cooper, Asahel W. Jr. Untitled. Address presented at the regular meeting of the Wyvern Club, New Orleans, Sept. 20, 1972. Wyvern Club Collection, Louisiana Historical Center, Louisiana State Museum, New Orleans. Typescript.

Cooter, Alice. "Pet Alligators, Owned by Negro Here, Are Used to Plow Back-Yard Garden." *Morning Advocate*, Baton Rouge, Mar. 2, 1941 or 1946 (poorly dated clipping).

Crain, Jim. "State Spending Myth Dies Hard." *Louisiana State Voice*, Baton Rouge, 2nd Quarter, 1989.

Creecy, Col. James R. Untitled poem, as quoted in Edward C. Carter II, ed., *The Papers of Benjamin Henry Latrobe*, quoting from Ulrich Bonnell Phillips, *Life and Labor in the Old South*. Boston: Little, Brown & Co.,1929.

Crispin, A. C. *V*. New York: Pinnacle Books, 1984.

Cumming, W. P., R. A. Skelton and D. B. Quinn. *The Discovery of North America*. New York: American Heritage Press, 1972.

Cuvier (Baron). *The Animal Kingdom*, Vol. IX. London: Whittacker, Treacher & Co., 1831.

Dabney, Thomas Ewing. "Alligator Hunting No More at New Orleans." *Inn Dixie*, July 1955.

Daley, Robert. *The World Beneath the City*. New York: Lippincott, 1959 (as cited by Brunvand, 1981).

Daly, Katharine. "Orleanian Runs Alligator Farm as Hobby; Tony Mullet Lives Quiet Life There with Hundreds of Saurians as Pets." *Item*, New Orleans, Nov. 21, 1937.

Darby, William. *A Geographical Description of the State of Louisiana*. Philadelphia: John Melish, 1816.

Daudin, François-Marie. *Histoire naturelle des reptiles*, Vol. 2. Paris, 1803.

Davis, Frank. "Do They Really Hunt Alligators?" *Louisiana Woods & Water*, Vol. 2, No. 7, 1973.

——. *The Frank Davis Seafood Notebook*. Gretna: Pelican Publishing, 1983.

Dawson, Sarah Morgan. *A Confederate Girl's Diary*. 1913. Reprint, James I. Robertson, Jr., ed. Bloomington: Indiana University Press,1960.

Dawson, Victoria. "Bayou greenbacks lay 'golden eggs.' *Times-Picayune*, New Orleans, July 2, 1989.

——. "Rifle-toting Gator Hunters Stalk Data for Researchers." *Times-Picayune*, New Orleans, July 24, 1989.

Deak, Gloria. "Picturing Mrs. Trollope's America." *The Magazine Antiques*, Nov. 1988.

Denuzière, Jacqueline and Charles Henri Brandt. *Cuisine de Louisiane, Histoire et recettes*. Paris: Editions Bonoël, 1989.

Diderot, Denis and Jean le Rond d'Alembert, co-comps./eds. *Encyclopédie, ou Dictionnaire Raisonné des Sciences des Arts et des Métiers*, Vols. I, IA, IV, VI, VIII, IX, and Planches. Paris and other cities: volumes issued 1751, 1754, 1762, 1765, 1768, 1771, and 1789.

Didier, Karen. "Ponchatoula's Alligator Mascot, Hardhide Jr., Dies." *Morning Advocate*, Baton Rouge, undated clipping, [Jan. 1990]. Vertical file "A," Louisiana and Lower Mississippi Valley Collections, Louisiana State University, Baton Rouge.

Diehl, William. *Thai Horse*. New York: Ballantine Books, 1989.

Ditmars, Raymond Lee. *The Reptile Book*. Garden City: Doubleday, Page & Co., 1920.

——. *Reptiles of the World*. 1910. Reprint. New York: The Macmillan Company, 1959.

Dorson, Richard M.. *American Folklore*. Chicago: University of Chicago Press, 1959.

——. *America in Legend: Folklore from the Colonial Period to the Present*. New York: Pantheon Books, 1973 (as quoted by Coleman, 1979).

Dowler, Bennet, M.D. "Contributions to the Natural History of the Alligator [1846]." Offprint from *New Orleans Medical and Surgical Journal*, Nov. 1846. New Orleans: B. M. Norman, 1846.

Duffy, Joan I. "La. Alligators Enter Computer Age." *State-Times*, Baton Rouge, Nov. 21, 1980.

DuFour, Charles "Pie." "Alligators Won Battle of New Orleans,. *Times-Picayune*, New Orleans, Jan. 7, 1951.

Dundee, Harld A. and Douglas A. Rossman. *The Amphibians and Reptiles of Louisiana*. Baton Rouge and London: Louisiana State University Press, 1989.

Dunnavant, Bob. "Alabama to Deport Alligators Received from Louisiana *State-Times*." Baton Rouge, June 12, 1980.

Duvallon, ed. *Vue de la Colonie Espagnole du Mississipi [sic] ou des Provinces de Louisiane et Floride Occidentale, en L'Année 1802*. Paris, 1803.

East, Charles. "BR Man Recuperating After Bout with 'Gator." *State-Times*, Baton Rouge, June 27, 1956.

Ehrenberg, Herman. *With Milam and Fannin: Adventures of a German Boy in Texas' Revolution*, Charlotte Churchill, trans., Henry Smith, ed. Austin: The Pemberton Press, 1968.

Elsey, Ruth M., Ted Joanen, Larry McNease and Valentine Lance. "Stress and Plasma Corticosterone Levels in the American Alligator— Relationships with Stocking Density and Nesting

Success." *Comp. Biochem. Physiol.*, Vol. 95A, No. 1, 1990.

English, Terry. " 'Gator Farm Raided, 155 Reptiles Stolen." *State-Times*, Baton Rouge, July 15, 1963.

Erickson, Bruce R. "*Albertochampsa Langstoni*, Gen. Et. Sp. Nov., A New Alligator From the Cretaceous of Alberta." *Scientific Publications of The Science Museum of Minnesota*, N. S., Mar. 31, 1972.

——. "Alligator Ancestors." *The Explorer*, Fall 1972.

——. "The Gators of Hobcaw." *Encounters*, Mar. –Apr. 1986.

——. "The Wannagan Creek Quarry and Its Reptilian Fauna [Bullion Creek Formation, Paleocene] in Billings County, North Dakota." in Don L. Halvorson, *Report of Investigation No. 72, North Dakota Geological Survey, 1982*, Grand Forks: Associated Printers, Inc., n.d.

——. "*Wannaganosuchus*, A New Alligator from the Paleocene of North America." *Journal of Paleontology*, Vol. 56, Mar. 1982.

"Experience Annie Miller's Swamp Tour." *New Orleans Tourist News*, Mar. 1990.

Faciane, Valerie M. "Gator Off Endangered List in 9 More Parishes." *Times-Picayune*, New Orleans, Jan. 28, 1979.

Farrell, Diane. "When You're 90, Will You Hunt Alligators?" *Times-Picayune*, New Orleans, Dec. 7, 1947.

Fergus, George. "More on Alligators in the Sewers." *Journal of American Folklore*, No. 93, 1980 (as cited by Brunvand, 1981).

Ferguson, M. W. J. and Ted Joanen. "Temperature of Egg Incubation Determines Sex in *Alligator mississippiensis*." *Nature*, Apr. 29, 1982.

"Finger Lickin' Alligator Ribs." *Cooks*, Apr. 1989.

"First Alligator Arrest of 1951." *Roosevelt Review*, Feb. 1951.

Fitzmorris, Tom. "How to Enjoy Alligator." *Go-New Orleans*, Apr. 1989.

Flint, Timothy. *A Condensed Geography and History of the Western States in the Mississippi Valley* (aka *Flint's Geography*) Vol. 1. Cincinnati: E. H. Flint,1828.

Forest, P. "Forest's Voyage aux Etats-Unis de l'Amerique en 1831," Georges J. Joyaux, ed. *Louisiana Historical Quarterly*, Oct. 1956.

Frederick, Donald J. "Alligators Use Smell to Find Meals, Mates." *Sunday Advocate*, Baton Rouge, Nov. 19, 1989.

Fundaburk, Emma Lila and Mary Douglass Fundaburk Foreman, eds. *Sun Circles and Human Hands: The Southeastern Indians' Art and Industries*. Luverne: Emma Lila Fundaburk, 1957.

Garcia, Chris. "Exotic Animals Lure Teachers to Folsom Area." *The Picayune*, New Orleans, Aug. 16, 1990.

Gator Lager Beer. "Gator Lager Beer Among First Beer Manufacturers to Stress Responsibility, Moderate Consumption [ca. 1988]." Special Projects alligator research files, Louisiana Historical Center, Louisiana State Museum, New Orleans. Press release.

——. "Tastes Great, Less Fattening—All Natural Gator Jerky [1990]." Special Projects alligator research files, Louisiana Historical Center, Louisiana State Museum, New Orleans. Press release.

"Girl's Battle with Alligators." *Chicago Tribune*, undated clipping [1900], Research files, Lake County Museum, Wauconda, Ill.

Glasgow, Vaughn L. "Caught [1989]." Narration for conceptual piece by Elizabeth Shannon, performed at the annual meeting of the American Association of Museums, New Orleans, June 1989. Special Projects alligator research files, Louisiana Historical Center, Louisiana State Museum, New Orleans. Typescript.

——. "The Earth Trembles with His Thunder." *Image File*, Vol. 6, No. 1, 1990.

Glazier, Willard. *Down the Great River; Embracing an Account of the Discovery of the True Source of the Mississippi*. Philadelphia: Hubbard Brothers, 1892.

Graham, Frank and Ada Graham. *Alligators*. New York: Delacorte Press, 1979.

Graves, Ralph A. "Louisiana, Land of Perpetual Romance." *National Geographic Magazine*, Apr. 1930.

Gray, John Edward. Synopsis reptilium; *or Short Descriptions of the Species of Reptiles, Part I—Cataphracta*. London, 1831.

Gray, Leonard. "Paradis Residents Say 'No!' to Alligators." *River Parishes Guide*, St. Charles Parish, Louisiana, May 28, 1989.

"Great South—Louisiana (The)." *Scribner's Magazine*, Nov. 1873.

Gross, Ruth Belov. *Alligators and Other Crocodilians*. New York: Four Winds Press, 1976.

(de) Grummond, Jane Lucas. *The Baratarians and the Battle of New Orleans*. Baton Rouge: Louisiana State University Press, 1961.

Guérin, M. F.-E.. *Dictionnaire Pittoresque D'Histoire Naturelle et Des Phénomènes de la Nature*, Vol. 1. Paris, 1834.

Gunther, Albert C. L. G. *The Reptiles of British India*. London: Robert Hardwicke, 1864.

Haas, Edward F. "Black Cat, Uncle Earl, Edwin and the Kingfish: The Wit of Modern Louisiana Politics." *Louisiana History*, Louisiana Historical Association, Lafayette, Louisiana, 1988.

Hansen, Harry, ed. *Louisiana, A Guide to the State*, rev. ed., American Guide Series. New York: Hastings House, 1971.

Harris, Joel Chandler. *Nights with Uncle Remus*. Detroit: Singing Tree Press, 1971.

Henry, Tom. "First There Was a T-shirt, Then There Was Gator Lager." *The Tampa Tribune*, Tampa, Aug. 26, 1990.

"*A Herpetological Cookbook* Tells How to Cook Amphibians and Reptiles." *Terrebonne Magazine*, Sept. 1985.

Hiaasen, Carl. *Tourist Season*. New York: Warner Books, 1987.

Hill, Beron Earle. *Recollections of an Artillery Officer*, Vol. II. London: Richard Bentley, 1836.

Hines, T. C. and K. D. Keenlyne. "Alligator Attacks on Humans in Florida." In *Proceedings of the Annual Conference of the Southeastern Association of Fish and Wildlife Agencies*, Vol. 30. N.p.: Southeastern Association of Fish and Wildlife Agencies, 1976.

"His Majesty, the King of Alligators." *American Magazine*, May 1945.

Historical Sketch Book and Guide to New Orleans and Environs with Map. New York: Will H. Coleman, 1885.

Hoage, R. J., ed. *Perceptions of Animals in American Culture*. Washington, D.C.: Smithsonian Institution Press, 1989.

Hodgson, Adam. *Remarks During a Journey Through North America in the Years 1819, 1820 and 1821*. New York: Samuel Whiting, 1823.

Holbrook, Dr. John Edwards. *North American Herpetology; or, A Description of the Reptile Inhabitants of the United States*, Vol. II. Philadelphia: J. Dobson, 1842.

Holy Bible, Containing the Old and New Testaments Translated Out of the Original Tongues and with the Former Translations. Newburyport: E. W., Wm. B. & H. G. Allen, 1813.

Horn, Jack. "White Alligators and Republican Cousins—The Stuff of Urban Folklore." *Psychology Today*, Nov. 1975 (as quoted by Coleman, 1979).

Hot Jazz & Alligator Gumbo Society. Bulletin #45, Plantation: Hot Jazz and Alligator Gumbo Society, Mar. 1984.

Hurd, Thacher. *Mama Don't Allow*. [New York]: Harper & Row, 1984.

——. "Is Alligator a Friend of Fish?" *Louisiana Department of Conservation Review*, Nov. 1931.

Joanen, Ted and Larry McNease. "Alligator Farming Programs in Louisiana." Paper presented to the I.U.C.N. Survival Services Commission, Crocodile Specialist Group. Lae, Papua, New Guinea, Oct. 1988.

——. "Culture of the American Alligator." In *International Zoo Yearbook*, Vol. 19. Dorett, England: Henry Ling, Ltd., Dorset Press, 1979.

Joanen, Ted, Larry McNease, Johnie Tarver and John Behler. "Captive Propagation of Alligators in Louisiana." *ASRA Journal*, Vol. 2, No. 1, 1983.

Johnson, Clifton. *Highways and Byways of the Mississippi Valley*. New York: Macmillan Co., 1906.

Johnston, Mrs. William Preston (née Margaret Avery). "Trouble, Trouble, Brer Alligator." *Journal of American Folklore*, Vol. 9, 1896.

"Joseph" [pseud.] *Cajuns of Louisiana Bayous . . . the People and the Legends*. New Orleans: Authentic American Art, 1984.

Kalmbach, Fred. "Officials Say Glut of Alligator Hides Choking Industry." *State-Times*, Baton Rouge, Jan. 8, 1991.

Kane, Harnett T. *The Bayous of Louisiana*. New York: Bonanza Books, ©1943.

——. *Deep Delta Country*. Erskine Caldwell, ed. New York: Duell, Sloan & Pearce, 1944.

Katz, Shelley. *Alligator*. New York: Dell Publishing, 1977.

Kellog, Remington. "The Habits and Economic Importance of Alligators," U. S. Department of Agriculture Technical Bulletin No. 147. U. S. Department of Agriculture, Washington, D. C., 1929.

Kerrigan, Anthony. "Dixie Dinosaurs." *Inn Dixie*, Mar. 1948.

King, Edward. *The Great South*. Hartford: American Publishing, 1875.

Kirkland, Mike. "Pet Gators." *Louisiana Conservationist*, Sept. 1957.

Kleinpeter, Jim. "New Swamp Tour Gives Alligators the Top Billing." Unidentified newspaper clipping [probably *Times-Picayune*, New Orleans,] n.d. [ca. 1982].

Kniffen, Fred B. *The Indians of Louisiana*. Gretna: Pelican Publishing, n.d.

——. *Louisiana, Its Land and People*. Baton Rouge and London: Louisiana State University Press, 1968.

Kniffen, Fred B., Hiram F. Gregory and George A. Stokes. *The Historic Indian Tribes of Louisiana.* Baton Rouge: Louisiana State University Press, 1987.

Kushlan, J. A. and J. C. Simon. "Egg Manipulation by the American Alligator." *Journal of Herpetology,* Vol. 15, No. 4, 1981.

(de) Lacépède, G. E. deLaV. (Comte). *L'Histoire Naturelle des Quadrupèdes Ovipares, des Serpens, des Poissons et des Cétacés.* Paris: P. Dumenil, 1836.

Laney, Rex, ed. *Do You Know Louisiana?* Baton Rouge: Tourist Division, [Louisiana] State Department of Commerce and Industry, Baton Rouge, [1938].

———. *This Is Louisiana.* Baton Rouge: Tourist Bureau, [Louisiana] Department of Commerce and Industry, Baton Rouge, 1940.

Latour, Major A. Lagarrière. "Plan of Attack." Map, 1815. Louisiana State Museum, New Orleans.

Lauber, Patricia. *Who Needs Alligators?* Champaign: Garrard Publishing, 1974.

(de) Laudonnière. *A Notable Historie Containing Voyages made by Certaine French Captaines into Florida* . . . Paris: 1586 (as quoted by W. P. Cumming *et al.,* 1972).

LeBlanc, Olen. "Alligator Trapping Industry Maintains Steady Pace In La." *Journal,* Baton Rouge, Apr. 2, 1950.

Lee, Candace. "Alligator Meat 'Delicacy' Rotting in Louisiana Swamps." *State-Times,* Baton Rouge, Sept. 22, 1979.

Leon, Warren and Roy Rosenzweig, eds. *History Museums in the United States: A Critical Assessment.* Chicago and Urbana: University of Illinois Press, 1989.

LePage du Pratz, Antoine Simon. *Histoire de la Louisiane,* Vol. II. Paris: 1758.

Levasseur, A. *Lafayette in America in 1824 and 1825: Journal of a Voyage to the United States,* Vol. II. Philadelphia: Carey and Lea, 1829. Reprint. New York: Research Reprints, 1970.

Lewis, Meriwether and William Clark. *Travels in the Interior Parts of America; Communicating Discoveries Made in Exploring the Missouri, Red River and Washita, by Captains Lewis and Clark, Doctor Sibley, and Mr. Dunbar.* London: Richard Phillips, 1807.

Lightfoot, Linda. " 'Gator Meat: Swamp Beast on Its Way to Louisiana Supper Tables." *State-Times,* Baton Rouge, June 30, 1982.

Liner, Ernest A. *A Herpetological Cookbook*[:] *How to Cook Amphibians and Reptiles.* Houma: privately printed, 1978.

Lippmann, Peter. *The Great Escape, or The Sewer Story.* New York: The Golden Press, 1973 (as cited by Brunvand, 1981).

Lockwood, C. C. *The Gulf Coast; Where Land Meets Sea.* Baton Rouge: Louisiana State University Press, 1984.

Louisiana Film and Video Index, Vaughn L. Glasgow *et al.,* comps. Office of Special Projects, Louisiana State Museum, New Orleans. Extensive research and informational files.

Louisiana Fur and Alligator Advisory Council. "Louisiana's Alligator Industry [1989]." Special Projects alligator research files, Louisiana Historical Center, Louisiana State Museum, New Orleans. Leaflet.

Louisiana Seafood Promotion & Marketing Board. "Louisiana Alligator Recipes [ca. 1989]." Special Projects alligator research files, Louisiana Historical Center, Louisiana State Museum, New Orleans. Brochure.

Louisiana Revised Statutes of 1950.

Luke, Margie Laws, ed. *Gator Gourmet.* Franklin: International Alligator Festival, 1982.

Luxuriant Louisiana. Baton Rouge: [Louisiana] Department of Agriculture and Immigration, 1947.

Lyell, Sir Charles. *A Second Visit to the United States of North America,* Vol. II. London: John Murray, 1849.

Malik, Tom, and Barbara Malik, eds. *"Gator."* Morgan City: privately published, 1980.

Maltin, Leonard, ed. *TV Movies,* 1979–80 rev. ed. New York: Signet Books, New American Library, 1978.

Manhattaner in New Orleans (The). New York: A. O. Hall, 1851.

Martin, Lisa. "Gator Aid: Hunters Put Hides on Auction Block." *Times-Picayune,* New Orleans, Oct. 10, 1986.

Martin, Margaret. "Charlie the Alligator Tells All." *The Shreveport Times,* Shreveport, undated clipping, [ca.1985].

Mason, D. P. Manuscript letter, Camp Parapet (Carrollton, near New Orleans) to mother and sister (Northwood, New Hampshire), Mar. 24, 1863. Louisiana Historical Center, Louisiana State Museum, New Orleans (LSM 1975.18, LHC RG 68).

Massey, Phil. "Louisiana: With More Hectares Devoted to Aquaculture Than Any Other State, Louisiana Claims a Prominent Role in U. S. Aquaculture." *World Aquaculture,* Mar. 1, 1989.

Matsuura, Patsy. "Alligator for Dinner?" *The Honolulu Advertiser*, Honolulu, Apr. 6, 1986.

Mazel, Jean. *Louisiane, Terre d'Aventure*. Paris: Robert Laffont, 1979.

McIlhenny, E. A. "Ned." *The Alligator's Life History*. 1934. Reprint. Berkeley: Ten Speed Press, 1987.

——."Nature Ramblings." *The Progress*, Hammond, July 8, 1938.

——. "Notes on Incubation and Growth of Alligators." *Copeia*, July 30, 1934.

McNealy, Martel. "Alligator Hunting Another Source of Jefferson Parish Wealth." Unidentified clipping [possibly *Jefferson Parish Review*], ca. 1945. Vertical file "A," Louisiana and Lower Mississippi Valley Collections, Louisiana State University, Baton Rouge.

McNease, Larry and Ted Joanen. "A Study of Immature Alligators on Rockefeller Refuge, Louisiana." In *Proceedings of the Twenty-Eighth Annual Meeting, Southeastern Association of Game and Fish Commissioners*, White Sulphur Springs, West Virginia, 1974. N.p.: Southeastern Association of Game and Fish Commissioners, n.d.

McNeely, Martel. "Merchandising Mr. Gator's Hide." *Roosevelt Review*, 30 Jan. 1947.

——. "Merchandising Mr. Gator's Hide." *New Orleans Port Record*, June 6, 1946, (slightly lengthened version of article by same author and title appearing in *Roosevelt Review*).

McSherry, Julia Murchison. "The Return of the Gator: Louisiana's Management Success Story." *Louisiana Conservationist*, July–Aug. 1981.

——. "The Gator Man of Bayou Blue." *Louisiana Conservationist*, July– Aug. 1981.

Medlin, Faith. *A Gourmet's Book of Beasts*. New York: Paul S. Eriksson, n.d.

Merrill, Ellen C. "The Swiss and German Connection: The First Migration to the Gulf Coast Under French Colonial Rule." *Gulf Coast Historical Review*, Spring 1988.

Michaels, Pat and W. McFadden Duffy. "Suicide Boys of the Bayou." *Men*, May 1953.

Miller, Annie. "They Stay Young Grabbing 'Gators." *Times-Picayune*, New Orleans, May 8, 1960.

Minton, Sherman A. and Madge Rutherford Minton. *Giant Reptiles*. New York: Charles Scribner's Sons, 1973 (as quoted by Coleman, 1979).

(de) Montigny, DuMont. "Historical Memoire on Louisiana, 1753." Louisiana Historical Center, Louisiana State Museum, New Orleans. W.P.A. translation in typescript.

Moody, Michael W., Paul D. Coreil and James E. Rutledge. "Alligator as Food." *Louisiana Agriculture*, Fall 1980 (reprinted in Moody and Coreil, comps., *Alligator Production Manual*).

——. "Alligator Meat: An Evaluation of a New Seafood [n.d.]." Special Projects alligator research files, Louisiana Historical Center, Louisiana State Museum, New Orleans. Louisiana Cooperative Extension Service typescript.

Moody, Michael W. and Paul D. Coreil, comps. *Alligator Production Manual*. Baton Rouge: Louisiana Cooperative Extension Service, Louisiana State University, n.d. [ca.1980].

Moss, Jeffrey, Norman Stiles and Daniel Wilcox. *Sesame Street ABC Storybook*. New York: Random House, Inc. 1974.

Mullen, Patrick B. "Modern Legend and Rumor Theory." *Journal of the Folklore Institute*, No. 9, 1972 (as quoted by Brunvand, 1981).

"Munson's Cypress Bayou Swamp Tour." *New Orleans Tourist News*, Mar. 1990.

Myers, [?]. "The Heat Is On." *Greenpeace*. May-June 1989.

Navigator (The): Containing Directions for Navigating the Monongahela, Allegheny, Ohio, and Mississippi Rivers; with an Ample Account of These Much Admired Waters . . . to Which Is Added, an Appendix, Containing an Account of Louisiana . . . 7th ed. Pittsburgh: Cramer, Spear & Eichbaum, 1811.

Nelson, Carolyn. "Louisiana State Museum/Shreveport." *Parishscope*, Oct. 1989.

New Orleans. souvenir booklet. N.p.: n.d. [ca. 1884].

Nichols, James D., Lynn Viehman, Robert H. Chabreck and Bruce Fenderson. *Simulation of a Commercially Harvested Alligator Population in Louisiana*. Baton Rouge: Louisiana State University Agricultural Experiment Station, 1976.

Nicolosi, Michelle. "Quick Bites." *Times-Picayune*, New Orleans, Sept. 15, 1989.

1980 Alligator Festival Cookbook. Luling: Rotary Club of West St. Charles Parish, 1980.

Nolan, Nell. "Gaston the 'Gator Pays a Visit to Twelfth Night Revelers Ball." *Times-Picayune*, New Orleans, Jan. 14, 1990.

Norman, B. M. *Norman's New Orleans and Environs*. New Orleans (printed in New York): B. M. Norman, 1845.

"Old and New Louisiana—II." *Scribner's Magazine*, Dec. 1873.

Oliver, Mike. "Gator Jaw Door Must Be Moved." *Orlando Sentinal*, Orlando, Nov. 4, 1989.

O'Neil, Ted. *The Fur Animals, the Alligator and the Fur Industry in Louisiana.* Baton Rouge: Louisiana Department of Wildlife and Fisheries, 1977.

——. *The Muskrat in the Louisiana Coastal Marshes.* New Orleans: Louisiana Department of Wildlife and Fisheries, 1949.

Pendley, Marian "Pie." "Pie's Potpourri." *Louisiana Conservationist,* July– Aug., Sept.–Oct. 1982.

Petty, Kate. *Crocodiles and Alligators.* New York: Franklin Watts, 1985.

Picou, Jean H. and Windell A. Curole. "Alligator Recipes." In *Alligator Production Manual,* Moody and Coreil, comps., *q.v.*

——. "Perk Up Your Meals with 'Gator." *State-Times,* Baton Rouge, undated clipping [possibly June 30, 1982]. Vertical file "A," Louisiana and Lower Mississippi Valley Collections, Louisiana State University, Baton Rouge.

Pictorial Museum of Animated Nature (The). London, n.d. [ca. 1900].

Pittman, Philip. T*he Present State of the European Settlements on the Mississippi.* London: J. Nourse, 1770.

Poe, Edgar. "The Washington Scene[:] Gulf Coast Alligator Population Shows Increase." *Times-Picayune,* New Orleans, Nov. 6, 1949.

Pol, Warren I. (Chairman, Louisiana Wildlife and Fisheries Commission). "Alligator Season Regulations." *Louisiana Register,* July 20, 1990.

Pope, John A. A *Tour Through the Southern and Western Territories of the United States of North America.* Gainesville: University Presses of Florida, 1979.

"Prime of Lauren Hutton (The)." *Vanity Fair*, May 1989.

Pynchon, Thomas. *V: A Novel.* Philadelphia: J. B. Lippincott, 1963.

Reed, Julia. "People Are Talking About . . . ." *Vogue,* Jan. 1990.

Reese, Albert M. *The Alligator and Its Allies.* New York and London: G. P. Putnam's Sons, 1915.

Rice, James. *Gaston Goes to Mardi Gras.* Gretna: Pelican Publishing, 1977.

Riegel, Stephanie. "Bayou Sauvage Refuge Still Months from Reality." Gambit, New Orleans, Aug. 22, 1989.

Ringling Brothers and Barnum & Bailey Circus. "Ringling Brothers and Barnum & Bailey Circus,118th ed. souvenir program & magazine [Blue Unit]." [Vienna, Va.]: Ringling Brothers and Barnum & Bailey Circus, 1988.

Robichaux, Mark. "Alligator Farming Shows There's a Lot to Be Said for Cows." *Wall Street Journal,* Aug. 2, 1989.

Robin, C. C. V*oyage to Louisiana*[,] *1803–1805,* abridged trans., Stuart O. Landry, trans. New Orleans: Pelican Publishing,1966.

——. *Voyages dans L'Intérieur de la Louisiane, de la Floride Occidentale, et dans les Isles de la Martinique et de Saint-Domingue,* Vol. III. Paris: F. Buisson, 1807.

Ronstrom, Maud O'Bryan. "From Bayou Mud to Luxury Leather." *Times-Picayune,* New Orleans, Aug. 25, 1946.

Rothe, Aline. *Kalita's People.* Waco: Texian Press, 1963.

(du) Ru, Paul (Fr.). "Journal de Voyage en Louisiane [1700]." As published by Baron Marc De Villiers, 1925.

Schmidt, Karl P. *The American Alligator.* Chicago: Field Museum of Natural History, 1922.

Schultz, Christian. *Travels on an Inland Voyage through the States of New York, Pennsylvania, Virginia, Ohio, Kentucky, and Tennessee, and through the Territories of Indiana, Louisiana, Mississippi and New Orleans*, Vol. II. New York: Isaac Ripley, 1810.

Scott, Jack Denton. *Alligator.* New York: G. P. Putnam's Sons, 1984.

Seatsfield, [?]. *Life in the New World; or Sketches of American Society,* G. C. Hebbe and James Mackay, trans. New York: J. Winchester, New World Press,1844.

Shufeldt, Dr. R. W. *Chapters on the Natural History of the United States.* New York: Studer Brothers,1897.

Skinner, Cornelia Otis. *Madame Sarah.* Boston: Houghton Mifflin and Cambridge: The Riverside Press,1967.

Smith, Harold R. "Alfred the Alligator, and His Descendants." *Louisiana Conservation Review,* Winter 1939.

Smith, J. F. D. Voyage dans *les Etats-Unis de l'Amérique, fait en 1784.* Paris: Buisson,1791.

Smith, Robert. "Entrepreneur Takes Aim at Europe's Tanneries." *Times-Picayune,* New Orleans, June 5, 1990.

Smyth, J. F. D. *A Tour in the United States of America.* London: G. Robinson, 1784.

Snow, Constance. "Quick Bites: Nothing Greater Than a Gator." *Times-Picayune,* New Orleans, Sept. 28, 1990.

Snyder, Howard. "A Louisiana Alligator Hunt Turns

into the Battle of Big Bull." *Times-Picayune*, New Orleans, Magazine Section, Feb. 3, 1945.

———. "Vanishing Alligator." *Times-Picayune*, New Orleans, Aug. 31, 1947.

"South Louisiana Swamplands Give Up Alligator Hides, New Business." *Times-Picayune*, New Orleans, Nov. 17, 1947.

Southern Biological Supply Co., Inc. "Price List No. 15 [Sept. 15, 1926]." Louisiana Historical Center, Louisiana State Museum, New Orleans. Brochure.

Stevenson, James. *No Need for Monty*. New York: Greenwillow Books, 1987.

Sugarman, Carole. "Double Duty: A Gator Cop and Cook." *Washington Post*, Washington, D. C., April 14, 1989.

(de) Surgère. *Journal of the Voyage Made to the Mouth of the River Mississippi by Two Frigates of the King*, Henri de Ville du Sinclair, trans. Biloxi: Committee for the Celebration of the 275th Anniversary of the Biloxi Bay Colony, 1973.

Swanson, Betsy. *Historic Jefferson Parish from Shore to Shore*. Gretna: Pelican Publishing, 1975.

Swanton, John R. *The Indians of the Southeastern United States*. Washington, D. C.: U. S. Government Printing Office for the Smithsonian Institution, 1946.

Tenth Biennial Report of the Department of Conservation, State of Louisiana [,] 1930–31. New Orleans: [Louisiana] Department of Conservation, 1931.

"Thank You, Chicago, But We Have Some Alligators." *Louisiana Conservationist*, May 1943.

Tomkins, Calvin. "The Crocodile and You." *The New Yorker*, Jan. 7, 1974 (as quoted by Brunvant, 1981).

"Trosclair" [James Rice]. *Cajun Night Before Christmas*, James Rice, illus., Howard Jacobs, ed. Gretna: Pelican Publishing, 1973.

Troth, Henry. *Journal of Henry Troth, 1799* [1799], manuscript, Clinton Lee Brooke and Tyrrell Willcox Brooke, transcribers. Louisiana Historical Center, Louisiana State Museum, New Orleans. Typescript.

"True Craftiness." *Vogue*, May 1989.

United Press International. "Gator Lager: Florida's Beer, Michigan Born [Aug. 28, 1989]." Special Projects alligator research files, Louisiana Historical Center, Louisiana State Museum, New Orleans. Wire service release.

———. "Gator Lager: Logo Comes Before Beer [Feb. 24, 1989]." Special Projects Alligator research files, Louisiana Historical Center, Louisiana State Museum, New Orleans. Wire service release.

(De) Villiers, Marc (Baron). "Extrait d'un journal de voyage en Louisiane du Père Paul du Ru." *Journ. Soc. Amér.*, Paris, n.s., Vol. 17, 1925.

Viosca, Percy Jr. "Elusive 'Old Fire Eyes' Gave Hunters of Frogs, Alligators Wide Berth." *The Progress*, Hammond, July 7, 1939.

———. *Louisiana Out-of-Doors, a Handbook and Guide*. New Orleans: Percy Viosca, Jr., 1933.

———. "The Sun Worshiper." *Louisiana Conservationist*, May-June 1960.

———. "The Tale of 'Old Fire Eyes': An Encounter with a Giant Alligator in the Swamps of Louisiana." *Natural History* (American Museum of Natural History, New York), Vol. XXV, No. 4, 1925.

"Vogue Point of View: Style That Works . . . " *Vogue*, Aug. 1989.

Waldo, Ednard ["Edward"?]. "Mr. Gator, King of the Swamps." *Louisiana Conservationist*, Dec. 1957.

Warner, Coleman. "N.O. Sausage Maker Catches Gator Fever." *Times-Picayune/States-Item*, New Orleans, Sept. 11, 1986.

Weigel, Christophe. "Geographische Beschreibung der Provinz Louisiana/in Canada von dem Fluss St. Lorenz bis an den Ausfluss des Flusses Mississipi [*sic*]; samt einen kurtzen Berich von dem jetzt florirenden Actien-Handel. [Leipzig, 1720]." As published by Merrill, 1988. Broadside.

Welch, Walter Wade. *Ballooning Alligators and Other Louisiana Anecdotes*. New Orleans: Dilettante Press, 1990.

Weldon, Michael and Charles Beesley. *The Psychotronic Encyclopedia of Film*, Bob Martin and Akira Fitton, contributing authors. New York: Ballentine Books, 1983.

Wheeler, C. Gilbert. *Hand-Colored Illustrations of the Beautiful and Wonderful in Animated Nature*. Chicago: S. J. Wheeler, n.d. [ca. 1890?].

Wilhelm, Paul (Duke of Württemberg). *Travels in North America [,] 1822–1824*, W. R. Nitske, trans., Savoie Loffinville, ed. Norman: University of Oklahoma Press, 1973.

Williams, John Lee. A *View of Florida*. Gainesville: University Presses of Florida, 1976.

Williams, L. A. S. *Outlines of Chinese Symbolism and Art Motives*. Rutland: Charles E. Tuttle, 1974.

Wilson, Austin. "Seafood Salesman Hopes for Gator Meat as a Family Menu Staple." *State-Times*, Baton Rouge, Aug. 18, 1980.

Wilson, J. C. "Gator's Appetite Problem Cured." *The Shreveport Times*, Shreveport, July 3, 1975.

Wortley, [Lady] Emmeline Stuart. *Travels in the United States, etc., During 1849 and 1850*, Vol. 1. London: Richard Bentley, 1851.

Writers' Program of the Works Progress Administration in the State of Louisiana. *Louisiana, A Guide to the State.* New York: Hastings House, 1941.

Yancey, Richard K. "Alligator in the Marsh," *Louisiana Conservationist*, July–Aug. 1959 (re-issued as "Alligator in the Marsh," Wildlife Education Bulletin No. 55, Louisiana Wild Life and Fisheries Commission, New Orleans, 1962).

Yockey, Hal. "Catches Five-Foot 'Gator in Less Than a Minute." *Times-Picayune*, New Orleans, July 24, 1948.

Young, Perry. *The Mystick Krewe, Chronicles of Comus and His Kin.* [1931]. Reprint. New Orleans: Louisiana Heritage Press, 1969.

Zacharie, James S. N*ew Orleans Guide* (aka *Hansell's New Orleans Guide*). New Orleans: F. F. Hansell & Bro., [1893].

Zim, Herbert S. *Alligators and Crocodiles.* New York: William Morrow and Company, 1978.

Zola, Melanie and Katherine Grier. *Alligators* (in the "Getting to Know . . ." Nature's Children Series). Canada: Grolier Educational Corporation, n.d.

Newspapers

Signed newspaper articles are presented by author in preceding listings to facilitate coordination of chapter texts with citations. Unsigned newspaper articles are presented below by publication name and date.

Chicago Citizen, Chicago, Ill., Feb. 22, 1892.

Daily Reveille, Louisiana State University, Baton Rouge, Louisiana, Sept. 29, 1953.

Gambit, New Orleans, Louisiana, May 1 and Aug. 29, 1989.

Morning Advocate, Baton Rouge, Louisiana, Feb. 9, 1968; Feb. 25 and July 15, 1973; Mar. 12 and Sept. 15, 1986.

New York Mirror, New York, New York, Mar. 1, 1834.

New York Times (The), New York, New York, Feb. 10, 1935; Nov. 12, 1989.

Progress (The), Hammond, Louisiana, Nov. 12, 1937.

Rooster (The), New Orleans, Louisiana, May 3, 1989.

Shreveport Journal, Shreveport, Louisiana, July 15, 1966.

States-Times, Baton Rouge, Louisiana, Dec. 22, 1943; July 22, 1965; May 14 and Aug. 5, 1970; May 25, June 24 and Oct. 5, 1972; July 6 and Aug. 5, 1974; Mar. 14, Sept. 1 and Oct. 12, 1979; Oct. 1, 1980; May 5, Aug. 12, Sept. 4 and Oct. 14, 1982; Mar. 28, 1986; Oct. 4 and 10, 1989; Jan. 25, 1990.

States-Item, New Orleans, Louisiana, Dec. 2, 1978.

Sunday Advocate, Baton Rouge, Louisiana, Oct. 17, 1943; July 13, 1969; Nov. 16, 1986.

Times (The), Shreveport, Louisiana, July 28, 1967; Sept. 21, 1969; Apr. 18, 1975.

Times-Picayune, New Orleans, Louisiana, Nov. 27, 1938; Apr. 18 and 26, 1942; Dec. 12, 1943; Nov. 17, 1947; Sept. 5, 1948; Aug. 5, 1951; July 22, 1956; Aug. 2, 1965; Oct. 15, 1985; Sept. 28 and Dec. 4, 1986; June 16, 1989; Sept. 13, 1990.

Winfield News-American, Winfield, Louisiana, Sept. 9, 1938.

ABOUT THE AUTHOR

Vaughn L. Glasgow has been committed to documentation and popularization of Southern culture since high school days. Raised in Baton Rouge, Louisiana, he was educated at Louisiana State University and Pennsylvania State University, as well as at European programs in France, Italy, and England. Glasgow assimilated a remarkably rich and diverse methodological background that he stringently applies to professional involvements. Son of prominent forester, wildlife biologist, and pioneering ecologist Dr. Leslie L. Glasgow, he watched as his father faced the challenges of preserving species and habitats in an era and area of ever-increasing exploitation of the natural environment by the petro-chemical industry. His family and professional backgrounds provided unique preparation to undertake *A Social History of the American Alligator: The Earth Trembles with His Thunder.* Vaughn Glasgow found the outlet for his interests and commitments at the Louisiana State Museum in New Orleans, where he joined the staff in 1975 and has researched and directed numerous exhibitions that have traveled in-state, nationally, and internationally. He has been decorated twice by the French government for international cultural exchange activities.

ABOUT THE LOUISIANA MUSEUM FOUNDATION

The Louisiana Museum Foundation, created in October 1981, was organized exclusively for the purpose of supporting the Louisiana State Museum system. As such, the foundation is charged with the responsibility of soliciting and administering gifts, grants, bequests, and property (real and personal) in order to subsidize and promote projects of the museum and is recognized by the IRS as a 501(c)(3) organization.

In recent years, the foundation has sought to publish books growing out of manuscripts accompanying exhibits and projects at the State Museum in New Orleans. *A Social History of the American Alligator* is just such a tome but is especially significant because it is the first LMF manuscript to be published and distributed by a major commercial publishing house.

Major funding for the accompanying museum exhibit was furnished by

Additional support was provided by the Louisiana Fur and Alligator Advisory Council.